Theology from the Womb of Asia

Theology from the Womb of Asia

C. S. Song

Maryknoll, New York 10545

Published by Orbis Books, Maryknoll, NY 10545

Manufactured in the United States of America

Manuscript editor: William E. Jerman

Except where indicated otherwise, Bible quotations are from the *New English Bible;* RSV = *Revised Standard Version;* JB = *Jerusalem Bible*

Library of Congress Cataloging in Publication Data

Song, Choan-Seng
Theology from the Womb of Asia.

Bibliography: p.
Includes index.
1. Theology—Methodology. 2. Theology, Doctrinal—Asia. I. Title.
BR118.S68 1985 230′.095 85-31008
ISBN 0-88344-518-2 (pbk.)

To
Dr. Shoki Coe
and Dr. Aharon Sapsezian
former directors
and
Dr. Samuel Amirtham
present director
of the Programme of Theological
Education, the World Council of Churches,
for their tireless efforts in theological
developments in the Third World.

Contents

PART FOUR
VISION

Preface

My elder daughter Ju-Ping, who is fond of putting her thoughts in verse, wrote this poem when she was in the tenth grade (1984):

The Poet

The soft brushing of his pen
could be heard,
Through the thin wooden walls
of his tiny old room,
Through the ceiling,
Through the floor,
Through the darkness outside
covering his small cottage
like a huge blanket.
Endlessly, his pen raced on the paper,
forming words, phrases, sentences.
And finally, a poem.
He read it out loud
to all those who would hear—
The little bugs
crowding around the bright candle flame,
The dogs, the cats,
To all living creatures outside,
And to himself.
It was he who was judge of the poem,
He who wrote it over and over
until finally satisfied.
Then, after hours and hours of work,
He set paper aside,
To start again
—a new beginning.

This is how she goes about her poetry-making. Perhaps it can apply to theology-making too.

How many of us who write theology are conscious of the world outside us as we listen to the soft brushing of our pen, the loud noise of our manual typewriter, or the crisp sound of our word-processor? Most of us do not listen when we write. Writing theology is an exercise of the brain. It is an unloading of thoughts accumulated in our minds.

How many of us who are engaged in doing theology are aware of the ever-changing world of nature outside our workroom? Do we sense the presence of other beings, including persons from different walks of life and different backgrounds? Most of us leave them outside our theological confinement. They are not directly linked up with our abstruse theological statements, complicated arguments, and difficult metaphysical propositions.

And how many of us bring to our theological work our entire being: the body, the spirit, and the soul as well as the mind? Our theology is more likely to be a development of "objective" truths than an account of the faith that is in us—the faith to which women, men, and children bear witness in their daily lives. In our theology we are more concerned about the nature and authority of the church than about its mission and ministry in an unjust society, a conflict-torn community, a world exploited by greed and power. And we write to establish ourselves among the small circle of theologians who constitute only a fraction of the Christian community, and an even tinier fraction of the world community.

Perhaps a poet can tell us how we should go about theology. Look out the window of your workroom and imbibe the colors with which God has adorned nature! Then there will be more color in your theology. Listen to dogs bark, birds sing, and insects hum outside your workroom. Then your theology will become audible as well as legible. Read to them out loud what you have written on paper and attentively hear their responses! Then you will have to write over and over again before you will be satisfied.

Let our own heartbeats and the heartbeats of the world around us pulsate in tune with the heartbeats of God in creation! Then we shall not be satisfied with timeless theological constructs. We cannot stand still, repeating essentially the same thing again and again. We cannot close our mind's door to fresh insights and new possibilities. A new beginning has to be made.

What I have attempted to do in this book is a new beginning of this sort. It begins with the *imagination* that goes beyond the familiar territory of our theological efforts. It pleads that theology must be done with *passion* as well as with reason. It finds in *human community*, with all its tensions and hopes, the testing of our theological formulations—a testing in words and in deeds. And it finds nourishment in a *vision* of the future in which love and justice will prevail. Theology done with imagination and passion, in the midst of a human community, inspired by the vision of a better tomorrow, will have to be done over and over. It has to start again—a new journey, a new adventure, a new pilgrimage; in short, a new beginning.

Parts of what you will read in this book I first presented at a theological seminar-workshop held in Hong Kong, February-March 1983. To that seminar-workshop came young theologians and church leaders from various countries of Asia. We studied together, agonized over our theological poverty, and agreed to carve out a new theological path by doing theology not with books and essays imported from outside but with the abundant resources readily available in Asia. I am deeply grateful to those friends and colleagues at the seminar-workshop who responded to the challenge of building a theological community committed to doing theology with Asian resources—Asian cultures, religions, histories, stories of struggle for freedom, justice, and love.

Some chapters of this book were delivered as the Thatcher Lectures at the United Theological College in Sydney, Australia, in August 1984, and as the Birks Lectures at the Faculty of Religious Studies, McGill University, in Montreal, Canada, in October 1984. I want to thank Principal G. R. Ferguson of the United Theological College and Dean J. C. McLelland of McGill University and their faculties for the honor they did me in appointing me to those lectureships.

My conversations and discussions with faculty members and students on those two occasions were most rewarding. There were of course more skeptical frowns than enthusiastic smiles when I suggested to them a greatly expanded universe of theological discourse. But to my great surprise and joy, I seem to have touched the core of some theologians who are consciously trying to liberate themselves from the captivity of traditional theology, and wrestling with the task and responsibility of doing theology within their own communities. With them I have forged a theological comradeship. Theology that takes seriously the world that is God's and also ours is not monopolized by theologians in the Third World. There is going to be an increasing number of theologians in the West who will join the theological movements started by black theologians, feminist theologians, and Third World theologians. This is a heartening thought!

This book is dedicated to my three friends and colleagues in the Programme of Theological Education, formerly the Theological Education Fund, of the World Council of Churches: Dr. Shoki Coe and Dr. Aharon Sapsezian, its former directors, and Dr. Samuel Amirtham, the present director. The role that the Programme of Theological Education has played in the development of creative and independent theological efforts in the Third World will be writ large in the history of theological education. My own theological development has been greatly aided and supported by the Programme, especially by these three colleagues of mine. It is my distinct pleasure, therefore, to express my deep appreciation to them and through them to the Programme of Theological Education.

And, if what appears on the pages of this book vibrates with rhythms of the energy working unseen in the mysterious depths of creation, and with tunes of unsung songs in the hearts of troubled and aspiring humanity, it is because words, phrases, and sentences took shape and formed images in the midst of the music my wife, Mei-Man, and my daughters, Ju-Ping and Ju-Ying, make in our home. Music is a form of art eminently capable of responding to the infinitely mysterious movement of the Spirit in creation, eminently capable of echoing, with profound sensitivity, voices of the human soul striving to be set free from the shackles of finitude and transience. To my wife and my daughters, then, I wish to express my deep thanks for the appearance of yet another book.

A word of thanks also to the editorial staff of Orbis Books. Their undiminished commitment to letting Third World theological voices be heard helps to usher in a new theological era.

Geneva
Spring 1985

Introduction

How is one to describe the growth of theology in the Asian setting? What look did it have in the past? What shape does it have at present? As to its future, what has one to expect of it? Each one of us may have ready answers. But let us not too quickly turn to the diagnosis of its symptoms. Let us not too swiftly set out to analyze its conditions. Nor let us too confidently predict its developments. We should first of all listen to a folktale from the Philippines and see if it may shed some light on our theological endeavors in Asia.

The folktale is called "The Gungutan and the Big-Bellied Man," the Gungutan being one of the best-known characters in Manuvu and Matigsalug oral traditions and sometimes portrayed as a cannibal. The motif of the folktale is described in various ways but can best be said to be a "forced, feigned dream come true":

> There was once a big-bellied man who lived alone. One day the hairy Gungutan came to him. The big-bellied man asked the visitor, "What news do you bring me?"
>
> "I came to ask you to tell me about your dream," the Gungutan said. Big-belly replied, "But I have no dreams." "That is not possible," the Gungutan said, "you must have dreamed something, last night or the other night." And the big bully of the forest threatened Big-belly. Big-belly cowered, repeating he did not have any dream. "Do not fool me," the Gungutan insisted.
>
> "All right, I have a dream," said Big-belly, who had to fabricate one. "In my dream my spirit saw a big hog and a fishtrap full of fish." "That is good," the Gungutan said. "Let's go and see the hog and the trap." But Big-belly said that it was only a dream. "Never mind," the Gungutan said. Big-belly tried to excuse himself, saying he could not carry his body, for he was too fat. But the Gungutan forced him. Now they departed until they reached a big river. They went downstream until they reached a junction where they saw a fishtrap. "See," the Gungutan said, "your dream is true."
>
> They examined the fishtrap and found that it was full of shrimp and eel. The Gungutan told Big-belly to carry the trap of fish. Big-belly could hardly lift the trap, but the Gungutan helped him put it on his back. Big-belly complained he could not carry the load, but the Gungutan told him to stop his plaints. Big-belly carried the fishtrap, sometimes falling on his

knees and bruising himself on the stones in the riverbed as they trudged downstream.

Soon they found a big trapped hog as they went up the river bank. The Gungutan said "'Carry that hog, Big-belly." "I can't," Big-belly replied. "But that was your dream," said the Gungutan, who immediately lifted the carcass of the hog, throwing it on top of the fishtrap.

Big-belly dropped down on his knees and could only mumble words as he heard the Gungutan say, "That was your dream, fool!" . . .

After [some] days had passed the Gungutan came once more. . . . "Where is the rein and bit of your horse?" he asked Big-belly. "Come with me because we are joining the datu's [tribal chieftain's] hunting party."

The Gungutan took the rein and put the bit into the mouth of Big-belly. Then he rode on him. And he forced him to run. Soon they reached a wide grass land and they saw many people. . . .

They got to talking of [many] things. "We are here," [a] young man said, "to catch the deer with a golden antler as a bridewealth prize for the datu's daughter, for the datu said that whoever could catch the deer with a golden antler shall be married to my daughter."

The deer with the golden antler had run into the thick grass. So the suitors set fire to the grass to flush out the deer with a golden antler. And the deer indeed came out dismayed. The young suitors, on their horses, started to chase it. The other people watched them eagerly [try to] catch the deer with the golden antler, but the young men failed.

Now the Gungutan said, "Watch me, young men, for I shall take my turn to chase the deer, the bridewealth prize for the datu's daughter." The Gungutan leaped to Big-belly's shoulders and urged him, "Run fast, Big-belly." And the Gungutan's horse ran as fast as it could. Now the people saw the deer running around the world. It was a wonderful sight to behold Big-belly running like a swift striking lightning.

Soon the deer with the golden antler was overtaken. As soon as the deer was killed, the Gungutan disappeared. The big-bellied man now turned into a handsome young man whose forehead beamed like rays.

He carried the deer on his shoulders, directing his steps to the house of the datu. And the datu greeted him, "You have caught the deer with the golden antler, now you can marry my daughter and you will be my son-in-law."[1]

From a big-bellied man to a handsome young man—this is a long, painful journey. From an ugly, obese lazybones to a lively dashing prince—this is back-breaking work. And for a forced, feigned dream to come true, one has to obey an unreasonable command, to force oneself to dream, and to commit oneself totally to an adventure that at first appears frightful, intimidating, and unpredictable.

Theology is such an adventure. Christian theology in Asia has been overweight, like that big-bellied man. It could hardly walk or run with its huge belly of undigested food—a belly crammed with schools of theology, theories of biblical interpretation, Christian views of cultures and religions, all originating from the church in the West and propounded by traditional theology. It became even more obese when the vast space of Asia, with its rich cultures, vigorous religions, and turbulent histories, began to compete for room in that already over-loaded theological belly. The result is painful indigestion. Our chief concern must be how to cure its indigestion, reduce its weight, and regain its agility and dynamic to win the hand of theology authentic to the Asian mind.

But where is our Gungutan who may force us Christians and theologians in Asia to dream? How can we find him who makes us walk and run in pursuit of our dream? And who is this Gungutan of ours who has the magic of changing our big-bellied theology into a handsome youthful theology? Well, our Gungutan is a very complex creature. Our Gungutan is (1) the power of *imagination* given to us by God who created us human beings in the divine *image;* (2) it is the *passion* that enables us to feel the *compassion* of God in us and in others; (3) it is the experience of *communion* that makes us realize we are *responsible* for one another and for God; and (4) it is the *vision* of God's redeeming presence in the world, enabling us to *envision* a new course for theology.

This is an adventure of faith. This is an exploration of faith in the midst of the cultures, religions, and histories that are ours by birth or by heritage. I propose, then, to set out on our theological adventure and exploration in four parts: imagination, passion, communion, and vision, always keeping before us the folktale of "The Gungutan and the Big-Bellied Man." Let us hope that in the end we may gain freedom for our theological mind—freedom to meet God in Asian humanity, freedom to identify God's world within our Asian world, freedom to intertwine biblical history and Asian history, and freedom to encounter Jesus the savior in the depth of the spirituality that sustains Asians in their long march of suffering and hope.

PART ONE
IMAGINATION

1

Life Is Coded

A BATTLE OF CODES

The odds were against Japan in the Pacific theater of World War II. Japan had overextended itself in its quest for domination over the Asian land mass. In its war of aggression it had drained itself of its human and physical resources. A major setback came in June 1942 in the Battle of Midway—an island lying a thousand miles northwest of Hawaii. By seizing Midway, Yamamoto, Japan's great admiral commanding Japanese naval forces in the Pacific, hoped to deal a decisive blow to the American fleet and carry the war to the doorstep of the United States mainland. But victory was denied him. He lost two-thirds of his own carrier fleet, "a disaster from which the Japanese navy was never able to fully recover."[1]

In March 1943 Admiral Yamamoto himself was on the island of Rabaul deep in the South Pacific. Through his charismatic presence (in his death he was to be revered as a *gun-sin,* warrior-god) he sought to inspire his beleaguered troops and to bid farewell to the young fliers taking off on their suicide missions against enemy ships. Yamamoto must have known that the tide of war had decidedly turned against him and his country. Short of a miracle, no military genius, not even his, could avert the inevitable. But how could there be a miracle for a military government that had brought so much tragedy to millions and hundreds of millions of persons in China, in the Pacific, and to its own people? Yamamoto must have sensed his own imminent death too. On his flight from Rabaul to Bargainville, his plane was intercepted by American naval fighters and shot down over the Solomon Islands, thus ending the life of a great warrior and the tragic ambition of Japan to master the whole of Asia.

What was the direct cause of the Japanese defeat in the crucial Battle of Midway? Why was the plane carrying Admiral Yamamoto, the irreplaceable commander, intercepted? Superior American forces? Not exactly. The force Yamamoto threw into the Battle of Midway was larger and stronger. A miscalculation in Yamamoto's military strategy? Unlikely. With his uncanny military sense, miscalculation was most unlikely. The main reason is said to have been the ability of the Americans to decode Japanese naval signals. "Before the Battle of Midway," it was disclosed, "the United States scored one of the greatest triumphs of the war by cracking Japan's naval code,"[2] thereby enabling it to know Yamamoto's war plans in advance. And less than a year after the Battle of Midway, his flight from Rabaul to Bargainville, a heavily coded secret, was also decoded and ended in his death.

A battle of codes! This is what it was. The world in time of war is packed with codes and signals. Top military secrets—battle strategies, troop movements, deployment of land-air-sea powers—are all carefully guarded in codes. The fate of a nation, the destiny of a people, the success of a battle, are all packed into a few signals. Communication in plain language is suspended. To surprise enemies and defeat them, code language must be invented and employed. But enemies do not remain idle, waiting to be surprised and defeated. They spare no effort to crack *their* enemies' codes, interpret their signals, and penetrate their coded secrets. A fierce tug-of-war is joined between warring nations—the war of encoding and decoding. Japan lost the tug-of-war with the United States. It was defeated in the Battle of Midway and lost its most able military leader. The United States won the tug-of-war and turned the course of the Pacific War to its own advantage.

THE CODE-PACKED UNIVERSE

The world in time of peace is also packed with codes and signals. We live in a coded world. As a matter of fact, the whole universe is made up of codes and signals of all kinds. The language of the universe is code language. That is why the universe is such a huge mystery. It will remain a mystery even after parts of it have been invaded by us humans with our space ships and satellites. The universe, with its galaxies of stars and infinite space, has fascinated human beings and awed them, and it will continue to fascinate and awe them. The universe, most of it unknown to the inhabitants of tiny planet Earth, has aroused their curiosity and challenged their scientific perspicacity, and it will continue to do so. The universe at once beckons us human beings and obstructs our penetration of it. Its immense power overwhelms us but also draws us to it. And it yields bits and pieces of its secrets to the wisest among us who succeed in cracking some of its codes and deciphering its signals.

The universe, for example, has for centuries confronted earth dwellers with a certain code in the form of a falling apple. Countless apples have fallen from trees. Countless persons have seen them. An apple that falls from its tree! Can this reflect a code from the mysterious universe? Does it contain some truth about its vast space? To most viewers it did not seem likely. Such questions never occurred to them. It was beyond their wildest dream to think of a falling apple as fraught with a secret about the universe. An apple that falls from its tree is just a natural phenomenon. When an apple becomes ripe or overripe, it falls. It is as simple as that.

But it was not as simple as that. A falling apple embodied a code containing an important message from the universe. Through it one could catch a glimpse of the secret of inscrutable space. And it was for Isaac Newton to crack the code and interpret the message. We can imagine Newton sitting in his garden drinking his afternoon tea. It could have been a beautiful autumn day when fruit in the orchard and crops in the field were ripening for harvest. Newton saw an apple fall. That falling was no different from all the other fallings. But Newton suddenly realized that right in front of him was a code opening into the secrets of the universe. Contained in that falling apple was a universal force, the *dynamis* that keeps all things in the universe in their place. The force that pulls the apple to earth is the same force that keeps the moon in orbit! Just think of it: the code that opens a door to the mystery of the universe in classical physics was discovered in the commonplace phenomenon of an apple falling to the ground. But what a tremendous code it was! What an excitement it must have been for Newton to be able to decode it!

The universe confronts human beings as an enigma. It challenges human intelligence. Disclosure of its secrets piques human curiosity. From the dawn of human consciousness to the present era of nuclear physics, human beings have been engaged in a battle of codes with the universe. From a very early stage of human history, they have sought to make the universe yield its secrets through magic. Magic is "primitive" science. Beliefs, cultic expressions, rituals, and taboos of our ancestors, practiced in the great centers of early civilization—in China, in the ancient Near East, in Egypt—were mixtures of magic and primitive science. The universe was not self-explanatory. Life on earth was threatened by a source of power hidden in the depths of the mysterious universe. To understand the world around them was an urge as instinctive as it was persistent. Through magical devices, cultic practices, and ritual performances they hoped to gain glimpses of the secrets of the universe and the mystery of life. And in the thick of that quest they encountered powerful deities that they believed were clues to explain life and the universe. Their curiosity about the universe was coupled with what we call religion. They were engaged in religious quests and they found in their deities the key to decode life and the universe packed with enigmatic codes.

We begin to understand better why each tribe, each people, each nation, almost without exception, has creation myths. We have our creation story in the first two chapters of the Bible. It in turn is derived from the Babylonian creation epic of *Enuma Elish.* In Asia we have an abundance of myths and stories of creation, often supreme in their poetic forms, profound in religious insights, and resplendent in their power of imagination. In an ancient chant of creation, Io, the supreme being of the Maoris of New Zealand, causes light to shine in the darkness of the universe:

> Io dwelt within breathing-space of immensity.
> The universe was in darkness, with water everywhere.
> There was no glimmer of dawn, no clearness, no light.

And he began by saying these words,
That he might cease remaining inactive,
"Darkness, become a light-possessing darkness."
And at once light appeared.
He then repeated those self-same words in this manner,
That he might cease remaining inactive,
"Light, become a darkness-possessing darkness."
And again intense darkness supervened.
Then a third time he spake, saying,
"Let there be a darkness above,
Let there be a darkness below. . . .
Let there be one light above,
Let there be one light below. . . .
A dominion of light,
A bright light."
And now a great light prevailed.
Io then looked to the waters which compassed him
about and spake a fourth time, saying,
"Ye waters of Tai-kama, be ye separate.
Heavens be formed."
Then the sky became suspended.
"Bring forth thou Tu-pu-koro-nuku."
And at once the moving earth lay stretched abroad.[3]

Io, the supreme being, accounts for the light, the heavens, and the earth. Io is the key. In Io the Maoris found the answer to their "scientific" question about the universe. And on Io their religious mind came to rest. Does this not tell us that for our ancient ancestors "interpretation" is part and parcel of life and religion? Interpretation—hermeneutics—is not the invention of the modern critical mind.

But the codes of the universe are not always assuring and transparent. In fact they baffle and confuse us too. Here the religious mind engaged in understanding life and the universe gives way to doubt and perplexity. And what expresses better this doubt and perplexity than a creation hymn in the Rig Veda, the oldest collection of hymns in India, some of which date back as far as the fifteenth century B.C.? The hymn bears the title, "Who Can Say Whence It All Came, and How Creation Happened?" It runs in part:

Then even nothingness was not, nor existence.
There was no air then, nor the heavens beyond it.
What covered it? Where was it? In whose keeping?
Was there then cosmic water, in depths unfathomed?

Then there was neither death nor immortality,
nor was there then the torch of night and day.
The One breathed windlessly and self-sustaining.
There was that One then; and there was no other.

At first there was only darkness wrapped in darkness.
All this was only unillumined water.
That One which came to be, enclosed in nothing,
arose at last, born of the power of heat. . . .

But, after all, who knows, and who can say
whence it all came, and how creation happened?
The gods themselves are later than creation,
so who knows truly whence it has arisen?

Whence all creation has its origin,
he, whether he fashioned it or whether he did not,
he, who surveys it all from highest heaven,
he knows—or maybe even he does not know.[4]

If the One, the supreme God, does not know how creation came into being, then who knows? God, the key to unlock the mystery of life and the universe, is wrapped up in codes too. How to crack the codes that surround God? The question has inspired the human mind to spare no effort to find an answer. It has blossomed into philosophical schools, theological systems, and religious traditions.

But how are we ourselves to crack the codes that make God a remote, indifferent, and unknown entity? How are we to decode them? Can modern biblical scholarship help us? Will theories of biblical and theological hermeneutics help us? Will the history of Christian thought and traditions of the church enlighten us? Or can a comparative study of religions get us closer to the truth? They may and they may not. But we must also pose another question: where are the codes that disclose God to us? Are they in heaven? Or are they on earth? Are they tucked away in a cathedral or do they lie exposed in the marketplace? The question lies at the heart of our doing of theology. The answer we give to it shapes our theology, molds our faith, and determines our religious lifestyle. Let us hope that toward the end of our inquiry each one of us may find our own answer. For the present, let us continue to see how life—your life and mine and the life of the world—consists of bundles of codes. Deep awareness of this lies at the beginning of the doing of theology.

TWO MOONS I SEE

Isaac Newton, to continue our story of encoding and decoding, cracked a code of the universe as a scientist and ushered in the modern era of science and technology. But scientists are not the only ones to rise to the challenge of the code-packed universe. There are others who are no less equal to it. But they, especially artists and poets, read the code language of life and universe very differently. The reality of life and universe that they discover with their brush, explore with their colors, delineate with their stories, muse over in their verses, and sing with their melodies, is no less real than the reality that scientists such as Newton portray in equations, explain with hypotheses, and capture with their laws. A poem, "Two Moons," by Hsu Chih-Mo, a famous Chinese poet in the early decades of the twentieth century, may help us to appreciate this:

> Two moons I see,
> The same in shape, yet different in feature.
>
> The one's just in the sky
> Decked in a gown of bird-plumes.
> She does not stint her favours,
> Her gold and silver spread o'er all the earth.
> She does not forget the tiles on the palace-roof.
> And the Three Lakes brim and glisten with her beauty.
> Over the clouds she leaps, over the tree-tops,
> And hides herself in green shades of the vine.
> Even the fish within the lakes are rapt!
> And yet she has a flaw. . .
> The naughty habit of becoming thin:
> Sometimes the sparks of stars are seen aloft
> But not her round enchanting countenance.
> And though she may return at other seasons
> This absence is a torture too excessive.
>
> Another moon there is you cannot see,
> Despite the splendour of her radiance.
> She also has her dimple smiles
> And grace of movement;
> She's no less generous than the other moon. . . .
> What a pity that you cannot see my garden!
> Sublime her sorcery,
> Kindling and quickening my ecstasies:
> I love her sudden swell of silver waves
> Leaping with melodies of silver bells,
> Even her foam, blown white like horses' tails,
> Fostered more tenderly than deep-sea pearls.
> A full and perfect moon
> Who never wanes.
> Whenever I close these eyes of mine
> She rises and sails into the heavens.[5]

The moon never fails to captivate the sensitive mind of a poet. This is still true even after it has been invaded by astronauts from earth. Should it captivate a theological mind also? It certainly should. But poetry has been abandoned by our theologians. There is no sun, moon, and stars in our theological books. That is why theology has become arid and dry. It has become largely a matter of the head. It has lost the heart—the heart that feels, embraces, and communicates. The Old Testament psalmist who sang these words is different:

> Praise God, sun and moon;
> praise God, all you shining stars;
> praise God, heaven of heavens,
> and you waters above the heavens [Ps. 148:3–4].

Can sun and moon and stars praise God? Of course they can. Theologians must regain the ability to hear them sing and praise God. Then their theological mind will expand. There will be room in it for things other than Christian dogmatics, ecclesiastical laws, and church pronouncements.

To return to our Chinese poet. He speaks of two moons. Is this not strange? Why two moons? Is he not letting his poetic fantasy run wild? Well, our Chinese poet sees the moon in the dark sky. It is the moon seen by everybody, poet or not. That moon changes. It waxes and wanes. It can even disappear. The poet knows the moon functions in accordance with the laws of nature. This is common knowledge—a well-known fact.

Most persons stop here. The moon that waxes and wanes is to them a plain, natural phenomenon. It does not contain any secrets. It sends out no codes. It needs no decoding. But our poet sees differently. The moon does not just wax and wane. It "becomes thin." There must be a difference between "waxing and waning" and "becoming thin." The process of decoding has begun in the mind of the poet. The lunar "habit of becoming thin" is to him "a flaw and a torture." A scientist will say this is nonsense. Persons who insist on scientific logic for everything cannot see the poet's point. But they must know how much meaning of life they miss by not being able to see the poet's point.

The moon that endures the flaw and torture of becoming thin ceases, in the eyes of our poet, to be just a moon. To the poet in us all, the moon that becomes thin and even disappears belongs to a code related to human life and to all lives on earth and in the universe. That moon is life in transition, life in finitude, life under the threat of decay and death. The poet in us who gazes at the moon in the quiet of the night becomes a decoder of life.

But our poet has another moon hidden in his garden. That moon does not wax and wane. After the flaw and torture that the first moon brings to our life, our poet must be overjoyed to have the company of a moon that neither becomes thin nor disappears. It always retains its round shape. He can count on its abiding presence. That moon—the moon-shaped pond with its water glistening in the moonlight—echoes "melodies of silver bells" in his heart. It answers his longing for "a full and perfect moon"—for the meaning, power, and eternity without which life drifts away into nowhere. Here the poet in us all is not just a decoder of life. We are believers in life with its sorrows and joys, despairs and hopes. The cosmic moon and the moon in our hearts become united to rekindle our faith in eternity amid a world of temporality.

We begin to understand, do we not, that there must be two moons: the moon outside us and the moon inside us, the moon in the sky and the moon in our hearts, the moon that waxes and wanes and the moon that stays fully round always. The two moons are not the same, but they are related. They are not identical, but they overlap. They are in tension, one with the other, but they also inspire each other.

Do the two moons not tell us that our code-filled life has both external meaning and internal meaning? To get to internal meaning from external meaning, to penetrate the inner dimension of life, to reach the depth of meaning in the innermost recesses of history, and to hear and comprehend the longings of the human spirit in the grasp of the divine spirit—is this not what interpretation is really about? It is, in fact, much more than interpretation. It is confrontation. It is encounter. It is interpenetration. This is what we find in the Bible. This is the way history should be searched. This is how cultures and religions are to be explored. And above all, this is the way theology must be pursued. To be a scientific theologian is not enough. One has to be a poetic theologian.

DEEPENING THEOLOGICAL IMAGINATION

When a theologian penetrates God's creation with a poetic mind, creation begins to speak in human terms. Creation is the story of heaven and earth, but it is at the same time the story of human beings. It is about the sun, the moon, and the stars, but it is also about human life. It is a record of the struggle between the power of light and the power of darkness in the universe, but it is no less a record of the struggle between the power of good and the power of evil in human society. It discloses terrible conflicts between order and chaos in the heart of the cosmos, revealing at one and the same time conflicts between order and chaos in the human spirit.

What is more evident of this than the close link with which creation and the new year are related in the minds of ancient Near Eastern peoples? The old year with its good and evil is passing away, and a new year that must be fraught with good and evil is about to begin. At the new year festival people then turn to the creation for clues of the vicissitudes of the year to come. Creation story at the new year festival becomes human story and the story of the world. In the midst of rejoicing and anticipation at the turn of the year people are engaged in serious theological effort—an effort to discern the possibilities of life and history in relation to God the creator. Psalm 33 in the Old Testament is a typical example of such theological effort from a Jewish perspective as peoples of the ancient Near East participate in the new year celebrations.

The person who composed that new year festival hymn must have been a poet and a theologian. He must have been a poetic theologian and a theological poet. That important time in the life of human community must have inspired his poetic best and drawn out his theological best. The result is the hymn in which God's story and human story are brought into dynamic interactions. The hymn is a superb poetic art. It is also a profound interweaving of creation and history. We must see how this poet who has left us no name did it. The poet first affirms the God of creation:

> The word of the Lord holds true,
> and all the work of the Lord endures (v. 4).

Then he tells us at once how God is related to the world:

> The Lord loves righteousness and justice,
> God's love unfailing fills the earth (v. 5).

Love, justice, and righteousness—this is what God's creation is about. This must also be what the world of human beings is about. Heaven and earth endure because God's love and justice endure. It is then not a blind force but God's word that brings creation into existence:

> The Lord's word made the heavens,
> all the host of heaven was made at God's command (v. 6).

This God of creation is at the same time the God of history. God is personally involved in human history. That is why our poet moves from creation to history and says:

> The Lord brings the plans of nations to nothing,
> God frustrates the counsel of the peoples (v. 10).

There are conflicts and strifes in history. But again conflicts and strifes that make history paralyzed and render human beings helpless are not the final words. God remains in command of history as well as of creation:

> The Lord's plans shall stand forever,
> and God's counsel endure for all generations (v. 11).

This is a great affirmation of faith by someone who has observed closely how creation and history, God and humanity, are interlocked in the birthpangs of hope and future. The new year praise must then conclude with words of faith and hope:

> Let thy unfailing love, O Lord, rest upon us,
> as we have put our hope in thee (v. 22).

History has a future because of such faith. And life has meaning because of God's unfailing love. This is the way in which that ancient Hebrew poet did theology in the context of the new year festival celebrated throughout the Near East. Is this not illuminating for those of us who endeavor to do theology in Asia?

Asia is neither a theological vacuum nor a theological wilderness. What one finds are religious beliefs rooted in awe for a power that transcends the world and yet makes direct impacts on human affairs. One encounters there cultures shaped by religious experiences of that power. In Asia one is in the company of people whose life of toil and labor, hope and despair, is sustained by religions and cultures that deeply penetrate the fabric of their community. There are codes waiting to be decoded theologically. There are signs that attract our theological curiosity. And there are symbols that lift us from the depths of Asian humanity to the heights of God's redemptive dealings with the world.

Resources in Asia for doing theology are unlimited. What is limited is our theological imagination. Powerful is the voice crying out of the abyss of the Asian heart, but powerless is the power of our theological imaging. If we want to engage ourselves in theological decoding of those codes, signs, and symbols that make Asia Asia and shape the spirituality of Asian peoples, we must deepen our theological imagination and strengthen the power of our theological imaging.

There is, for example, a hymn in Rig Veda from ancient India called "What God Shall We Adore with Our Oblation." To quote it in part:

> In the beginning rose Hiranyagarbha, born only lord
> of all created beings.
> He fixed and holdeth up this earth and heaven.
> What God shall we adore with our oblation?
>
> Giver of vital breath, of power and vigour, he whose
> commandments all the gods acknowledge;
> Whose shade is death, whose lustre makes immortal.
> What God shall we adore with our oblation? . . .
>
> Who by his grandeur hath become sole ruler of all
> moving world and that breathes and slumbers;
> He who is lord of human beings and lord of cattle.
> What God shall we adore with our oblation?
>
> By him the heavens are strong and earth is steadfast,
> by him light's realm and sky-vault are supported;
> By him the regions in mid-air were measured.
> What God shall we adore with our oblation?

To him, supported by his help, two armies embattled look
while trembling in their spirit,
When over them the risen sun is shining.
What God shall we adore with our oblation?. . .

Ne'er may he harm us who is earth's begetter,
nor he whose laws are sure, the heaven's creator,
He who brought forth the great and lucid waters.
What God shall we adore with our oblation?

Prajapati! thou only comprehendest all these created things,
and none other beside thee.
Grant us our hearts' desire when we invoke thee;
may we have store in riches in possession.[6]

This is a hymn welling out of the depths of Indian humanity. What signs do we find in it? What are the codes that it challenges us to decode? With what symbols does it spellbind our theological mind?

A hymn such as this—and there are many many more, not only hymns, but dramas, stories, arts, that speak out of the life and history of Asian peoples—does it have no theological meaning? Does it not share some fundamental questions we Christians seek to answer in our faith? Is the hope expressed by it completely alien to the hope cherished by us Christians? Asia is in fact filled with theological codes. It is a rich field of theological signs. And it is a precious mine of theological symbols. Asia challenges us with the enormity of its theological power. It is with this enormous theological power that we will engage ourselves in the pages that follow.

Theology that seeks to deal with life and history in Asia with its theological depth cannot be found in the familiar traditions and teachings of the church. In pursuit of theological truths familiarity is a hindrance rather than a help. It confines us to the ideas, views, and practices to which we are accustomed. It makes us safe and comfortable in religious convention and mental habituation. It limits the sphere of our theological activity. It discourages adventure in faith and closes the door to new insights.

Jesus had to contend with the familiar traditions of his own religion. That religion, with its accretions of perfectionistic traditions, did not permit believers to do good on the Sabbath, but for Jesus to do good must be permitted even on the Sabbath (Matt. 12:12). Jesus based his "outrageous" breaking of the Sabbath on a conviction radically different from and unfamiliar to that of the religious authorities of the time: the Sabbath was made for the sake of human beings and not human beings for the Sabbath (Mark 2:27). This was an unheard of assertion. For such "blasphemy" alone Jesus could have been at once condemned to death.

Jesus' religion is so unconventional and his practice of faith so daring that he collided head-on with religious orthodoxy. He moved in the company of "sinners," ate with them, and offered God's forgiveness to them. When questioned, he said that it was not the healthy who needed a doctor, but the sick, that he had not come to call the virtuous, but sinners (Mark 2:17). To the ears of most of his hearers these words sounded refreshingly unfamiliar. They had to mull them over and over in their hearts to realize their full force. It was a revolutionary faith that Jesus tried to inculcate. And in the Sermon on the Mount there is the well-known formula that Jesus must have used on a number of occasions: "You have learned that they were told. . . , but what I tell you is this . . . " (Matt. 5:27–48). Ancient wisdom and faith must be tested in the fire of the present life. Untested faith is the opium of the people. Untested wisdom is a piece of dead wood.

What Jesus showed us is how to do theology with people daily involved in the joys and sorrows of this life. He must have then spent more time in the marketplace than in the sanctuary. Theology must be done at the place where the serious business of life is conducted, argued about, wrestled with. He was so much with the people outside the boundaries defined by the religious authorities that an accusing finger was always pointed at his back: "Look at him! A glutton and a drinker, a friend of tax-gatherers and sinners" (Luke 7:34). But it was in the company of these "undesirable people" that Jesus must have developed his theology of God's kingdom.

Does this not tell us that the theological truths we are after are to be found precisely in Asia? We may search for them in the history of doctrines developed in the West. We may look for them using methods and principles of hermeneutics advocated by different theologians outside Asia. But we tend to forget that the theological truths we are after are with us all the time in Asia. There are signs of them in the marketplace. Their codes are written on the faces of women, men, and children in Asia. And symbols of theological truths hide themselves in the masses of Asian people. Where else then can we get glimpses of them if not in our cultures and histories? Life in Asia is theologically coded. To decode it we must immerse ourselves in it. Reappropriation and reexperience of that life with its cultural manifestations, religious beliefs, and historical hopes are essential parts of doing theology from the womb of Asia.

2

Signs of the Times

A REMNANT SHALL RETURN

During the second half of the eighth century B.C., geopolitics was uppermost in the minds of the rulers of the ancient Near Eastern nations. Powerful Assyria was a threat to the peace of the entire region. How to check its power and frustrate its advance against other nations became the major concern of national policy and international politics.

In Isaiah 7 we have an account of power politics played to its bitter end under the menacing shadow of Assyria. It was a historical drama with a profound theological meaning. Involved in the drama was military pressure from the two kingdoms of Syria and Israel to force Judah into an alliance against Assyria the superpower. At center stage were the towering figure of Isaiah the prophet and the worried politician Ahaz, king of Judah (737–715 B.C.), meeting at the water conduit in Jerusalem. This had to do with the so-called Syro-Ephraimitic war in 733 B.C.

It was a time of national emergency. Martial law must have been proclaimed. Ahaz must have already mobilized his troops. Strengthening the defense of the city must have been the top military priority. Facing the beleaguered king and his people, Isaiah appeared with his son named Shear-jashub, meaning "a remnant shall return" (Isa. 7:3). Isaiah must have announced his son's name to the king and his retinue with a sonorous voice: "Shear-jashub! A-Remnant-Shall-Return!"

Shear-jashub was a code name to decode the danger threatening Judah. It was also a symbolic name symbolizing hope to the residents of Jerusalem. And it was a sign name, meant to reassure the king and the people that the nation had a future.

The history of Judah was at stake. The future of a people was in great danger. Out of this historical drama two ways emerged: a political way and a theological way. The king and his military and political advisors had opted for the political way. They were critically involved in power politics. On the one hand was Assyria, the nation on its way to being a decisive power in the region.

On the other was the coalition of Damascus and Samaria pressuring Jerusalem to defy Assyrian domination.

The political way chosen by Ahaz involved political strategy and military tactics to fend off the coalition and align Judah with Assyria. There was nothing mysterious about it. One had to be hardheaded. What had to be faced was an impending political crisis, not a code, a symbol, or a sign pointing away from the crisis. This political way does not lead to a theological way.

But Isaiah the prophet entered the historical crisis of his nation in a theological way. He came with a code for the king to decipher, a sign for the king's advisors to interpret, a symbol that would enable the people to see beyond the immediate crisis. In the eyes of the prophet there was no such thing as "mere historical fact." History has to do with life. History is the pilgrimage of a person, the journey of a people, the vicissitudes of a nation. Because life is coded, history must be coded too. This is how Isaiah saw the imminent attack of the enemy forces. That is why he brought his son with him, a son with the code name A-Remnant-Shall-Return.

This theological way led to a political way. Isaiah counseled Ahaz: Do not ask for military help from Assyria; that would be disastrous. Do not be afraid! Be firm in your faith in God! With that Isaiah gave his theological interpretation of that particular historical happening:

> This shall not happen, and never shall,
> for all that the chief city of Aram is Damascus,
> and Rezin is the chief of Damascus;
> within sixty-five years
> Ephraim shall cease to be a nation,
> for all that Samaria is the chief city of Ephraim,
> and Remaliah's son the chief of Samaria.
> Have firm faith, or you will not stand firm [Isa. 7:7–9].

This is a marvelous combination of theological and political insight. The Assyrian King Tiglath-pileser would invade Syria and Israel anyway, with or without Judah. By rejecting Isaiah's call to faith, Ahaz lost his independence and became in effect a vassal to Assyria not only in political terms but also in religious terms. He and his political leaders were not able to understand the meaning that was within history but also transcended history. They failed to grasp the hope of A-Remnant-Shall-Return in the struggle for survival.

History is not mere facts. History is not mere chronology. It is not the past and nothing more, the past that one cannot do anything about. History has life. It is alive with meanings that defy the past, transcend the present, and envision the future. History is not to be memorized but to be interpreted. It is not just to be remembered but to be understood. It is not finished at any point in time but is created and re-created. History is the movement of life—life emerging from the dark past, struggling to live the present, and striving for fulfillment. And it is the task of theology to grasp, understand, and nurture this life within history. A theologian, must then, be an interpreter of history.

Politicians view history differently. For them history is a record of political maneuverings. It is an accumulation of political successes and failures. That is why they play *Realpolitik,* politics based on cold calculation of gains and losses in the struggle for power. For prophets such as Isaiah politics must be pursued with faith— not with faith in military power but faith in God's power.

Rulers, particularly those who practice totalitarian politics, have an illusion that they have the power to create history. Listen to these words Isaiah put into the mouth of Sargon, the Assyrian king who conquered Israel and made it disappear from history in 721 B.C.:

> Are not my officers all kings?
> See how Calno has suffered the fate of Carchemish.
> Is not Hamath like Arpad, and Samaria like Damascus? . . .
> By my own might I have acted
> and in my wisdom I have laid my schemes;
> I have removed the frontiers of nations
> and plundered their treasures,
> like a bull I have trampled on their inhabitants.
> My hand has found its way to the wealth of nations,
> and as a man takes the eggs from a deserted nest,
> so have I taken every land;
> not a wing fluttered,
> not a beak gasped, no chirp was heard [Isa. 10:8–9, 13–14].

These words are ominously modern. They express power in its most fearful, destructive, and antihuman form.

History taken as the arena of power politics has no code beyond that of brute power. History created out of a power struggle carries no sign beyond that of naked power. History written out of the barrel of a gun comports no symbol pointing to a meaning beyond itself. The appearance of the prophet Isaiah with his son, A-Remnant-Shall-Return, witnesses to the history that is not mere brute, naked power. As such a witness he was a theologian of history. The prophets in ancient Israel were all, without exception, theologians of history. Anyone who confronts history as codes, signs, and symbols, and attempts to penetrate the meaning hidden in its core, is a theologian of history. If this is true, then how can any of us engaged in doing theology not be a theologian of history?

Our question is: Is there theology of history in Asia? Have there been persons in our cultures who read history as code and sign? Are there persons who have sensed theological meaning of happenings in their personal lives and in the life of their nation? Or is theology of history confined to the Old Testament and the New Testament? Is it a special insight reserved for Christians and for those influenced by Christian faith one way or another?

We should not try to answer such questions in an abstract way. We must not deal with them on the basis of theological principles and presuppositions inherited from traditional theology. We must search hard in our own histories, letting them speak to us not only historically but theologically. It may be that theology of history—"theological" ways of looking at happenings in one's personal life and in the life of a community—is, to our surprise, already there. We may perceive that a link, a theological link, fashioned by God, the creator of the whole universe, does exist between biblical life and Asian life. Our theology, including of course the full range of theological sub-disciplines, then becomes an exciting effort to decode the codes God has implanted in the lives of Asian peoples and in the histories of Asian countries.

Let us go back, for instance, to the end of the third century B.C. when the first Chinese empire, Ch'in, came to a violent end. In the fierce struggle for power two rivals remained to compete for the dragon throne and to decide the fate of the empire. One was the shrewd peasant general Liu Pang; the other was Hsiang Yu, an experienced warrior, son of a general of Ch'u destroyed by Shih Huang Ti, the first emperor of Ch'in. The outcome of the struggle was in Liu Pang's favor. The decisive battle between the two contenders, leading to the downfall of Hsiang Yu, was fought at Kaihsia. Hsiang Yu, besides being a soldier skilled in military art, must have possessed a poetic soul sensitive to the power of destiny at work in the universe. In the moving account in the *Shih-chi* ("Historical Records") by Szuma Chien, the great historian in the second half of the second century B.C., equal in stature to Herodotus of ancient Greece, Hsiang Yu rose to drink in his tent. With him was the lovely Lady Yu, who followed him wherever he went, and Chui, the swift steed that he always rode. Hsiang Yu chanted a tragic air:

> My strength uprooted mountains,
> My spirit overtopped the world;
> But the times are against me,
> And Chui can gallop no more.
> When Chui can gallop no more,
> What can I do?
> And what is to become of Lady Yu?

Hsiang Yu fought his way out of Kaihsia with five thousand enemy horsemen in hot pursuit. He reached the River Wuchiang. The stationmaster there offered him a boat to make his escape. "Heaven is against me," replied Hsiang Yu with a laugh. "What use is it to cross the river?"[1] Then he turned back and plunged into the enemy ranks and died a valiant death.

Is this merely heroism of a brave warrior to be admired and sung again and again in verse by later generations? Is this only the tragic end of a great general to be immortalized in Chinese theaters? It is much more than that. "Heaven is against me," said Hsiang Yu. Even a fearless warrior such as Hsiang Yu had Heaven to contend with. And he knew the time had come for him to submit to the will of Heaven. Was this not his *theo*-logical understanding of history? Was it not his *theo*-logy of destiny?

Not only Hsiang Yu, but most Chinese in ancient times saw the meaning of history in terms of the will of Heaven. This was the code by which they evaluated the rise and fall of dynasties. This was a sign by which they interpreted the vicissitudes of their nation. And this was a symbol of which they understood the meaning and place of their lives within the space-time of China. Reverence for the will of Heaven created a deep spirituality in them. It fostered a profound sense of destiny. It also imbued in certain historians, scholars, and statesmen a prophetic spirit similar to that found in ancient Israel, defying tyranny, demanding justice, at the risk of their lives. Is it not our task as Christian theologians to explore—theologically—stories such as this in our own countries? Will it not enrich our understanding of biblical faith? Will it not deepen our ability to decode the codes of history whose Lord, we believe, is our God?

GOD-IS-WITH-US

Earlier I said that a theological way makes an impact on a political way, witnessing to signs that point to future meanings of the historical present. To do theology, in fact, is to gain the ability to be witnesses of such signs. No matter what branch of theology is your main concern and no matter what you do to become competent in it, your efforts must lead you to a theological understanding of the life and history of your own country, and you must be able to relate that understanding to your faith derived from the Christian Bible. Our theology must have enough room for the world of Asia as well as for the world of the Bible. It must have enough space for histories of Asian countries as well as the history of Israel and the history of the Christian church.

To return to the story of the encounter between Isaiah the prophet and Ahaz, king of Judah, we observed earlier that a political way as a rule bars a theological way. A political way does not deal with codes and signs. It deals with alignment of powers. It does not look toward the future but is preoccupied with the present. It is concerned with political parties and not with individuals who may nonetheless break into the political scene. This is as true in our world today as it was in the world of Isaiah many centuries ago. For Ahaz, Isaiah's son with the name A-Remnant-Shall-Return had nothing to do with the critical situation of his kingdom. It had no meaning for the national crisis. For Ahaz it was no time for codes and signs. It was a time for greater military strength, for more military help, for more armaments.

But Isaiah did not give up easily. The theologian Isaiah pressed the politician Ahaz further. "Ask the Lord your God for a sign," he demanded, "from lowest Sheol or from the highest heaven" (Isa. 7:10). What more can one ask of God? From Sheol to heaven and from heaven to Sheol! This covers the entire universe. This is the whole of creation. Even Sheol, that mysterious abyss of the creation, can be summoned from its depth to render service. Heaven, the height beyond the reach of mortals, can be called down to render help. Sheol and heaven, the infinite space beyond the limits of human imagination—if they are on your side, Ahaz, why are you afraid of Rezin of

Damascus and Pekah of Samaria, those two "smoldering stumps of firewood" (7:4)?

By calling to Sheol and invoking heaven, Isaiah put God on the line. The welfare of Judah is God's welfare. Its life and death is God's life and death. Its future is God's future. At stake is not just the kingdom of Judah. At stake is God, the creator of heaven and Sheol. The entire creation is at one's service. Even God is ready to be a sign for the survival of the people. Even God is there as a sign of hope "for the asking." Can there be a clearer sign than this sign? Is there a sign more assuring than this sign?

The history of a nation thus becomes related to God. The crisis of a people is God's crisis. This is how the prophets in ancient Israel understood the history of their nation. This is how they interpreted the struggle of their people. From the exodus to the exile, from Moses to Ezra and Nehemiah, no historical happening was theologically neutral. Whether kings liked it or not, whether governors and generals wanted it or not, God did not leave Judah alone. The political way had always to reckon with the theological way. Kings and rulers could not do without prophets and theologians urging them to ask for a sign as deep as Sheol or as high as heaven.

Judah was a nation closely bound with Yahweh its God. It was a nation that had to do with God at each and every turn. But is Asia any different? Does it not have to do with God as Judah had? Are the nations in Asia left alone by God to forge their own destiny? Can we not find theological ways in them? Is their historical coursing purely and simply political? Christian thinkers in Asia can no longer put off answering such questions.

How are such questions to be answered? On the basis of some preconceived principles? Using the concepts and framework of traditional theology? Such a conceptual approach will not enable us to detect signs of God in Asia. Such a propositional method will not get us near to the depth of the spirit of Asians who have never lived outside the presence and care of God. We must go to the roots of our own nation. We must search the history of our own people. We must become part of the historical dramas entered into by our Asian brothers and sisters. Then we may be able, like Isaiah, to point to the signs of God's presence in the long history of our own nation in the past, in the present, and also in the future.

Mahatma Gandhi, for instance, was such a sign of God to the people of India in their struggle for political independence. Gandhi called his political movement Satyagraha (from *satya,* meaning "truth," "love," "God"), the movement of "the force which is born of truth and love."[2] Armed with faith in love-force and truth-force, Gandhi led his people to independence by way of *ahimsa* (nonviolence). In Gandhi we find a political way determined by a theological way. Politics deals with power. But that power does not have to be brutal, naked power. It can be, and has to be, truth-power and love-power. It was Gandhi, a Hindu, who demonstrated this. It is small wonder that he was able to say:

For me, there is no politics without religion—not the religion of superstition and the blind religion that hates and fights but the universal religion of tolerance.[3]

Religious force behind political force must be the force of tolerance. Tolerance here is not compromise in the matter of truth and love. Far from it. The religious force of tolerance is that of "trusting one's opponent in spite of betrayals."[4] It would be a humbling experience for a Christian theologian to reexamine the history of Israel, particularly in the period of the conquest of Palestine, in the light of Gandhi's politico-religious basis of *ahimsa.* It would also be a sobering experience to study conflicts of religions on that basis. How mistaken Christians have often been in their understanding of the Asian spirit of tolerance on the ground of their exclusive claim to God's truth! The faith that underlines Gandhi's politics is a faith that does not hate one's enemies, that does not fight them with physical force or with divine wrath. This is one of the reasons why Gandhi was profoundly fascinated by the Jesus portrayed in the Sermon on the Mount and not by the Jesus preached by doctrinaire Christians.

Who is then the God of Gandhi? This is what he said:

I recognize no God except the God that is to be found in the hearts of dumb millions. They do not recognize His presence, I do. And I worship the God that is Truth which is God through the service of these millions.[5]

Does this not sound familiar to us Asian Christians? Is this not the very heart of "people theology"?

People theology or popular theology was not invented by us Asian theologians. It was there before us. It has been always in the hearts of millions of Indians, hundreds of millions of Asians. If popular theology has to be invented by a handful of Christian thinkers, then it is no longer theology of the people. The most fundamental thing about popular theology is that the people, the masses, the undertrodden, are *theo*-logical beings. They are human beings with whom God dwells. God is in "the hearts of dumb millions," as Gandhi put it. Gandhi found God in the hearts of silent millions in India and Gandhi served that God. Is he not a sign of God for us Christians also—a sign that God is with us, that God is with struggling humanity in Asia?

And it is that God who was with the people of Judah when faced with personal and national danger. The refusal of Ahaz the king to ask for a sign did not deter Isaiah. If the king would not ask for it, the prophet must give it. And there came from his mouth these stirring words:

The Lord himself shall give you a sign: A young woman is with child, and she will bear a son, and will call him Immanuel [7:14].

These are dramatic words, words that come from the intense interaction between deep faith and a historical crisis. But who was the woman the prophet pointed out here? Was she his own wife? Was she one of the king's consorts? Was she one of the prominent ladies in the audience? Or was she all mothers-to-be in Judah? One can guess on and on. We shall never be able to identify the pregnant woman Isaiah referred to, but we cannot fail to grasp the meaning of the code name of the child to be born. Immanuel was to be the child's name. God-is-with-us was the name the child was destined to carry for the beleaguered nation. What a code! What a sign! Who can exhaust its meaning?

Life without Immanuel is an illusion. It comes from nowhere and goes nowhere. It drifts like an abandoned ship in a vast ocean. It has no home. It has no destination. History is a terror without God-is-with-us. It is an eternal darkness devouring all truth, goodness, and beauty. But life is God-is-with-us. History is Immanuel. That is why in Asia we also have Gautama Buddha, Mo Ti, Shinran, Gandhi. That is why we have those who, Christians or not, fight for human rights, strive for freedom and democracy, in Asia. Immanuel is an enormous sign for us in Asia, as it was for the people of Judah in the days of Isaiah the prophet. A crucial task of Christian theology is to identify signs of Immanuel in Asian history and culture, and wrestle with them in the life and history of the "silent millions." This is Immanuel theology, God-is-with-us theology.

SIGNS OF THE TIMES

Theology does not deal with mere phenomena, whether personal, historical, cultural, or religious. It asks the theological meaning of phenomena—the meaning of Immanuel in the world, the meaning of God-is-with-us in history. This is essentially the way the Bible was written. And this must be essentially the way our theology is done. Phenomena can be signs for those who have the theological eye to see them, the theological ear to hear them, and the theological mind to comprehend them. If this is what theology is about, it can never be dull, for phenomena that encounter us as signs are never dull. There cannot be a dull theology. Nor is theology an academic discipline mechanically controlled by logical reasoning, for phenomena, especially those related to God's ways with humanity, are not bound by our logic. Theology that seeks to interpret God's ways in the world will not forestall God by its own logic. It is prepared for bewilderment, surprise, and wonder. There can only be humble and yet exciting theology.

It is not without good reason that Jesus talked about the signs of the times. As usual it was one of those debates Jesus' opponents engaged him in. They were the Pharisees and Sadducees, the religious leaders of the day. They "came, and to test him they asked him to show them a sign from heaven" (Matt. 16:1–4). Yes, those religious teachers also talked about a sign. They could not have been serious about it, could they? A sign with deep theological meaning cannot become the object of testing. It refuses to disclose God-meaning through debate.

A sign ceases to be a sign when put on a theological table to be dissected and dismembered. A sign must be grasped as a whole. It must be apprehended from all possible angles. A sign is not historical, cultural, and religious in three or more separate parts. It is historical, cultural, and religious as a unit. In our traditional theological endeavors we have made a serious error here. We have divided theology into several disciplines and departments without close, internal bondings. History is one thing. Then there are biblical studies. There is also systematic theology, as if there might be such a thing as "unsystematic" theology. It is not better even when it is called dogmatics. Then there is practical theology, almost implying that historical studies, biblical studies, and studies in dogmatics, are not practical. There is of course ethics also, having little direct connection with studies in other disciplines. This has been the theology we inherited from the past and still teach in our theological schools.

How can we restore unity, integrity, and wholeness to theology? This is an urgent question. The answer to it must be found, if we are serious about signs with God-meaning—meaning that can be disclosed to us only when signs are not treated as dismembered entities.

Jesus knew what his opponents were after. He said to them: "When it is evening, you say, 'It will be fair weather; for the sky is red.' And in the morning, 'It will be stormy today, for the sky is red and threatening' " (Matt. 16:2–3a, RSV). Jesus read their minds correctly. By "a sign from heaven" they meant nothing but a weather forecast. They were not asking a *theological* question. What they asked was a meteorological question. They did not have to come to Jesus for an answer to their meteorological questions. They should have gone to a weather forecaster, or a sky gazer. Jesus was not a weather forecaster. He was a forecaster of God's reign. Natural phenomena as such were not his concern. He concerned himself chiefly with divine-human dramas played out in the arena of life and history.

Jesus continued: "You know how to interpret the appearance of the sky, but you cannot interpret the signs of the times" (16:3b, RSV). In his answer Jesus brought out a striking contrast. No one could have missed it. On the one hand there was a sign from heaven or the appearance of the sky. There was on the other hand a sign of the times. As far as the appearance of the sky was concerned, Jesus conceded that his opponents could be expert interpreters. When the sky was red in the evening, they could accurately predict that there would be fine weather the next day. When the sky looked red and threatening in the morning, they could tell without fail that a storm was approaching. But when it came to the signs of the times, they were completely out of their depths. They could not even recognize them, let alone interpret them.

What, then, are the signs of the times that Jesus was talking about? They have nothing to do with the appearance of the sky. The signs of the times *(semeia ton kairon)* are something entirely different. They have nothing to do with heaven and sky. They have to do with God and humanity. They are historical dramas filled with divine-human meanings. They have to be seen, heard, and grasped by a theologically sensitive mind. They are to be faced with reverence and awe, not with carelessness and absent-mindedness.

It is important to notice that the Greek word *kairos* instead of *chronos* was used in the account of the signs of the times. *Chronos* is an extension of time, a period of time. It is physical time. It is a unit we use to measure the passage of time. *Chronos* ticks away of itself, entirely oblivious of us. It tells us seasons, years, months, weeks, hours, seconds, not expecting any response from us and regardless of our feelings. Friends who have not seen each other for twenty years say: "Oh, your hair has turned gray!" There is a lot of emotion in that exclamation. There is much tender feeling in it. And there is in it a complex reaction to the change in the person with the gray hair. But *chronos* is not interested in our emotion, feelings, and reactions. It continues its course as if it did not hear our exclamation, as if we did not exist. This is *chronos.* We need it to tell the time, but it does not need us.

It is not the word *chronos* but the word *kairos* that is used here. *Kairos* is also time, but a special kind of time. *Kairos* overlaps with *chronos,* but it changes it from physical time to personal time. *Kairos* is *our* time, the time that has to do with our personal life. It tells us that the gray hair on our head is a reminder of our human finitude. It says to us that after we have done our duty, we must leave the rest to God.

There is a famous verse in Psalm 90:

> The years of our life are
> threescore and ten,
> or even by reason of strength
> fourscore;
> yet their span is but toil and trouble;
> they are soon gone, and we fly away [v. 10, RSV].

Years filled with toil and trouble—this is our *kairos,* our personal time. Our prayer must then be like that of the psalmist: "So teach us to number our days that we may get a heart of wisdom" (90:12, RSV).

Kairos, further, is an appointed time, time that does not just come and go but has a purpose, time that will be remembered for the serious consequences it brings. This was the time Ezekiel, for example, was referring to when he said:

> Behold, the day! the doom is here, it has burst upon them. Injustice buds, insolence blossoms, violence shoots up into injustice and wickedness. And it is all their fault, the fault of their turmoil and tumult and all their restless ways. The time has come, the day has arrived; the buyer has no reason to be glad, and the seller none to regret [Ezek. 7:10–12].

Ezekiel was probably speaking to the inhabitants of Jerusalem at a time of crisis when the news reached them that the Babylonian king, Nebuchadrezzar, was approaching with his army. The day of reckoning had come. The time of national catastrophe had arrived. That day and that time was not coming of itself. It was brought about by violence and injustice in Judah.

What was true in Ezekiel's time was also true in Jesus' time. Religion had become oppressive for the masses of the people. And those restless under the Roman rule were resorting to physical force to reverse the fortunes of the nation. It was a time filled with signs and portents, but the Pharisees and Sadducees were asking about a sign from heaven. They were testing Jesus about the appearance of the sky. He must have experienced extreme pain in his heart. Here was Jesus, the very sign of the times—Jesus appointed by God to play a decisive role in human history—but the religious leaders were not aware that the appointed time had come. They did not realize that they were confronting in Jesus the decisive time of God. *Kairos* eluded them.

3

Portents of Our Day

I AM BECOME DEATH, DESTROYER OF WORLDS

If what has just been said was true in Ezekiel's time, and in Jesus' time, can it also be true in our time? The fact is that it is perhaps *more* true in our time. In our world today there are powerful signs of the times for us to see, read, and interpret. There are portents of our day challenging Christian thinkers to bring all biblical scholarship, theological insight, and historical sensitivity to bear on them.

The portent of an apocalyptic dimension in our day is the threat of a nuclear war. It was in 1945 that the United States detonated the first atom bomb, at Alamogordo, New Mexico. "Stunned and horrified by what he and his fellow scientists had wrought . . . physicist J. Robert Oppenheimer recalled the incantations of the Hindu god Vishnu as he transformed himself into the avatar of [the] apocalypse: 'I am become death, the destroyer of worlds.' "[1] It is a strange coincidence, surely, that the Hindu god Vishnu became the decoder of the fatal meaning of nuclear weaponry for human survival, even for the survival of Mother Earth—weapons of death that took their origin in a nation that still uses money bearing the motto: In God We Trust.

It is an ominous portent, this power released from the atom and embodied in nuclear weapons. According to the "Comprehensive Study on Nuclear Weapons," a report of the secretary-general of the United Nations in 1980:

> The exact number of nuclear warheads in the world is probably not known by any single person or institution, and estimates cannot be verified officially. Published figures indicate, however, that the total may be in excess of 40,000. In explosive power these warheads are reported to range from about 100 tons up to more than 20 million tons equivalent of chemical high explosive. The largest weapon ever tested released an energy approximately 4,000 times that of the atomic bomb that levelled Hiroshima, and there is in principle no upper limit to the explosive yield that may be attained. The total strength of present nuclear arsenals may

> be equivalent to about 1 million Hiroshima bombs, i.e., some 13,000 million tons of TNT. It is often pointed out that this is equivalent to more than 3 tons for every man, woman, and child on the earth. The arsenals of the United States and the Soviet Union contain most of these weapons, with the known remainder belonging to China, France, and the United Kingdom.[2]

Just imagine three tons of TNT for each person on earth—for you and me! And think of the real possibility of that horrifying amount of destructive power exploding over the head of each man, woman, and child—over your head and mine! Confronted with such a monster let out from the nucleus of the atom, can Christians go on calmly reciting the ancient creed of Nicea as if no major change has occurred between the world of the fourth century and the world of the twentieth century? Can theologians coolly continue debating how divine nature and human nature can become united in Jesus Christ—as if the world would be spared a nuclear holocaust until they have debated the question to their hearts' content? When the world lives under the shadow of nuclear destruction, such faith is irrelevant and such theology is unethical.

The time for doing theology in a leisurely fashion is over. The day of indulging in speculation about the existence of God for days on end is gone. Whether we like it or not, we now live in a nuclear time whose distinctive characteristic is speed:

> The speed of the nuclear reactions is enormous. Both in a fission and a fusion explosive, the entire nuclear energy is released in about one millionth of a second. With today's technique, it is thus possible to release by one weapon more energy in one microsecond than that from all conventional weapons in all wars of history.[3]

Is this literally true, or is it an exaggeration? The word "exaggeration" does not exist in the dictionary used by scientists. It is really formidable, this monstrous power of the atom. In one millionth of a second, in one *micro*second, not even in one second, more energy can be released by one nuclear weapon than that from all conventional weapons in all the wars of history.

Translated into more graphic terms, what is likely to happen is something like this: "If . . . most of the weapons on both sides [i.e., the United States and the Soviet Union] were to be exploded, the earth would momentarily flicker back at the distant stars—and then perhaps go out, the very life of the planet extinguished."[4] For those of us who are Christians, does this not at once bring to our mind the apocalyptic picture of the end of the world depicted in that strange book of Revelation, the last book of the Bible? The seer on the island called Patmos saw in a vision:

> the seventh angel pour his bowl on the air; and out of the sanctuary came a loud voice from the throne, which said, "It is over!" And there

> followed flashes of lightning and peals of thunder, and a violent earthquake, like none before it in human history, so violent it was. The great city was split in three; the cities of the world fell in ruin [Rev. 16:17–19].

Two thousand years after the seer had this nerve-wracking vision, the world is faced with the destruction and disappearance of planet Earth. Will it be our fate to hear a loud voice from the throne saying: "It is over!"?

How do we do theology under this portentous sign of the nuclear destruction of the world? How do we talk theologically about human history? How are we to understand the "holy war" justified in our traditional theology when applied to the Hebrew tribes in their conquest of the land of promise? And what is the mission and task of the Christian church in a world confronted with an apocalyptic end as a real possibility?

Theology in this nuclear age of ours must be done with apocalyptic urgency. We cannot have horrified scientists, news-hungry journalists, and a worried world public do theology for us. We must do theology with them, and together with them search for a God-meaning in all this. The time of doing theology only for the church, and within the church, is over. The church continues to be central in our doing of theology, but not the church as a safe enclave in an unsafe world; not a church that monopolizes access to God's salvation, but a church that emulates God's ways with all humankind; not a church petrified by its own traditions and orthodoxy, but a church ready to relinquish outdated traditions and dream new dreams. Theology within this kind of church will be an exciting adventure. This nuclear age of ours is challenging us to bring this kind of theology into the world.

Theology of the nuclear age has made its belated appearance on the world scene today in different forms. Christians have begun to insert their interpretation of the portent of the atomic power into the rising tide of antinuclear movements. One example is the Christian wing of Mobilization for Survival launched in the United States in 1977. In a "pastoral letter" in 1978 its members declared:

> Sisters and brothers . . . the nuked conscience of political, military, and economic interests has seized on the lives of our people; with astonishing arrogance—it would seize on the sovereignty of our God. The spirit of money, the spirit of violence, symbolized in the boiling frenzy of nuclear weaponry, mocks the spirit of the Lord, blasphemously anoints not the servants of the Lord but the nuclear idols and their benighted adorers. They bring bad news to the poor, they proclaim enslavement of the free, they inflict blindness on insightful people, they tread underfoot the freedoms of all, they proclaim a demonic Year of the Neutron.[5]

The language is too religiously eloquent, too traditionally rhetorical, too theologically metaphorical and fundamentalistic. "The nuked conscience seizes upon the sovereignty of God." What does this mean? Is God still sovereign if God's sovereignty can be seized by anyone and by anything, even by the nuked conscience? But what does God's sovereignty mean in our time? Is God sovereign because God is like a king or emperor sitting on a throne, served by ministers and court officials in fear and trembling? And how can the spirit of the Lord be mocked by the spirit of money and violence?

Obviously this kind of language comes from the traditional interpretation of the story of the fall in Genesis 3 and the story of the tower of Babel in Genesis 11. There the end of human ignorance and innocence is supposed to be the result of human pride wanting to know everything, like God, and the division of one people into the different ethnic strains and language groups is taken as God's punishment on our ancestors for their pride—again the concept of pride, hubris—in wanting to build a tower that would reach to heaven.[6] Such traditional interpretations must be reviewed and challenged in the light of modern biblical exegesis. And this applies not only to these two well-known Old Testament stories; it applies to most of our inherited understanding of stories in the Bible. Let a new hermeneutical era begin!

But the message of this "pastoral letter" is strikingly contemporary. It proposes an end to nuclear weapons and the arms race. But it goes further. It relates the escalation of nuclear weaponry to poverty, militarism, and violation of human rights, especially in Third World countries. The chain of cause and effect here is both subtle and cruel. The world is not only involved externally in the process of destroying its own habitat. It also undergoes internal erosion of human relationships through ruthless economic exploitation and violent manipulation of the human person. Is it, then, not logical that the theology of antinuclear power should develop into theology against poverty, theology against militarism, and theology against the violation of human rights? Will such theologies not pose for us many questions that are not dealt with in traditional theology? Will they not compel us to look at our Bible in a new way, enabling us to appreciate the relationship between the life we live and the faith we believe, between theology and ethics, and between the world of the Bible and the world of Asia?

Political cartoonists are delightful artists. Under their pen the world of politics becomes populated with presidents and prime ministers depicted at their most vulnerable. It must be the envy of learned political analysts. With their simple lines that make politicians of world fame dance on a tightrope, they make political satire that outmatches that of accomplished political essayists. And the profound humor of their cartoons, carrying a message of hope in this dangerous world of geopolitics, is more eloquent than many learned writings on political theology.

Consider a cartoon (Fig. 1) depicting a diminutive President Reagan, a gun strapped on each side of his waist as in a western movie, standing between two gigantic nuclear bombs. One bomb has a grim angry face with a black hat on top, representing the Soviet Union, and the other with a smiling face wearing a white hat, standing for the United States. And this is what that personable Reagan is saying in the cartoon: "The bad guys have tricked some of you sincere, well-intentioned folks! C'mon, root for the white hats!! It's the American way."[7]

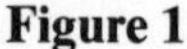

Figure 1

The question that at once comes to my mind is: Who is tricking whom? The answer seems to be: Reagan is tricking himself, because he is a prisoner of his own simplistic, one-track worldview fostered by his anticommunist ideology. Another question: Who is the good guy and who is the bad guy? For Reagan the answer is as clear as day on the basis of his Christian faith nourished in his Sunday school days and reinforced in the make-believe world of western movies. But the line between good and bad disappears when both the United States and the Soviet Union are in possession of nuclear warheads sufficient to blow up Mother Earth. The cartoon then hits you with a dreadful thought: a bomb that has the horrendous power to destroy the world looks innocuous standing beside the personable president. That bomb with a smiling face made in the USA appears personable too. And to confound the public further, Reagan calls his one hundred huge new MX (Missile Experimental) intercontinental ballistic missiles "Peacemakers." What a sad irony!

All this and much more is contained in that simple cartoon. There is a lot of politics in it. There is a lot of wisdom in it. And above all, there is a lot of theology in it. Without wasting any words, the simple cartoon brings home to us the message that we live in a world of a possible nuclear war from which no one would survive, no one would come out a winner. It forces us to look into the nature of the power we humans have acquired. It compels us to ponder deeply the destiny of humankind. And it prompts us to grasp the meaning of God's salvation not in black and white terms, not in good-guy and bad-guy logic, and not in Christian and non-Christian dogmatic.

We have a lot to learn from good political cartoonists. They are seers of our time. They are our "secular" prophets. It is about time we had theology based on political cartoons. Or even better, it is time we had theological cartoonists—theologians who can expose what is in the heart of humanity in humor, in passion, and in tears. We Asians, with our long history of suffering and with the ability to swallow bitterness without losing hope, seem particularly cut out to be theological cartoonists.

There is another reason why political cartoons are important for theology. They are a sign language signifying human dramas in the political world. They are the codes into which cartoonists pack their perception of the reality that confronts human community. In a sense they speak a kind of apocalyptic language that we come across in the Christian Bible—in the book of Daniel, the so-called "little apocalypse" in Mark 13:5–37, and above all in the book of Revelation. They were written not in plain language. Nor were they written to be read at face value. They were written to be perused, pondered, explored, interpreted, and understood in the light of the historical dramas taking place around them. That is why in the middle of that "little apocalypse" in Mark's Gospel where "the abomination of desolation" is mentioned, it is said in parenthesis: "Let the reader understand" (13:14). Understand the reader must. Decipher the reader must. And the author of the book of Revelation says at the very beginning: "Happy is the person who reads, and happy those who listen to the words of this prophecy and heed what is written in it" (1:3). It must be read and listened to with heeding, for what one finds there are earthly matters in unearthly language.

There is another cartoon that brings our thought closer to home in Asia (see page 36). The central figure in the cartoon is Deng Xiaoping, the strong man of China. Deng the political acrobat is balancing his small but stocky body with one leg on the seat of a tiny tricycle. In this balancing act his arms are spread wide, his right hand clutching an oversized dove with an olive branch in its beak and these words written on its chest: "goodwill (govt to govt)," and his left hand gripping a rifle with these words on its butt: "party to party." Tugged behind the tricycle is a placard: "BKK-KL-SIN Tour." The caption in block letters reads: "Of course, the left hand doesn't know what the right hand's doing." A little bird sitting at the bottom corner on the right chirps: "That's having his cake and eating it!"[8]

Deng was on his Southeast Asia tour in 1978. He visited Bangkok (BKK), Kuala Lumpur (KL), and Singapore (SIN), bringing the good will of his government to the capitals of these Asian nations. Hence that huge dove with an olive branch. He came to bring peace, not war. He promised good neighborliness, not hostility. He assured the peoples of these countries that China stood for national integrity, not for hegemony. But the leaders of the nations he visited were not so sure. For it is no secret that communist parties active in these

OF COURSE, THE LEFT HAND DOESN'T KNOW WHAT THE RIGHT HAND'S DOING.

Figure 2

countries have strong ties with the Chinese Communist Party, receiving material and military aid from it. In Kuala Lumpur, the prime minister of Malaysia, Datuk Hussein Onn, told his visitor: "Malaysia in particular would like to be left alone in peace, free from any form of interference, subversion, or incitement." In Singapore Prime Minister Lee Kuan Yew stressed that "Chinese and Singaporean Chinese were different peoples, that those in Singapore 'are in the midst of ensuring a separate and durable future for themselves in South East Asia.' "[9]

The message is loud and clear. The Chinese policy of good will from the Chinese government and subversion from the Chinese Communist Party will not work. Overseas Chinese in Southeast Asia owe their loyalty to the countries of their adoption. They are Thai Chinese, Singaporean Chinese, Malaysian Chinese. And as Lee Kuan Yew forcefully puts it, they and the Chinese in China are different peoples. This must be the basis of the foreign policy of China toward Southeast Asian nations. Deng and the leaders in Peking must know that it is wrong for their left hand not to know what their right hand is doing, and for their right hand not to know what their left hand is doing. It is nothing but a political pretense of the first order that either hand does not know what the other hand is doing.

The caption of the cartoon—"The left hand doesn't know what the right hand's doing"—comes of course from the New Testament: "When you do some act of charity, do not let your left hand know what your right is doing" (Matt. 6:3). Jesus was talking about doing good, not about doing *Realpolitik*. And Jesus was warning that advertising an act of charity is a self-defeating thing. It becomes charity to its doer and not to its recipient. It becomes corrupted by arrogance, by desire for respect and acknowledgment in society. The person at the receiving end of charity becomes a mere means to your own self-aggrandizement, a tool of your self-promotion. Your charity is then a demeaning act. It is an insult to those in need of help. It deprives them of human dignity. It destroys their personhood. Hence Jesus' admonition: "No; when you do some act of charity, do not let your left hand know what your right is doing."

Fearing that his listeners may not have fully understood him, Jesus added: "Your good deed must be secret, and your Father who sees what is done in secret will reward you." What is God's reward, then? God's reward is the persons themselves—the persons to whom you have done some good deed, the ones who have regained the ability to live in this difficult world, have their confidence in humanity restored, and their faith in God strengthened.

In the world of *Realpolitik* there can be no such thing as the left hand not knowing what the right hand is doing, and vice versa. This is a blatant political lie. The foreign policy of a powerful nation based on such a lie only brings about endless political struggles in other nations and creates a perpetual state of fear, suspicion, and unrest in the whole world. The cartoon is saying that China, or for that matter, any nation, must stop such deceptive conduct in relation to other nations. It is a plea to mind the welfare of other peoples and not regard them as objects of one's own ideological expansion.

The political cartoon we have been considering gives us another kind of thought and insight when applied to the domestic political scenes in most of the countries in Asia. The caption must then be slightly changed. It should read: "Of course, the left hand knows what the right hand's doing." Is this not the case in the autocratic nations in Asia? In these countries government and party are one and the same. Government is party and party is government. The good will of the government is the good will of the party. The ideology of the party is the ideology of the government. The dove and the rifle work together to coerce obedience, to force political opposition into silence, and to put advocates of human rights into prison. The party dictates what the government must do. And party loyalty is required of all those who aspire to positions in the government. Government and party are just two names for one and the same thing. This solidarity of government and party continues to be the fundamental malaise that makes political health impossible in most Asian countries.

Here our political theology must be based on the difference between the right hand and the left hand. It must affirm that government and party are not the same thing. A government has to be elected by the people and is accountable to the people and not to the party to which those in power happen to belong. For the health of the nation, governments must come and go. For periodic change of government to be possible, there must be more than one active, full-fledged political party. One-party rule destroys the very basis of government, the basis rooted in the will of the people. Here again in the heart of political theology is the people. Political cartoons can give us clues as to the kind of political system justifiable from the standpoint of political theology.

KAIROS IN ASIA

Our world is full of signs of the times and portents of the day. Political cartoonists can catch the present of these signs and portents with the ingenious use of their pen. The present captured in a cartoon is a kairotic present—a present that affects the life of a people, the destiny of a nation. Each nation and each people can look back into the past for such a kairotic present—or more than one. They can also look forward into the future for such a kairotic present. History becomes intelligible because of a kairotic present. It is on its account that we remember our past, do not despair in the face of present adversity, and continue to hope for a better future. And for this reason we go on investing in history the best we have, envisioning the fulfillment of what we hold to be true, good, and beautiful. In this way we live in history with faith. With courage we create history. And we dedicate history to God who brings it to its ultimate destination.

Israel, as we know from the Old Testament, had a kairotic time in the middle of the thirteenth century B.C. What made that time in history of Israel kairotic was, of course, the exodus. A group of Hebrew slaves made good their escape from Egypt, the land of their oppressors. For them it was not just another historical experience. It was a divine miracle. It was the triumph of their God over their enemy. The short but exuberant song of Miriam, Moses' sister, said it all: "Sing to the Lord, for he has risen up in triumph; the horse and his rider he has hurled into the sea" (Exod. 15:21).

The exodus remained *the* kairotic event throughout the subsequent history of Israel. It is to that time of the exodus that succeeding generations of Israelites went back in memory from time to time, renewing their faith in God and hoping for God's deliverance in the critical times of their nation. It is small wonder that in the very heart of the famous Shema, the soul of Old Testament faith—Hear, O Israel: The Lord our God is one Lord . . . (Deut. 6:4–7), we find the exodus remembered. When the Israelites finally were settled in the land of promise, they must "be careful not to forget the Lord who brought you out of Egypt, out of the land of slavery" (6:12). The role played by the exodus in their faith cannot be underestimated. One would only wish that they were also able to appreciate the spirit of the exodus at work in other nations and peoples.

If the history of Israel began with a kairotic event, it also came to an end with no less than a kairotic event, but tragic in contrast to the exodus. The kingdom of Israel came to an end in 721 B.C. and that of Judah in 582 B.C., unable to withstand Assyrian and Babylonian invasions. The exile that ensued shattered the dream of the promised land and dispersed the Jews in foreign lands. The lament of those in captivity wrenches even our hearts:

By the rivers of Babylon we sat down and wept
when we remembered Zion.
There on the willow-trees
we hung up our harps,
for there those who carried us off
demanded music and singing,
and our captors called on us to be merry:
"Sing us one of the songs of Zion."
How could we sing the Lord's song
in a foreign land? [Ps. 137:1–4].

A tragedy of such magnitude—the end of a nation—gives rise to poetic eloquence. In the heart of tragedy is poetry. Poetry seems to spring from the power that knows how to stimulate the saddened heart to weep, cry, and sing. What a traumatic *kairos*—the exile! Even today pious Jews who have a long memory pay an annual visit to the Wailing Wall in Jerusalem to lament over the Babylonian captivity more than twenty-five hundred years ago.

Israel had its *kairos* years, and all other nations have had them too. The year 1945 was a kairotic year for Asia. World War II, which devastated modern civilization and took countless human lives, came to an end in Asia with the explosion of the first atom bombs in Hiroshima and Nagasaki, dealing a death blow to the ambition of imperial Japan and giving the world a foretaste of the monstrous power of destruction hidden in the heart of the atom. That tragically kairotic year was a watershed in the history of Japan. From being a totalitarian warmongering nation, it became a nation with a democratic system of government.

For other nations in Asia under Western colonial rule, the year 1945 signaled a call to political independence. One nation after another rose up in struggle against its colonial rulers and won back national sovereignty. Indonesia issued its Declaration of Independence on August 17, 1945, ending more than three centuries of Dutch rule. Korea ended the 36-year rule of Japan in 1945, but the country was then partitioned into the south and the north beset with political and ideological tensions and conflicts. The Republic of the Philippines was proclaimed in 1946 after centuries of Spanish domination succeeded by U.S.A. colonialization. In 1947 India recovered its independence. The Union of Burma won its independence in 1948, to be followed in 1962 by the "Burmese Way of Socialism" under the Ne Win government.

As for China, the road to independence was singularly tortuous and bloody. Into the modern history of China is compressed the whole range of tragedies that can befall a nation, the abysmal depth of all human sufferings, and the silent longings of downtrodden peoples. In 1911 the Ching dynasty was overthrown by the revolutionary forces of Sun Yat-sen who established a fragile republic and nominally ended semicolonialism. But the Japanese invasion from Manchuria into the heart of China in 1937 thrust it again into a life-and-death struggle for survival. The whole of China became engulfed in an inferno of human atrocities that brought suffering and death to millions of its citizens. The end of World War II did not end the tragedy of the nation, however; it only gave it a respite. It was soon to be swept into the Civil War between the Nationalist government, which sought desperately to consolidate its power, and the communist forces waging a revolution from the countryside. The devastation wrought on the nation and its people was staggering. Millions of lives were lost in the ruthless Civil War. Finally came 1949, the year in which the People's Republic of China was established under communist rule.

These years, and there are many other years for the nations mentioned and for other Asian nations, are kairotic years. Citizens of each nation cannot look back on those years without their hearts being moved, their emotions stirred, and their souls pained. Those years are years of exodus and exile, deliverance and enslavement, fall and salvation. They are signposts in the history of their nation and in their own life, affecting for better or worse their journey toward the future as individual persons and as communities.

There is so much theology that could be done with those years. But how well do we understand them as part of our own history? How capable are we of giving an account of them in relation to our Christian experience? How well equipped are we theologically to appreciate them in the history of God's involvement in the world? And how much of all this are we able to incorporate into our faith derived from the Bible and appropriated from the history of Christianity? These questions do not instantly yield a new theology. But they compel us to read the Bible again and again, with deep imagination, and to reorientate our theology with courage and foresight.

1997

Our historical perimeter gets narrower and denser as it comes closer to us. It catches us in the middle of it and surrounds us with kairotic portents that will be decisive for life and history in Asia. One of those portents is the year 1997, the year in which the British lease on the New Territories, which accounts for 89 percent of the Hong Kong land area, will expire. The year 1997 has been there all along in black and white in the nineteenth-century treaties that ceded Hong Kong Island and the Kowloon Peninsula to Britain in perpetuity and gave Britain control of the New Territories until 1997. But it was forgotten by all parties involved even before the ink on the treaties became dry. And as time went on, it came to be buried out of sight. In the meantime Hong Kong became a prosperous crown colony, the most enterprising free port in the world. Colonizers and colonized alike, bent on profit and gain, preferred to let the ominous year 1997 remain buried in the depth of the past, wishing it would pass into oblivion forever.

The year 1997 proved to be a genie bottled up but not dead. It had been waiting to burst out of its captivity to startle the world once again. Its time finally came. China recovered from the frenzy of the Cultural Revolution. The ideological fanaticism cultivated by Mao Zedong (Tse-tung) was replaced by the pragmatism of Deng Xiaoping. Technocrats were rehabilitated and ideologues were packed off to reform camps to languish and repent. China has freed itself from self-imposed isolation and set out on a long march of modernization. It has also regained confidence so as to champion the Third World cause. As all this was happening, how could Hong Kong remain unaffected? The genie in the bottle began to stir. To keep Hong Kong bottled up as a British crown colony would be a historical anachronism. To have it remain under British rule is an affront to Chinese sovereignty. The genie finally burst out of the bottle. The year 1997 has become the hottest subject of conversation in private and in public in Hong Kong. Everywhere it is on the lips of the people. It leaps into their eyes as they move about in that small crowded space. It flows into their ears day in and day out.

Nineteen ninety-seven! It is a magic number. It is an ominous year. It is a frightening sign. After 1997 "people in China drive on the right," says the senior Chinese representative in Hong Kong, "but people in Hong Kong would be allowed to continue driving on the left."[10] This is an allusion to Peking's noninterference in the internal affairs of Hong Kong even after China has regained sovereignty over it in 1997. But driving on the left? Does this not make one nervous?

At any rate, who will believe in it? The examples of Tibet and Inner Mongolia as autonomous regions under Chinese sovereignty are neither encouraging nor reassuring. To no surprise of anyone, "an opinion poll [in Hong Kong] showed that a return of the colony to China was 'unacceptable' to 67% of the respondents, and that only 5% of those questioned would accept any change in the status quo."[11] As one Hong Kong businessman put it rather heatedly: "We don't want to be Chinese nationals. We would not accept restrictions on travel, speech, and human rights."[12] So, it is not a matter of economics. Nor is it simply a matter of survival. It is a matter of identity. It is a matter of human rights. Ultimately, it is a matter of self-determination for the people of Hong Kong, the political cause that some Taiwanese Christians have been advocating on the basis of Christian faith—a cause that has drawn objections from and even incurred the wrath of most overseas Chinese, including Hong Kong citizens of Chinese origin.

Nineteen ninety-seven is indeed a huge portent of our day, not only for the people of Hong Kong and for others of Chinese extraction outside China, but also for the world as a whole. It involves the future of the people of Hong Kong. It will have repercussions for Taiwan, where the Taiwanese have been growing restless under Nationalist rule and actively seeking the freedom and democracy that would lead to the self-determination of their political destiny. It has important implications too for peace and security in the Pacific. And what will it mean for the world polarized by ideological orthodoxies and endangered by settlement of political conflicts with more and more sophisticated arms?

Nineteen ninety-seven! This is a code. It challenges us to decipher it with all our theological sensitivity and ingenuity. We recall that Isaiah began his theological reflection on the destiny of Israel in the Jerusalem temple "in the year that King Uzziah died" (Isa. 6:1, RSV). That was 740/739 B.C. Should not theology in Hong Kong have these words in its preface: "In the year 1997 when change in the political situation of Hong Kong is to be effected"? Will 1997 be like a magnifying glass showing us a clearer picture of where history is moving? Will it not help magnify our Bible too, enabling us to discover many details we have not been able to see, and to perceive nuances we have failed to notice?

Each one of us Christians, and in particular theologians, must look for our own 1997 in the history of our nation and in the life of the community to which we belong. We may discover more than one 1997 in it. But the point is that our theology should deeply reflect and decisively act on the kairotic moments of our history. A moment, a year, a time is kairotic because its encounter brings with it signs for the future—signs that may speak to us God's thoughts and disclose to us God's ways.

4

Speaking in Parables

THOSE WHO HAVE EARS TO HEAR

Who does not have ears to hear except those born deaf? Who have ears that do not hear, apart from those who have lost their hearing through illness or old age? But Jesus said to the large crowd that gathered about him: "Those who have ears to hear, let them hear" (Mark 4:9). Was Jesus assuming that there might be some deaf persons in the crowd? Was he worried that some of those listening to him were hard of hearing? Was he making sure that everyone present heard him?

Jesus was not of course referring to the capacity of their auditory organs. He was talking about a special kind of hearing—hearing with the ears, responding with the heart, and understanding with the mind. It is hearing with your entire self, soul and body. You hear, needless to say, with your ears. But Jesus' message does not come home to you through that kind of hearing. Your heart must be all ears. Your soul should also be at the service of your ears. Your mind should be at the service of your ears. Then, only then, can you hear Jesus. Then, only then, can what he says penetrate you. Then, only then, can his words pierce you like a two-edged sword. Are we all ears? Is our theology all ears?

Jesus has just told the crowd the parable of the sower (Mark 4:3–8; par. Matt. 13:3–8; Luke 8:5–8). This is how he began: "Listen! A sower went out to sow" (Mark 4:3). Their interest must have been aroused instantly, for they were familiar with the sight of sowers in the fields. And some of them could well have been sowers themselves. Intently they listened to Jesus, trying to follow every word. Jesus then drew, with his story, a vivid picture of what happened to the seeds the sower was sowing. Some fell on the footpath and were eaten up by birds. Others landed on rocky ground and had their life nipped in the bud. Some seeds fell among thistles and failed to grow. But there were still others, most of the seeds as a matter of fact, that were sown in good soil, sprouted, grew, and bore fruit thirtyfold, sixtyfold, even a hundredfold.

From what we know from the four Gospels, Jesus is a marvelous storyteller.

He does not teach as do most of the rabbis. Jesus has inherited a profound sanity from the Old Testament prophets—the sanity that enabled them to penetrate the surface of everyday things and everyday happenings, and grasp the divine meaning in them. At once the prophet Isaiah comes to our mind. He castigated the ways in which priests and self-styled prophets went about teaching the people:

> . . . it is precept upon precept,
> precept upon precept,
> line upon line, line upon line,
> here a little, there a little [Isa. 28:10, RSV].

Precept upon precept and line upon line! They represent mere sounds, *tsawletsaw tsawletsaw qawleqaw qawleqaw* in Hebrew, not only unintelligible to their listeners but to themselves also.[1] Sounds without meaning—this is what their teaching is. Words not spoken from their hearts—this is all there is to their religion. They use elaborate concepts to impress innocent minds. They heap argument upon argument to prove what they believe is right and what others believe is wrong. Their empty words and hollow sounds are in defense of the traditions that make them secure and earn them a living. Jesus called such religious teachers hypocrites (Matt. 23) and blind guides (Matt. 15:14).

Does our own theology fare any better? Is it intelligible to our audience? Is it intelligible to ourselves? By intelligible I do not mean understandable. Most theological textbooks are intelligible in this sense. They are written in correct grammar. Their syntax is sound. Mobilized in them are "scientific" words and concepts. And they are built on solid traditions of theological scholarship. But still we must ask: Are they intelligible? Does their grammar correspond to God's grammar? Does the compilation of words and concepts reflect God's thoughts and ways? And above all, does the theological syntax emerge from the syntax of everyday life? Is it syntax of the heart? Is it the semantics learned in the depths of the longing soul?

If our theology does not reflect in some way God's grammar, if it does not arise from the syntax of the suffering and longing heart, and if it is not the semantics that touches the agonizing and hoping soul, then our theology is still unintelligible. It is still a theology of precept upon precept and line upon line. It is still just the sound of *tsawletsaw tsawletsaw qawleqaw qawleqaw*. It may satisfy all the criteria of truth laid down for us in traditional theology. It does not, however, satisfy the passion of love with which Jesus went about doing theology with the people.

Jesus had a tremendously important message to proclaim—the message of God's reign. He could have gone back into the history of his nation to find ample evidence to establish whatever credentials anyone might demand to authenticate his mission. It was there written large in the pages of history—the Davidic kingdom that gave the Jews national pride and inspired in them a messianic kingdom of a political nature. In fact even the earliest Christian community went out of its way to trace Jesus' genealogy back to King David (Matt. 1:6; Luke 3:32). And Jesus had to be born in Bethlehem, the city of David (Luke 2:5; Matt. 2:1). His lineage was impeccable. He could have exploited it fully and rekindled messianic hope in the coming of God's kingdom in the form of a Jewish kingdom restored to its power and glory as in the days of King David.

But Jesus did not invoke the ghost of King David. He did not hark back to the good old days in the history of the nation. Instead, he went to the people—those who toiled in the fields, men who begged in the streets, women who had to swallow a lot of bitterness as victims of social and religious prejudices. Jesus went to those who were crippled, disfigured by disease, or mortally sick. He even went to children, embracing them and saying, "Let the children come to me; do not try to stop them; for the kingdom of heaven belongs to such as these" (Matt. 19:14). His hearers exclaimed, dumbfounded: "A new kind of teaching!" (Mark 1:27). Surely it is. It is startlingly new. It is liberatingly fresh. It is a new kind of theology! It is a theology that breaks out of the confinement of orthodoxy. It is a theology that tears itself free from the conceptual games of traditional theology. And it is a theology that speaks out of life and speaks back into it—life not as a mere word or sound, but life that is lived in tribulation and expectation, in despair and hope, in anxiety and in a longing for peace.

That is why Jesus has to speak in parables and not in ideas and concepts. What is a parable? The dictionary tells us that a parable is "a short, simple story, usually of an occurrence of a familiar kind, from which a moral or religious lesson may be drawn."[2] But Jesus' use of parables goes far beyond the dictionary definition. To be sure, for Jesus also a parable is a short and simple story taken from a familiar occurrence in daily life. The parable of the sower is such a short, simple story of a familiar occurrence. But it is not just a moral or religious lesson that Jesus draws from it. Between Jesus' parables and God's reign, between his stories and God's ways in the world, there is a deeply inherent relationship. They do not overlap; they coalesce. They do not simply pass one into the other; they impact upon each other.

A parable that is rooted in life and derived from it brings the message it conveys into life itself. Jesus' parables, many of them, bring God's reign into human life, into the real world, full of problems and fears. When a parable makes human life and God's reign penetrate into each other, it ceases to be a metaphor, an allegory, or a parable in the usual sense. It is no longer mere parable. When such interpenetration happens, life itself becomes parabolic of God's reign and God's reign cannot be seen, heard, and grasped apart from real life.

The deeper we live our life, wrestling with it in agony and hope, the more thoughtfully we experience our own life and the life of others, struggling with ambiguity and tension, and the further we reach into fear and longing in the depth of the human spirit in our own life and the life of others, the more we live and experience parables of God's reign in that life of ours and of others.

Is Jesus' parable of the sower not such a parable in its deepest sense? A farmer who works his land diligently and produces a good harvest—is this not already a foretaste of God's reign? Is it not already God's reign, however incomplete and fragmentary, for the farmer? Can God's reign have a *personal* and *existential* meaning for him unless he can have glimpses of it in the fruits of his labor, in the yields he takes from his land?

And the kind of parable we are interested in here expands. It is not limited to its original setting. It moves into the lives of those who have the ears to hear and understand what they hear. Jesus himself seems to have intended his parables to extend beyond their immediate surroundings. His "normal practice . . . was deliberately to end the parable and to leave his hearers to grasp the point and to find the parallel or analogy for themselves."[3]

How could Jesus safely leave his parables with his hearers, most of whom were simple folk with not much religious education? How could he be sure those farmers and laborers with no theological training would not misinterpret and misapply his parables? This is the worry of professional theologians, not of Jesus, the paramount parablemaker and storyteller. Jesus seems to have the basic conviction that "the parables impart to their hearers something of his vision of the power of God at work in the experience of the people confronted by the reality of his proclamation."[4]

The power of God at work in human experience—this is what Jesus wants to let others know through his parables and through what he does with them. This is the key to interpreting his parables. This is the clue to understanding the signs of God's reign. And this is the sole factor that controls the application of the meaning of his parables. Life is packed with codes and signs of God's power at work in the world. To the life of the people, then, Jesus must go—life in suffering and hope, life in sorrow and joy, and life struggling to face death and conquer it. Life must be the stuff of Jesus' parables. And out of that life Jesus makes parables of God's power at work, enabling his followers to realize that God's reign is in the midst of their lives. To feel life intensely, to live life expectantly, and to experience life deeply—is this not, then, the way to understand and interpret Jesus' parables? And is this not the way we should be doing theology? Should our theology not be a theology in parables and stories, testifying to God's power at work in human experience?

THREE PARABLES OF A FATHER'S LOVE

A parable comes from the real life of a people and returns to it. The more deeply it is related to life, the more powerfully it makes its impact. The more genuinely it stands for what really happens in life, the more strongly it echoes God's thoughts and actions in human community. And what can bring to light more forcefully, truly, and profoundly what is in the human heart possessed by God than love? It is no wonder that parables of love abound in many cultures and religions. After all, life is what all persons—regardless of race, sex, culture, or religion—have in common; and the power that gives birth to life, sustains it, and gives it hope is the power of love. The following three parables of a father's love, taken from three different religious traditions, will fascinate our theological mind and reinforce our faith in God's love at work in humanity.

It Is Like a Man Who Leaves His Father . . .

The first parable is found in the Buddhist Sutra of the Lotus Flower of the Wonderful Law.[5] In the presence of the Buddha, the Enlightened One, are his three disciples, "the wisdom-destined Subhuti [disciples], Maha-Katyayana, Maha-Kasyapa, and Maha-Maudgalyayana," who are on their way to enlightenment. How best can they express their grasp of the truth imparted to them by the Buddha? In what way can they tell the Buddha they have experienced, understood, and embraced the law the Buddha preached to them? "Thereupon they rose from their seats, and, arranging their garments, humbly baring their right shoulders, placing their right knees on the ground, with one mind folding their hands, bending their bodies in reverence, and gazing upon his honored face, addressed the Buddha saying . . . 'Now let us have the pleasure of speaking in a parable to make plain' " the teaching of the law. They begin:

> It is like a man who, in his youth, leaves his father and runs away. For long he dwells in some other country, for ten, twenty, or fifty years. The older he grows, the more needy he becomes. Roaming about in all directions to seek clothing and food, he gradually wanders along till he unexpectedly approaches his native country. From the first the father searched for this son, but in vain, and meanwhile settled in a certain city. His home became very rich, his goods and treasures incalculable. . . .
>
> At this time the poor son, wandering through village after village and passing through countries and cities, at last reaches the city where his father has settled. . . . Meanwhile the poor son, hired for wages here and there, unexpectedly arrives at his father's house. Standing by the gate, he sees from afar his father seated on a lion couch, his feet on a jewelled footstool, revered and surrounded by Brahmans, Kshatriyas, and citizens. . . . The poor son . . . was seized with fear, regretting that he had come to this place, and secretly reflected thus: "This must be a king or someone of royal rank; it is no place for me to obtain anything for the hire of my labour. . . ."
>
> Having reflected thus, he hastily runs away. Meanwhile the rich elder on his lion seat has recognized his son at first sight and with great joy in his mind has thus reflected: "Now I have the one to whom my treasuries of wealth are to be made over. Always have I been thinking of this my son, with no means of seeing him; but suddenly he himself has come and my longing is satisfied. Though worn with years, I still yearn for him. . . ."
>
> Instantly he dispatches his attendants to rush after him and fetch him back. Thereupon the messengers hasten forth to seize him. The poor son, surprised and scared . . . thinks to himself that though he is innocent yet

he will be imprisoned, and that will certainly mean his death, so that he is all the more terrified, faints away, and falls on the ground. The father, seeing this from afar, gives the messengers his word: "There is no need for this man. Do not fetch him by force. . . ." The father, knowing that his son's disposition is inferior, knowing that his own lordly position has caused distress to his son, yet profoundly assured that he is his son, tactfully says nothing to others that this is his son. . . . A messenger says to the son: "I now set you free; go wherever you will." The poor son is delighted . . . rises from the ground and goes to a poor hamlet in search of food and clothing.

Then the elder, desiring to attract his son, sets up a device. Secretly he sends two men of doleful and undignified appearance, saying: "You go and visit that place and gently say to the poor man: 'There is a place for you to work here; you will be given double wages. . . .' " Then the two messengers went in search of the poor son and, having found him, placed before him the above proposal. Thereupon the poor son, having received his wages beforehand, joins with them in removing the dirt heap. His father, beholding the son, is struck with compassion for and wonder at him.

Another day he sees at a distance through a window his son's figure, gaunt, lean, and doleful, filthy and unclean from the piles of dirt and dust; thereupon he takes off his strings of jewels, his soft attire and ornaments, and puts on again a coarse, torn, and dirty garment, smears his body with dust, takes a dustpan in his right hand, and with an appearance of fear (or sternness) says to the laborers: "Get on with your work, don't be lazy." By such a device he gets near his son, to whom he soon afterwards says: "Aye, my man, you stay and work here, do not go again elsewhere; I am as it were your father; do not be worried again. . . . From this time forth you shall be as my own begotten son."

Thereupon the elder gives him a name anew and calls him a son. Then the poor son, though he rejoices at this happening, still thinks of himself as a humble hireling. For this reason, for twenty years he continues to be employed for removing dirt. After this period there is confidence between them and he goes in and out and at his ease, though his abode is still the original place . . . .

Then the elder becomes ill and . . . on seeing that his own end is near, commands his son to come and at the same time gathers together his relatives, and the kings, ministers, Kshatriyas, and citizens. When they are all assembled, he thereupon addresses them, saying: "Know, gentlemen, this is my son begotten by me. It is over fifty years since, from a certain city, he left me and ran away to endure loneliness and misery. . . . At that time in that city I sought him sorrowfully. Suddenly in this place I met and regained him. This is really my son and I am really his father. Now all the wealth which I possess belongs entirely to my son."

This is a long, winding story-parable. It has taken fifty years for the father and the son to find each other again. It has taken twenty years more for the father to reveal his identity to his son.

The parable moves slowly from one city to the next. In it the son's status is elevated step by step. It is not hurried. Even the father, overwhelmed by the joy of regaining his lost son, is not hurried. But, after all, the story takes place in Asia where bullock-carts in India move at a slow and steady pace with the movement of nature; where a foolish old man in China could move a mountain with his children, his children's children. . . . And the parable comes from the Buddhist faith, which measures time in terms of *koti*s, one *koti* being variously interpreted as ten million, or one hundred million, years, and in relation to *kalpa*s, one small *kalpa* alone being likened to the period required to remove all the poppy seeds from an area the size of a ten-square-mile city if one removed one poppy seed every three years, or the period required for a celestial maiden to wear away a ten-cubic-mile stone if she brushed it once with her garments every three years.[6]

But there is so much beauty in the parable—the beauty of the father's tenderness toward his impoverished son. And what a sensitive inner world of the oriental soul the parable shows behind the impassive facade of Asian faces! Above all, underneath the placid posture and the calm appearance of the Buddha is a heart pining for the multitudes suffering in the world, and a soul aching for the human beings lost in the sea of bitterness. This is a parable of the Bodhisattva's love. It comes from the drama of life—the drama of a father seeking his lost son, a drama that cannot fail to move profoundly the men, women, and children hearing it told or watching it played in the village square, or in the temple yard.

For us Christians the parable bears a striking resemblance to the famous parable of the prodigal son in Luke's Gospel. But it was "in existence well before Christian ideas could have found their way to India via Persia [and] it is unlikely that this parable owes anything to the Christian one."[7] Is this not amazing? The religious mind capable of such a drama of life must be closely linked to the mind of God that Jesus shows us in all tenderness, patience, and love. Parables growing out of real life and not doctrines concocted in a contentious spirit enable us to catch a glimpse of the heart of God. Our theology, to be Christian and also to be Asian at one and the same time, must learn to be sensitive to such glimpses and to respond to them.

There Was Once a Man Who Had Two Sons . . .

The setting of the drama is now different. This time it is the Semitic world. The Semitic mind has much in common with the Asian mind, but it also differs from it in many ways. It seems, for one thing, more direct in social conduct. It moves actively to shorten the space and time that separate human beings. Its expression of passion and emotion is more spontaneous and compulsive. But the theme is the same. It revolves around the love of a father for his wayward son. This is the parable of a father's love told by Jesus:

> There was once a man who had two sons; and the younger said to his father, "Father, give me my share of the property." So he divided his estate between them. A few days later the younger son turned the whole of his share into cash and left home for a distant country, where he squandered it in reckless living. He had spent it all when a severe famine fell upon that country and he began to feel the pinch. So he went and attached himself to one of the local landowners, who sent him on to his farm to mind the pigs. He would have been glad to fill his belly with the pods that the pigs were eating; and no one gave him anything. Then he came to his senses and said, "How many of my father's paid servants have more food than they can eat, and here am I, starving to death: I will set off and go to my father, and say to him, 'Father, I have sinned, against God and against you; I am no longer fit to be called your son; treat me as one of your paid servants.' " So he set out for his father's house. But while he was still a long way off his father saw him, and his heart went out to him. He ran to meet him, flung his arms around him, and kissed him. The son said, "Father, I have sinned, against God and against you; I am no longer fit to be called your son." But the father said to his servants, "Quick! fetch a robe, my best one, and put it on him; put a ring on his finger and shoes on his feet. Bring the fatted calf and kill it, and let us have a feast to celebrate the day. For this son of mine was dead and has come back to life; he was lost and is found." And the festivities began [Luke 15:11–24].

What a deeply moving human drama is the love that even a human father can be capable of! If such love can be real in our sinful world among sinful persons, how much more God is capable of it!

The parable as Jesus tells it is compact. It cuts a long story short without losing any essential element. In fact all essential elements are there and its brevity and compactness only heighten its dramatic quality. It is a story one can listen to breathlessly. The father must have been sad to see his son turning his share of the property into cash. The son must then have passed many days and nights of merrymaking and pleasure-seeking in self-abandonment in a foreign land. The father must have spent all this time "washing his face with his tears, swallowing his tears as his staple rice," as one would say in Taiwan.

But the parable does not linger on these details as does the Buddhist parable of the father's love. It moves on and shows us what a miserable sight the son has been reduced to. Then forced by a hungry stomach, the son in rags sets out on a sad return journey. At this point the pace of the parable quickens. There is the father's instant recognition of his miserable son. The father, hardly able to wait even one more second, runs to the son, embracing him and kissing him. The outburst of the father's love is uncontrollable. Then comes the father's order for a great feast, reaching its pinnacle of joy in the exclamation: "This son of mine was dead and has come back to life; he was lost and is found!" There is no embracing and kissing in the Buddhist parable. There is no outburst of emotion and spontaneous acceptance of the lost son in it. But, is the father's love here not essentially the same as there? Is the world of divine love manifested in human love not the same there in that Buddhist parable as here in this parable of Jesus?

These two parables from different cultural backgrounds and religious traditions show us how a parable is to be interpreted. They tell us that life—that is, the life we live in human community—is possible because of the power of love at work in it. The kind of love the father shows in the Buddhist and the Christian parable is not witnessed every day. Of course not. But there are instances of it. And when we become aware of it, it also enables us to have an idea of what God's love for us is like. Life then can be a parable of God's love. Life interprets the parable, and the parable interpreted by life in turn deepens our understanding of life and strengthens our faith in God.

For this reason, it is to be regretted that parables and stories have no place in traditional theology. Theology without parables and stories is like a robot without a soul and without life. Robots may make better cars, but they cannot make better drivers. Robotlike theology may tell us many things about God, humanity, and the world. But one thing it cannot tell us: love that brings God and human beings together in the drama of life. Is theology still theology without that love?

A King's Son Went Out in Evil Courses . . .

Jesus was born, lived, and died within a cultural milieu shaped and conditioned by Jewish religious traditions. His penchant for parables must have been nurtured within those religious and cultural frameworks. It must also have made a deep impression on the religious communities, Christian and Jewish, that came after him. It is, then, no surprise that we find a parable attributed to Rabbi Meir of the second century A.D. comparable to the Christian parable:

> A king's son went out into evil courses, and the King sent his guardian (*paidagogos*) after him. "Return, my son," said he. But the son sent him back, saying to his father: "How can I return? I am ashamed." His father sent again saying: "My son, art thou indeed ashamed to return? Is it not to thy father that thou returnest?"[8]

Short as it is, the parable manifests the Jewish understanding of God's love. One does not see in it the father in the Buddhist parable, going out of his way, even putting on coarse clothing, just to get near his son, scheming to get him reinstated. Nor does one feel in it the heart of a father in great excitement as in Jesus' parable. But one sees a father repeatedly urging his son to return. And in his question, "Is it not to thy father that thou returnest?" there is no trace of reproach. The father's forgiveness is evident. His acceptance of his son is indisputable.

A parable of love such as this has to be commended. It shows how love can become a redeeming power in a community defined by the strict observance of the Law. It tells us that life is more than the Law, that love can achieve what the Law cannot. After having said this, however, one is reminded of a limitation imposed by the faith of the Jewish community of those days on the application of the love pointed up in the parable. An apocalyptic passage from 1 Enoch (5:6f.), for example, will tell us what that limitation is:

> And there shall be forgiveness of sins,
> And every mercy and peace and forbearance:
> There shall be salvation unto them, a goodly light.
> And for all of you sinners there shall be no salvation,
> But on you shall abide a curse.
> But for the elect there shall be light and joy and peace,
> And they shall inherit the earth.[9]

A clear distinction between sinners and the elect—this is the limitation that the faith of a religious community is prone to place on the love it strives to teach and practice. Salvation is for the elect only, the repentant ones who were already members of that community. As to sinners, in the case of the Jewish community, Gentiles and the Jews who "had made themselves as Gentiles," that is, tax collectors, harlots, swineherds, thieves, and so on, cursed will be their lot.[10] There is no hope of God's forgiveness for them. They are beyond the pale of salvation. The son in the Jewish parable cannot be a Gentile or a Gentile-Jew. He must be an elect-Jew capable of re-admission into the community of his origin.

Jesus challenged this kind of limitation imposed on God's saving love. He was at pains to show that God is God because God is not conditioned by categorization of human persons on the basis of race, creed, sex or color. He stressed over and over in parables, in stories, and in actions, that it is premature for a religion to make a final judgment on a person's relation with God. It is not only premature; it is presumptuous. Such a judgment underestimates what God can do with sinners, with those outside the pale of a certain religious community.

It is evident that the parable with which we are concerned here is interpretative within the traditional Jewish faith and within the life shaped by it. But, when set in other religious traditions and in other communities, it becomes uninterpretative. At most it turns into a parable of what God is not and what God's love is not like. It does not bear out what is happening in the whole of the world. It does not testify to the love of God at work in the totality of God's creation.

All this indicates that there are at least two ways to test a parable told out of a certain religious background. Firstly, a parable has to be tested as to its validity within its immediate setting. It has to grow out of that setting to drive its point home to the people to whom the parable is addressed. But this is not enough, particularly in the multi-religious and multi-cultural world of our day. So secondly, a parable has to be tested in a wider setting—beyond the immediate context of its origin. If a parable does not stand the test posed by cultural and religious realities that shape life in other communities, its claim to point to God and to speak for God's thoughts and ways with humanity has to be discredited.

Jesus discredited much of what he inherited from the faith held by his own religious traditions. He associated with tax collectors, prostitutes, and other outcasts—those excluded from the community of the elected ones. He did not hesitate to commend non-Jews when they showed deep faith in God. And he told the parable of the father's love (note that the prodigal son was reduced to being a swineherd, that is, a Jew who made himself a Gentile!) to make the point directly to the people.

We must also pose the same test to the traditional theology we have inherited. How much of it, we must ask, can stand the test of religious-cultural and social-political realities in Asia? How much of the interpretation of the Bible we have learned in the theological classroom can bear out the lived experiences of people with whom we share a common history? And how deeply can our theological effort conditioned by traditional theology speak to the despair and agonies of the people around us?

Questions such as these point up the urgent need to do theology in a different way. Perhaps we must learn to speak theology more in the parables taken out of the life of people in Asia. We must let the stories of men, women, and children who make and live histories in our countries speak to our theological mind. Then, we may discover that God speaks to us in ways we have not known before, and discloses to us thoughts about salvation for humankind—thoughts we have never suspected before. Did not God put these words in the mouth of a prophet a long time ago?

> For my thoughts are not your thoughts,
> and your ways are not my ways. . . .
> For as the heavens are higher than the earth,
> so are my ways higher than your ways
> and my thoughts than your thoughts [Isa. 55:8–9].

What a humbling thought for us Christians and theologians in Asia! But, what an encouraging thought too! It makes doing of theology an exciting effort. Our age-old Bible becomes to us a *new* Bible.

5

Imaging Theology

HIBIKI

A parable that enables us to grasp God's ways in the world is one that echoes the everyday life of the people. The parables of Jesus are powerful because they powerfully echo the longings in the hearts of those who suffer injustice of various kinds. And parables that we find in abundance in religious cultures in Asia can also theologically reflect God's power at work in Asians when they echo strongly the aches and pains inflicted on the hearts and persons of millions and millions of their fellow Asians.

Echo, *hibiki* in Japanese, is important in *haiku,* the shortest form of Japanese poetry, consisting of seventeen syllables. *Haiku* is an echo of what is in the heart of nature. It is the resonance of humanity in the busy life of the marketplace and the village square. It is the *hibiki* of what lies deep in the human heart, responding to impacts from the world seen and unseen. *Haiku* is the *hibiki* of life. It is an echo of history in the grip of destiny. And it is the resonance of the world in the presence of the powers that affect it. *Haiku* is a poetic art. It is an expression of an inner world hidden from the naked eye. It is a work of the human spirit reaching out to the source and origin of life and being.

Basho, an unsurpassed master of *haiku,* lived in seventeenth-century Japan. He speaks of *hibiki,* the soul of *haiku,* in this way: "When you hit something, the noise comes back to you in a matter of an instant. This is what I mean by *hibiki.*"[1] *Haiku* is the *hibiki* of life surrounded by the mysterious universe. That is why it always consists of two pairs of short verses, with one pair hitting something and the other pair echoing its resonance.

In this sense, the soul of a parable must also be *hibiki.* With a parable you hit the deepest spot in the life of a people, and in an instant you get the *hibiki* of it in their hearts. In this sense the soul of theology must also be *hibiki.* You hit the theological core of life—the innermost recesses of the human heart where a person senses God and struggles with God, and you get *hibiki* from that core to be transcribed into theology. Theology without *hibiki* is a lifeless theology. It does not touch the core of being where the human and the divine meet in search of the meaning of life. How much of our theology has been without *hibiki.* That is why our theology cannot touch the Hindu heart, the Buddhist heart, the Confucianist heart. That is why it cannot touch the heart of Asia and get to its *hibiki.* Should we not learn something about *hibiki* from the art of *haiku*-making?

How does one then get that *hibiki* from life without which theology remains lifeless? How is one to learn how to hit something and hit it right so that one's theology becomes resonant with it? Let us once again turn to Basho, the master, and learn from him. A poet of his stature has truths to share, even truths with far-reaching theological significance. How to get that *hibiki* at the heart of things? This is what he says:

> Go to the pine if you want to learn about the pine, or to the bamboo if you want to learn about the bamboo. And in doing so, you must leave your subjective preoccupation with yourself. Otherwise you impose yourself on the object and do not learn. Your poetry issues of its own accord when you and the object have become one—when you have plunged deep enough into the object to see something like a hidden glimmering there. However well phrased your poetry may be, if your feeling is not natural—if the object and yourself are separate—then your poetry is not true poetry but merely your subjective counterfeit.[2]

Basho was talking about poetry, of course. But will not what he said about poetry apply to theology also?

"Go to the pine if you want to learn about the pine," says Basho, "or to the bamboo if you want to learn about the bamboo." It is as simple as that. Learn from the pine if you want to say something about it. Go to the bamboo and let it tell you about itself before you start singing about it. This is how *haiku* must be made. This is also how landscape paintings have to be painted. Asia—especially China, Japan, Korea, and Taiwan—is noted for its nature poems and nature paintings. The degree to which they impress you is the degree to which the poet and the painter have learned from mountains, rivers, trees, and birds. If Asian cultures can produce masterly nature poets and nature painters, how can they not produce theologians who can learn from the pine and the bamboo?

We do not know whether Jesus learned from the pine and the bamboo. But he learned a lot from the fig tree, olive tree, and cedar tree—trees that give food to sustain human life in Palestine and trees that are the pride of the land. There is unmistakable evidence that he learned a lot from the birds of the air and the lilies of the field. We are all familiar with what Jesus said about them. It can be arranged in pairs, resembling *haiku*:

> Look at the birds of the air;
> they do not sow and reap and store in barns.
>
> Your heavenly Father feeds them.
> You are worth more than the birds! [Matt. 6:26].

Jesus hits on something—birds of the air, the birds fed by God. The hitting produces *hibiki*, echoing back to Jesus and his listeners: you are worth more than they! For that *hibiki* to occur, Jesus must have been a keen observer of birds. His is also a life of risk and deprivation. That is why that *hibiki* sounds genuine, comforting, and encouraging. He is a nature theologian of the first rank! There is more theology in this "*haiku*" of Jesus than in many learned volumes of Christian doctrine.

If Jesus turns his thoughts to the birds of the air, he does not forget to look at the fields where beautiful lilies grow:

> Consider how the lilies grow in the fields;
> they do not work, they do not spin.
>
> Even Solomon in all his splendor was not attired like them.
> Will not God all the more clothe you? [Matt. 6:28–30].

Do you have any idea how splendidly Solomon was provided for? Perhaps no words would be adequate to describe it. But let the queen of Sheba, herself fabulously wealthy, tell it all. Having heard of Solomon's fame, she arrived in Jerusalem with a very large retinue from her kingdom in southwest Arabia. When she saw "the house which Solomon had built, the food on his table, the courtiers sitting around him, and his attendants standing behind in their livery, his cupbearers, and the whole-offerings which he used to offer in the house of the Lord, there was no more spirit left in her" (1 Kings 10: 1–5).

If even the queen of Sheba was daunted into speechlessness by Solomon's splendor, who would not be? But Jesus was not. For him the lilies of the field are in greater splendor. Then comes *hibiki* from the depth of Jesus' faith: Will not God all the more clothe you? From the lilies in the fields to Solomon in his splendor, and then to you and me—who have little faith! There is forceful *hibiki* in this. Jesus caught each sound of the *hibiki*. He grasped every nuance of the echo. He understood each and every tonality of the resonance. And all this became the stuff of his theology—faith in God's love for human persons, for you and me.

Jesus could have surpassed Basho as a master of *haiku*. He had the natural instinct to learn from nature and apply it to human life. He had the intuition to instantly grasp the meaning of what he encountered. His theology emerged from the *hibiki*s he heard and felt in his own life and in the lives of others. He made us see not the beauty of God but the beautiful God in the beautiful lilies. He drew our attention not to the providence of God but to the provident God in the birds well provided for. It is this Jesus who could say to the woman to be stoned for her sexual misconduct: "Neither do I condemn you; go and do not sin again" (John 8:11, RSV), and to Zacchaeus, the tax collector: "Salvation has come to this house today!" (Luke 19: 1–10). Theology that is imaged out of *hibiki* from the depth of a troubled life is so human yet so divine, so simple yet so profound.

A DEEP RESONANCE

There is something very important in this business of *hibiki* for theology. We must learn more about it. And how could we learn it better than from Basho, the master of *haiku*, especially from the best known of all his *haiku*s:

Furuikeya, kawazu tobikomu, mizu no oto.

Breaking the silence
of an ancient pond,
A frog jumped into water—
A deep resonance.

Just close your eyes and let your mind and heart open to these words. You will hear the silence. You will see an old pond that makes the silence deeper and louder. Enveloped in that silence, you hear a small but crisp and clear sound caused by a frog jumping into the pond. That sound breaks the silence, creating a deep resonance in the depth of nature and in the bottom of your heart. Then you see with your mind's eye something of the mystery behind the silence and feel with your heart the *hibiki* from your humanity responding to the resonance of that mystery. This is poetry as a deeply religious art.

To appreciate more this *haiku* of Basho, let us listen to how it was composed as told by one of his disciples:

> This poem was written by our master on a spring day. He was sitting in his riverside house in Edo, bending his ears to the soft cooing of a pigeon in the quiet rain. There was a mild wind in the air, and one or two petals of cherry blossom were falling gently to the ground. It was the kind of day you often have in late March—so perfect that you want it to last forever. Now and then in the garden was heard the sound of frogs jumping into the water. Our master was deeply immersed in meditation, but finally he came out with the second half of the poem,
>
> A frog jumped into water—
> A deep resonance.
>
> One of the disciples sitting with him immediately suggested for the first half of the poem,
>
> Amidst the flowers
> Of the yellow rose.
>
> Our master thought for a while, but finally he decided on
>
> Breaking the silence
> Of an ancient pond.

> The disciple's suggestion is admittedly picturesque and beautiful but our master's choice, being simpler, contains more truth in it. It is only he who has dug deep into the mystery of the universe that can choose a phrase like this.[3]

This account should make us theologians sit up and think deeply. It is richly suggestive of the way we should *image* theology.

The master's phrase "a deep resonance" is the key to unlocking the mystery. His disciples only *saw* a frog jump into water; they did not *hear* the deep resonance the jumping made. The master's mind had already gone beyond the jumping frog to the deep resonance in the water. But the disciples went on to look for something they could see. And they saw the flowers of the yellow rose. They moved from the frog to the flowers, completely losing the deep resonance vibrating in the heart of the master and echoing in the air of the garden. The mystery escaped them.

But how masterfully Basho grasped the mystery! He *saw* a frog jump into the water and he *heard* a deep resonance. The flowers and trees of the garden disappeared from the garden of his mind and heart. He saw an ancient pond and heard a deep resonance. The pond had to be ancient and the resonance had to be deep. A perfect match of reality and mystery! A new pond may also make a resonance when a frog jumps into it, but it will not be a *deep* resonance. There will be no inscrutable silence to break. But the master *heard* the silence even before the frog jumped into the water. The frog only provided the occasion for him to hear the deep resonance from the deep silence of the ancient pond. The hearing disclosed to him in that instant the mystery of nature and the mystery of life.

We as Christians and theologians in Asia see many things each and every day. We see the stockmarket rise and fall. We see currencies devalued. We see men, women, and children on busy streets and in crowded department stores. We see them in restaurants, in trains, on buses. We also see Vietnamese men, women, and children, in refugee camps, in dilapidated mud houses. But do we hear silence in the heart of a noisy metropolis? Do we hear silence in the hearts of men, women, and children competing, struggling, and trying to survive in the rigor of this harsh world? Do we also hear silence in our own hearts?

Perhaps most of us are more like Basho's disciples who see the frog and then see the yellow flowers. We do not hear the deep resonance breaking the silence of an ancient pond. That is why our theology breaks no new ground. It does not grasp new insights. It does not echo the deep resonance in the heart of silence underneath our busy life in this noisy world. But Gautama the Buddha heard it. Mo Ti heard it. Gandhi heard it. St. Paul heard it. Did he not write to the Christians in Rome that "the whole creation has been groaning in travail until now" (Rom. 8:22, RSV)? And above all, Jesus heard it. That is why he was able to say to those who came to hear him: "Come to me, all who labour and are heavy laden, and I will give you rest" (Matt. 11:28).

But what is the secret of seeing the silence when a frog jumps and hearing a deep resonance in an ancient pond? We quoted Basho earlier who said that if one wants to learn about the pine, one must go to the pine, and to the bamboo if one wants to learn about the bamboo. He went on to advise the aspiring *haiku*-makers: "Your poetry issues of its own accord when you and the object have become one—when you have plunged deep enough into the object to see something like a hidden glimmering there." This is very important. The greatness of Basho's poetic art comes from his losing himself in the objects of his attention. He does not try to hear what he wants to hear. He does not try to see what he wants to see. He lets them speak to him and lets them show him what he must see and hear. Then his poetry rises of itself from them. He does not originate it. He does not force it out of his brain. The depth of poetry depends on how deeply one has plunged into the silence at the heart of nature and at the heart of human nature, and on how well one hears a deep resonance breaking out of that silence. Poetry that does not plunge into that silence and echo that resonance is counterfeit poetry, as Basho calls it.

Is this not the same with theology? Is there not much counterfeit theology going around in Asia? Our theology becomes counterfeit when it says Hinduism does not know the true God because it is lost in a pantheon of many gods and many lords; Buddhism has no God because it teaches salvation by one's own power; Confucianism is simply a humanism that keeps away from God's involvement in human affairs. But have we ever plunged into the aching spirit of the Hindu believer who longs for deliverance from the shackles of karma? How deeply have we gone into the heart of the Buddhist who yearns for the divine love? And how much have we been able to penetrate the Chinese mind behind the Confucianist exterior—a mind freed to commune with the spirit that animates nature and makes life livable? If we have not done this, or have not even begun to do this, then our theology about them is counterfeit. We are just perpetuating counterfeit theology taught to us by makers and teachers of counterfeit theology.

Even in dealing with familiar subjects of theology, we are not entirely freed from counterfeit theology. Take the time-honored concept of covenant in the Old Testament. We have sacralized it to such an extent that we do not stop to think that it might have had strong political and ideological overtones in the history of Israel. We are so accustomed to regarding the history of Israel as sacred that we tend to regard covenant as a purely religious concept. But do we not have to relearn the history of Israel as a *profane* history, the history of a people seeking a land of its own and consolidating its political gains in the midst of other nations and peoples? Is, then, covenant not also to be seen as central in the political ideology unifying contentious member tribes and creating a national unity vis-à-vis outside forces?[4]

And what about Saul in his desperate struggle for power against David, the future king of Israel? How should we evaluate him? Against him was the formidable priestly power represented by Samuel. He was no match for the politically cunning David set up by Samuel as his rival. Saul, this young warrior, the hero who cleared the hill country of Philistines and rescued the people of Jabesh-gilead (1 Sam. 11:1–11), was destined to die a tragic death on Mount Gilboa in a fight against the Philistines (1 Sam. 31:1–7). The tragedy of Saul is made even more tragic by the account of his meeting with the witch at En-dor, shortly before his death on Gilboa, disguised and under cover of night. It must have been a pathetic sight, a man anointed king but removed by the same religious power that had made him king to make room for his rival. By the time he visited the witch, Samuel had been long dead. But he was still haunted by the king-maker. It was the spirit of Samuel that Saul asked the witch to call from its rest. And Samuel, who terrified him in life, also denounced him in death. "Why do you ask me," came the voice of Samuel from the depths of the spirit world, "now that the Lord has turned from you and become your adversary?. . . the Lord will let your people of Israel fall into the hands of the Philistines and, what is more, tomorrow you and your sons shall be with me." This was Samuel's death sentence for Saul. A dramatically tragic scene! "Saul was overcome and fell his full length to the ground" (1 Sam. 28:3–20). Our hearts cannot but go out to Saul, the tragic hero. He must have died on Mount Gilboa with *deep bitterness* in his heart, *han yuan er su*, as one would say in Chinese, or with *han* in Korean—"a feeling of defeat, resignation, and nothing" on the one hand and "a feeling with a tenacity of will for life which comes to weaker beings."[5]

Do we, then, understand the conflict between Saul and Samuel, and Saul and David, only in terms of God's purpose for Israel interpreted and represented by the priestly power of Samuel? Do we not have to plunge more deeply into the history of that conflict in terms of a political power struggle as well? Does not the same thing apply to the conflict between Esau and Jacob? Can we continue to accept the ancient verdict that "Jacob I loved and Esau I hated," as St. Paul did (Rom. 9:13)? This concerns the doctrine of election that has been at the center of Christian teaching. As we plunge more deeply into the spirit, the heart, and the soul of our Asian humanity embodied in religions, cultures, and histories outside the sphere of Christian influence, do we not have to rethink radically the Christian doctrine of election?

Let our theology come from a deep resonance in the heart of Asia. Let our theology be the *hibiki* of the Asian soul. And let our theology echo the silence broken by human suffering that grips most Asian peoples. With that theology let us turn once again to our own Bible, to the Christian faith. We may then become aware that we are standing beside an ancient pond, hearing deep resonance from human hearts touched by the Bible, by the Bhagavad Gita, or by the Sutra of the Lotus Flower of the Wonderful Law. What we encounter there are not cold doctrines, rigid laws, and menacing taboos, but human beings powerless before the power of fate and gripped by the touch of death; human beings in need of divine grace to sustain their hope in this world and beyond it. To be able to *image* such human beings is the beginning of theology in Asia.

POWER OF THEOLOGICAL IMAGING

Poets image their poems. Painters image their paintings. Should theologians too image theology? They not only should, they must. Especially theologians in Asia must be able to image their theology and not conceptualize it, for they live in the midst of rich cultures to which the power to image has greatly contributed. Ours is a culture shaped by the power of imaging, not by the capacity to conceptualize. It is a culture vibrant with the rhythms of life that cannot be abstracted into definitions, logic, and formulas. Such culture must lend itself to theological imaging. Unfortunately, a culture created in the West by the power of abstraction has taken control of the Asian theological mind. To regain our ability to image theology as a poet images poetry and a painter images painting is fundamental to theological efforts in Asia.

As a matter of fact, the Bible shows us how the power to image is at work in faith. The two creation stories in the book of Genesis exemplify it. Let us take the story told in the second chapter of Genesis first. It has come from the so-called Yahwist source, reflecting a mundane, down-to-earth mentality more attuned to vivid description than to orderly reasoning. It mirrors a poetic mind close to that of Basho, the *haiku* master. This is how the storyteller images God's creation of humankind:

> then the Lord God formed a man from the dust of the ground and breathed into his nostrils the breath of life. Thus the man became a living creature [2:7].

What a marvelously realistic picture of the emergence of a human being! Humankind does not emanate from the intellect of the creator, the all-wise God. Humanity is not an abstraction of divinity.

The dust of the ground! How could one think of it as worthy material for the creation of humankind—humankind endowed with special qualities of life and spirit not shared by other creatures, animate or inanimate? The dust of the ground—this is what we stand on, out of which plants grow. Why is God imaged as stooping so low as to make human beings from it? The dust of the ground—things dead and useless are buried in it. Why was it chosen to create human life from?

The dust of the ground is something like the frog in Basho's poem. A frog jumping into water is such a commonplace thing that to an unpoetic mind no deeper meaning is attached to it. But as we have seen, from the frog Basho images an ancient pond and hears a deep resonance in the midst of silence. Similarly, our storyteller, a poet of the first rank, images something in the dust of the ground and hears something echoing in it. What is it, then?

This question brings us to the story of the fall in chapter 3 of Genesis. For our purposes here we do not have to go into the story in all its detail, although it is a most fascinating story that never ceases to yield new thoughts and insights to the mind attuned to capturing images. Let us just turn to the final part of the verdict pronounced on Adam and Eve after they were found to have eaten the forbidden fruit:

> You shall gain your bread by the sweat of your brow until you return to the ground; for from it you were taken. Dust you are, to dust you shall return [3:19].

"The ground!" "Dust!" Do you see it? Do you hear it? Does it not remind us at once of the dust of the ground out of which God made humankind? We do not have to assume that the creation account in the second chapter of Genesis must have been written before the account of the fall in the third chapter. If one were to insist on chronological order, the story of the fall was probably told before the story of creation.

At any rate, as the storyteller images it, the dust of the ground into which the human body decomposes after death becomes the dust of the ground out of which human life emerges! What a power of theological imaging! Sickness, old age, and death follow after human beings everywhere. They are facts of life in the East and in the West, in ancient times and in the present day.

In Buddhist scriptures we have the classic story of how the future Buddha, a young innocent prince sheltered from the suffering world, encountered these inevitable facts of life. In his excursions from the palace he saw "old age, the destroyer of beauty and vigor, the source of sorrow, the depriver of pleasure, the slayer of memories, the enemy of sense organs." Next he came across a man afflicted with "the great misfortune called disease, developed from a disorder of elements by which this man, though he had been strong, has been disabled." Already profoundly disturbed, the young prince was yet to encounter the sight of a man "being carried by four others, followed by persons in distress . . . being mourned." He was then dutifully informed: "This is the last of all human beings. Death is certain for all, whether they be of low, middle, or high degree."[6] Deeply shocked and moved, the young prince set out on a journey to enlightenment.

The experience of the future enlightened one is the daily experience of us all. And no doubt it must have been the experience of the storyteller also. The dust of the ground is that to which human beings return after having been overcome by disease, old age, and death. "To dust you shall return." Why dust and not something else? The simple reason is, as the storyteller puts it, "dust you are." But the storyteller did not stop there, content to report what everyone already knew and experienced. For our storyteller that was where the power of theological imaging was put to work. The dust of the ground was not just the dust of the ground. "Dust you are." Precisely. *Therefore* God must have formed you from it! Now we see the connection between the story of the fall, giving an account of death, and the story of the creation, telling the origin of humankind.

But this still does not explain life. Dust may take a human form. It may be molded into a human figure. But dust cannot give life. It cannot generate life. Here the storyteller's theological imaging makes an astonishing leap. And this is what we hear next: "God breathed into his nostrils the breath of life." The storyteller's theological imaging reaches its peak. It images the human form from the dust of the ground, then images life not from the dust of the ground but from God. Theological imaging that emerges from the realities of the world will transcend the limitations inherent in these realities and reach God, the source of life. But theological imaging must begin with the dust of the earth, not with the rainbow in the sky. It must gaze at death deeply enough to grasp life that overcomes it.

Why do we turn to theological imaging? Why are we not content with viewing human life as just a series of natural processes? Why is it that we can image life out of the dust of the ground? Questions such as these take us to the account of humankind in the first creation story in Genesis 1:1–2:4a, the story from the priestly tradition several centuries after the story we have just studied.

In the earlier story humankind made its appearance at the beginning of God's creation. Here, in contrast, it emerged, as it were, out of the depth of God's being. Nature and all things in it came into being through God's commanding words. They are commanded into existence. They are ordered into being. But when it comes to human beings, command becomes invitation and order becomes mobilization of God's own being: "Then God said, 'Let us make human beings in our image and likeness' " (Gen. 1:26). This is an astonishing invitation. And it is a formidable mobilization of the very being of God. This invitation, this mobilization, is to result in the creation of humankind.

I shall not go into the theology of *imago Dei* here. Nor shall I dwell on the tremendous impact it has been making on the struggle against racism, classism, and sexism. For our purposes here I want to turn the word "image" from a noun into a verb and see what it will speak to the matter of theological imaging.

God *images* the human being out of God's own self. This seems to me what "Let us make human beings—in our image" means. Mobilizing the power of imaging, God images God's own self in humanity. "To image" as a verb is not the same as "image" as a noun. It does not lead us to anthropomorphic fantasy about God. It does not tempt us to reverse the process and make us envision God in our own image. But by imaging God's own self in humankind, God imparts to us the ability to image all created things in relation to God. God has given us the power of *theo*-logical imaging. With that power of imaging, a poet hears *hibiki* coming from the depth of an ancient pond and makes it resound in poetry. With that power of imaging, a painter discerns *hibiki* in the heart of mountains and rivers, and re-creates them in lines and colors on the canvas. And with that same power of imaging, a theologian perceives divine *hibiki* from the abyss of creation and from the rough and tumble of human life in the world of suffering and hope. It must have been with such power that the storyteller was able to image God breathing life into the nostrils of a human figure made from the dust of the earth and making it a living being.

What power! And what an act of imaging! This power of imaging must be the energy that enables us to do theology. And what is most important, this must be the power making us *image* theology and not conceptualize it, *hear* theology and not theorize about it, *see* theology and not turn it into a mechanism for argumentation. With this power of *theo*-logical imaging, can we also not image God in the heart of Asian peoples—God making *hibiki* in the centuries-old religious beliefs and practices? Can we not hear that *hibiki* in all those Asians who struggle to live a truly human life? And can we not see that *hibiki* in the faces of silent millions exposed to the heat of the day and bearing the burdens of life? Then, and only then, shall we recognize in all these resonances the *hibiki* of God coming from the cross on Golgotha where Jesus died. What a deep resonance that death on the cross can have, breaking into the silence of the ancient culture of suffering in Asia! Our theology must be a response to that deep resonance.

PART TWO

PASSION

6

Rhythms of Passion

INTESTINES, LUNGS, AND LIVER

Theology is a deep resonance of God's *hibiki* echoed in *hibiki*s from the heart of nature and from the innermost recesses of the human soul. Poetry, painting, and music seem to have been invented to sing and paint that *hibiki*. And *theology* is inherent in human beings because God has imaged God's own self in them and enabled them to image God in creation and human community. That is why poetry, painting, and music, at their best, pass into theology, and theology, at its best, passes into poetry, painting, or music. Just listen to this marvelous psalm and you will see what I mean:

> When I look up at thy heavens, the work of thy fingers,
> the moon and the stars set in their place by thee,
> what is man that thou shouldst remember him,
> mortal man that thou shouldst care for him?
> Yet thou hast made him little less than a god,
> crowning him with glory and honor. . . .
> O Lord our sovereign,
> how glorious is thy name in all the earth! [Ps. 8:3-5,9].

This is poetry. This is painting. This is music. And above all, this is theology! Is this not another strong evidence that theology is not so much a matter of concepts and doctrines as a matter of heaven and earth, a matter of creation and life?

There is passion in that psalm. You cannot read psalms in the Old Testament without feeling human passion bursting out of them. You cannot read many stories in the Bible without being affected by their human passion crying out to heaven. And you cannot read the accounts of Jesus' life and work in the New Testament without sensing that human passion is about to tear open the womb of the earth. "My God, my God, why hast thou forsaken me?" These passionate words of Jesus on the cross embody the passion of humanity from the beginning of history to its end.

Rhythms of creation are rhythms of passion. Rhythms of life are also rhythms of passion. Poetry without such rhythms is no poetry. It does not sing; it just mumbles. Painting without them is no painting. It does not paint life; it paints death. Music without them is no music. It makes no melody and tune; it just makes a noise. And theology without rhythms of passion is no *theo*-logy at all, for how can theology still be theology when it has no human passion echoing God's passion?

Where, then, do rhythms of passion come from—rhythms without which theology is not *theo*-logy? Where are they to be found? How are they to become the power, the energy, of our theology? I have talked a lot about poetry and painting. They have a lot to tell us theologians. The reason is already obvious to us from what has been said. So, at this point, let me once again refer you to a painter and poet, this time the famous Chinese scholar poet-painter Su Tungp'o (A.D. 1035–1101) of the Sung dynasty. Once he scribbled a poem on his host's wall:

> Sprouts come from my dry intestines, moistened by wine,
> and from my lungs and liver grow bamboos and rocks.
> So full of life they grow that they cannot be restrained,
> and so I am writing them on your snow-white wall.[1]

A poet capable of such passion cannot but be a superb artist!

"Sprouts come from my intestines, and from my lungs and liver grow bamboos and rocks," says Su Tungp'o. He did not compose this poem with his head only. It was his intestines, lungs, and liver that wrote and painted with the passion that lives in bamboos, rocks, and sprouts. His whole being was consumed in passion, and that passion bodied forth in bamboos and rocks. That passion became transformed into sprouts. That is why his sprouts, his bamboos, and his rocks spoke of his passion—passion for life, passion for something beyond life.

Our Western friends tell us they are puzzled by the passive faces of millions and millions of Asians. They cannot understand us because we do not show emotion. This is especially true of persons of Chinese origin. It has been pointed out that our Western friends often fail to appreciate "the extreme sensitiveness and fine feeling of the Chinese soul hidden behind a somewhat unprepossessing exterior." They cannot penetrate "behind the Chinese flat, unemotional face concealing a deep emotionalism."[2] Traditional Western theology has of course no inkling of "the extreme sensitiveness and fine feeling of the Asian soul." It cannot feel "a deep emotionalism" behind the unprepossessing exterior of the Asian mind. And Asian theologians, long under the tutelage of traditional theology, have also failed to realize their own extreme sensitiveness and fine feeling. They have also been apologetic about their own unprepossessing exterior—concealing in fact a deep passion.

But we Asians are capable of having sprouts come from our intestines and bamboos and rocks grow from our lungs and liver! What a feat! And what wonder! But, is this not what people in our Christian Bible were also capable of? Is this not the way the prophets of ancient Israel wrote the history of the rise and fall of their own nation? One recalls the words of anguish from Jeremiah when Jerusalem was seized with panic at the imminent Babylonian invasion:

> My anguish, my anguish! I writhe in pain!
> Oh, the walls of my heart!
> My heart is beating wildly;
> I cannot keep silent;
> for I hear the sound of the trumpet,
> the alarm of war [Jer. 4:19, RSV].

Compare this translation with that of the *New English Bible:*

> Oh, the writhing of my bowels
> and the throbbing of my heart!
> I cannot keep silence.
> I hear the sound of the trumpet,
> the sound of the battle-cry.

These two renderings of the same verse from Jeremiah explain each other. Jeremiah, anticipating the destruction of Jerusalem by the Babylonian army, feels extreme anguish. His heart beats wildly in pain. That is why his bowels writhe and his heart throbs. The bowels are in anguish and anguish is in the bowels. What a powerful way to express pain and anguish! Jeremiah wrote the last chapter of his history of Israel with his writhing bowels and his throbbing heart. Does this not enable us to see why Su Tungp'o, the Chinese poet, says in his poem that bamboos grow from his lungs and rocks from his liver?

Jesus must have often felt pain and agony in his stomach, his lungs, and his heart during his ministry. In the Garden of Gethsemane, so Luke, the author of the Gospel that bears his name, tells us, Jesus prayed:

> "Father, if it be thy will, take this cup away from me. Yet not my will but thine be done.". . . and in anguish of spirit he prayed the more urgently; and his sweat was like clots of blood falling to the ground [Luke 22: 42–44].

It must have been a terrible anguish. That anguish gripped Jesus with extreme pain. His anguish then became sweat like clots of blood falling to the ground. "Father, if it be thy will." These were words coming from his stomach, lungs, and liver. To capture that Jesus on canvas must be nearly impossible. Perhaps an Asian artist gifted with passion of the heart could do it.

Asians possess an extreme sensitiveness of the soul and a deep emotionalism of the heart. Their internal organs hidden behind their not so expressive exteriors seethe with emotion and writhe in pain in the rigor of life in the turbulent Asian world. To give another example, there is the Okinawan word *chimugurisa.* Its root is *chimu,* meaning "lungs" and "intestines." *Chimugurisa* means "to be moved to pain in one's intestines by a neighbour's pain and sorrow."[3] The English word "pity" is of course too weak to express such a strong emotion. In fact there are no words adequate to express such feelings of pain seizing one's body and gripping one's spirit. You can only imagine it, or better, you yourself have to feel it within yourself. A Chinese mother weeps over her dying child, "Oh, my treasure child, my heart, and my liver!" This is *chimugurisa.* This is anguish of the intestines.

For us Asians life is rhythms of passion internalized in our soul and heart. Our theology must catch those rhythms and express them. It must bring those rhythms out of the depth of our being and externalize them. It must be spoken to by those rhythms in order to be able to speak to them. It is most certain that our theology will then be able to recognize in those rhythms of passion the rhythms of Jesus' passion. In them we will surely be hearing rhythms of God's passion. Such theology reflecting rhythms of Asian passion has begun to appear. It will be the predominant theology out of the depths of Asian spriritual soil. And how fertile that soil is! The theology that grows out of such Asian soil must be a passionate theology—theology with passion, theology done not in our head but in our bowels and in our lungs, theology imaged in our liver and in our heart. It has to be a forceful theology.

THEOLOGY OF *HAN*

One example of such a forceful theology in tune with rhythms of passion is the Korean theology of *han. Han* is the rhythm of passion welling out of restless souls in the world of the dead, the wrongs done to them unrequited. *Han* is the rhythm of passion crying from the hearts of those who have fallen victim to social and political injustices. The last stanza of "Slave Diary" by Yang Sung-woo, for instance, grips those who read it with powerful *han*:

> Even though you survive for a million years
> like worms in dying petals;
> I will look down, waving my hands in the air,
> being torn like a rag.
> Even though you vanish as dew on a sword
> the blood scattered when you rolled and rolled;
> I will wet the scars of the swords, the gunshot wounds,
> wet your stained hearts
> as a shower falling down in May.
> Even though you thrash without stopping
> like the sleet in mid-winter;

I will shout out
breathing as roots of grass
which sleep not under the ground. . . .

Do you hear, you poets,
the thick voice which echoes to the end of the earth
hitting the air with fists,
fists from inside graves,
sorrowful graves of 5,000 years.[4]

Just think of the *han* which "has been absorbed into the bones and muscles of the people of the country for 5,000 years"! [5]

The *han* accumulated for five thousand years must be powerful *han*. It has been accumulating from one generation to the next. It has been accumulating in Korean stomachs, lungs, livers, and hearts. It has been filling the entire being of the Korean people. It has been filling the air of the nation. And the time comes when human bodies cannot contain it any longer, when the fabric of society can no longer stand it, when the texture of the nation cannot endure it. That is the time when *han,* brewing in the soul of the people and seething in the abyss of the nation, breaks out into revolt and revolution. The power of *han* is transformed into the power of revolution. *Han* as the prime mover of revolution becomes the soul of a new history and a new era.

This power of *han* is of course not the monopoly of the Korean people. It is a universal power dormant in the inmost part of the human soul biding its time. But in Asia, where a culture of suppression has prevailed for centuries and is still ruling today, that power is particularly strong and evident. What we have in many countries in Asia is a culture of suffering within a culture of domination. It is in a culture shaped by suffering and bitterness of life that we come to know and experience the suffering and passion of a people, the dynamics of its history. And it is in its folk stories, folk songs, folk drama, and folk music that *han* grips us with its demands, sorrow, or anger.

In the traditional Chinese family system, the culture of suffering concentrates on the daughter-in-law. It is she who absorbs centuries of deep bitterness in her bones, muscles, and heart. The story of her suffering, living under the same roof as her parents-in-law, her husband's brothers and sisters, is endless. And there are many, many folk songs that sing about such suffering and bitterness of life. Here is one from Taiwan:

So difficult to be a daughter-in-law:
Though rising before dawn they still say it is too late,
Washing face with warm water causes their displeasure.
I cook with rice white as snow,
but they say it is black as charcoal.

I make dress for them with silk,
but they find fault with it
saying it is too coarse. . . .[6]

How many daughters-in-law in Chinese-speaking societies sing this folk song with tears in their hearts? It is sung by street singers and in folk dramas. But how many parents-in-law understand the infinite pathos and passion buried deep in the hearts of their daughters-in-law?

Even in this kind of traditional society there have been some open outbursts of pent-up bitterness from oppressed daughters-in-law. They can no longer contain it in their hearts and have to let out the passion caused by their suffering. The "Story of the Sharp-tongued Li Ts'ui-lien" from the late thirteenth century in China is both hilarious and sober.[7] There must have been other liberated women like Li Ts'ui-lien who waged a courageous but fruitless war against the oppressive family system in feudal China.

Li Ts'ui-lien was an unusually independent-minded daughter. When she was married, she proved to be a total novelty to her husband's home. With her sharp tongue and her independent mind she refused to be submissive. Things finally came to a head. On the occasion of the visit of Ts'ui-lien's mother, Mrs. Chang, the mother-in-law gave vent to her fury and "recounted from beginning to end how Ts'ui-lien had inflicted blows on the astrologer and how she had abused the match-maker, how she had insulted her husband, and how she had slighted her parents-in-law." Being a product of the feudal society herself, Ts'ui-lien's mother was greatly alarmed and started to scold her daughter. But Ts'ui-lien answered:

Mother, don't start a row yet;
Listen while I relate it in each particular.
Your daughter is no untaught peasant woman;
There are some matters you little know about.
On the third morn the new daughter-in-law enters the kitchen
(to prepare her first meal for the family in accordance with custom),
Two bowls of thin rice porridge with salt was all they provided.
And, to serve with the meal, not even tea but plain boiling water!
Now you, their new relation, make your first call,
At once they start their tittle-tattle:
Regardless of white and black, true or false,
Harassing me is all they are bent on.
My mother-in-law is by nature too impetuous,
The things she says are none too proper.
Let her beware—lest driven to my last resource,
With a bit of cord and a swing from the noose
I leave her to answer for my corpse.

She was well before her time. She could wage a revolution only with "a bit of cord and a swing of the noose." But how many daughters-in-law in China and elsewhere in Asia have gone to their death waging their war of liberation "with a bit of cord and a swing of the noose"! The deep bitterness of these daughters-in-law alone could have turned a feudal society upside down!

Ts'ui-lien's answer made her parents-in-law angry. The father-in-law said in a rage: "A female person should be gentle and staid, and sober in speech: only then is she fit to be a daughter-in-law." The mother-in-law, who had driven her daughter-in-law to open revolt, cried: "Have done! Have done! Such a daughter-in-law would one day bring down the family name and be a reproach to the ancestors." Ts'ui-lien was quickly packed into a sedan chair and sent home with the certificate of repudiation, to the infinite shame and dismay of her own parents.

But Ts'ui-lien was undaunted. She comforted her parents and said:

Dad, do not shout; Ma do not shout. . . .
It is not that your lassie would sing her own praises,
But from childhood she has been of high mettle.
This day I left their household,
And rights and wrongs of the affair I will leave off.
It is not that my teeth are itching to speak,
But tracing patterns and embroidering, spinning and weaving,
Cutting and trimming garments, in all these I am skilled.
True it is, moreover, I can wash and starch, stitch and sew,
Chop wood, carry water, and prepare choice dishes;
And if there are silkworms, I can keep them too.
Now I am young and in my prime,
My eyes are quick, my hand steady, my spirits bold;
Should idlers come to peep at me,
I would give them a hearty, resounding slap.

The parents must have stared at their liberated daughter in total confusion and utter incomprehension. Unable to get their approval for what she had done, there was only one thing she could do apart from resorting to "a bit of cord and a swing of the noose"—that is, become a nun. She said to them:

I will cut off my hair and become a nun,
Wear a straight-seamed gown and dangle a gourd from a pole,
And carry in my hands a huge "wooden fish."
In the daytime from door to door I shall beg for alms;
By night within the temple I shall praise the Buddha . . .

A Bodhisattva I might not become:
To be Buddha's least handmaid would still content me!

Is there not plenty of feminist theology in this Chinese folk drama? We do not have to turn to the West for it. Here in Asia feminist theology has deep roots in the culture of suffering. We must explore that culture in lives narrated in stories, dramas, songs, and poems. We then will discover that feminist theology has been a *living* theology in Asia for thousands of years.

And there is something else in Li Ts'ui-lien's story. Hers was a robust and combative soul. She fought for her rights at home and in her husband's family. But she had all the social traditions against her; even her own parents were captive of those traditions. She chose finally the life of a nun in a Buddhist temple.

Does this ending of the tale not tell us that we must look at Buddhism, for instance, from the perspective of the culture of suffering instead of just as a body of teachings to be studied and to be compared with Christianity? How many men and women with unrequited suffering have sought the peace and justice offered in Buddhist temples, convents, and monasteries? Behind their enclosed doors, millions of persons must have tried to transcend the culture of suffering to overcome it and to attain the peace of Buddhahood. Perhaps no Asian historians of religions have explored in any depth this culture of suffering in Buddhism. Has any Christian historian of religions done it?

I'LL OPEN A MUSEUM

If personal life in Asia is immersed in the culture of suffering, history too is fed by that culture of suffering. After all, history cannot be separated from persons. It is persons who make history. History without persons is an abstraction. It is the creation of an imperial power. It is a plaything in the hands of dictators. Dictators can impose history on a people. They can rewrite it. They can construct it the way they want to. But such history, without the consent and approval of the people, is a false history. It is a fiction.

A people has its own history. Or better, its constituent members are themselves history. And their history grows out of the culture of suffering. That is what makes their history genuine, powerful, and passionate. History is their lives of love fulfilled and betrayed. It is the stories of their faith heightened and shattered. It is the dramas of their dreams come true and torn into shreds. In a word, history for them is the lived experience of their suffering. It is this kind of history that we theologians must explore. We can leave the study of empires and republics, ancient or modern, their systems and structures, to "scientific" historians and political scientists. But the study of a people's history informed by the culture shaped by suffering is the task of theologians.

The history of Asian nations and peoples is the history of people's suffering and their experience of deep bitterness of life. It has been demonstrated from the history of Korea. The same is true of the Philippines, Taiwan, Indonesia, Thailand, China, Kampuchea, and Vietnam. A poem entitled "Exhibition," by Muong Man, gives a Vietnamese example:

I'll open a museum
to display all the possessions of a man's life
the way they exhibit works of art
or trophies of war

we'll set your love in a glass case
to hang by my younger years like an amulet
next to loneliness and a rusty saber
the vestiges of our heroic race
surviving the past like so many medals
to decorate the crumpled tunic of life

the future—I'll fashion that into a naked statue
a statue with just one arm
(enough to hold a switchblade)
and I'll pin a statement on its chest
a statement listing the crimes of war
and the names of friends who died at Pleime
Doc Co, Ba Long
and a promise of revenge for all
(the paper is smeared with tears and blood). . . .

no need to put price tags on each item—one sign
will do to let visitors know
we're willing to part
with the whole collection.[8]

I can hear someone protesting, "This is poetry, not history!" But can poetry that rises out of a culture of suffering be anything but history? And, couched in subdued language, pent-up bitterness in the heart of this poem.

The poem has to do with the history of the suffering of the Vietnamese people during and after the Vietnam war. "I'll open a museum," says the poet. He wants to house the tragic history of his beloved country in a museum for everyone to see. A fantastic idea! His museum begins to be filled with mementos of the past—vestiges of loneliness and suffering. What about the future? A museum does not house the future; it houses only the past. But the poet's museum is different. It can house the future. But the future of his nation is its past. That is why he fashions the future into a crippled naked statue with only one arm.

Why is the statue crippled? It is crippled by the past, by that hideous Vietnam war. The poet's country has become a crippled nation inhabited by men, women, and children maimed and destroyed by bombs. Why is the statue naked? It is stripped naked by the past, by that horrendous proxy war of foreign powers fought in the heart of his nation. Then comes the deepest expression of suffering in the poem. On the chest of that naked crippled statue called future is pinned a statement listing war crimes and the names of friends and dear ones killed in that war. That statement, smeared with tears and blood, is "a promise of revenge" to those souls cut off from the world of the living by human atrocity.

The poet wants to build a museum to house the suffering of his people. His museum is going to be a monument dedicated to the Vietnamese culture of suffering. Perhaps this is what he means when he, at the beginning of the poem, sets "your love in a glass case" beside those memorials of the tragic past and the statue of the naked future. Pent-up bitterness consumed with hate can become a dangerous power wreaking vengeance in fury and destruction. But it can be transformed by love, when it picks up the broken pieces from the past to clothe the naked future. Then suffering becomes redemptive. Theology in Asia should be alert and sensitive to manifestations of redemptive suffering experienced in Asian communities.

HE HAS BORNE OUR GRIEFS AND CARRIED OUR SORROWS

Turning then to our Bible with what has been said, we cannot help realizing that the faith it has given to us is also nourished within the culture of suffering. The story of the exodus at once comes to mind. It is the story of the suffering that mercilessly gripped the Hebrew slaves living in the land of their oppressors. Their lot was back-breaking hard labor and ruthless treatment from their masters. They were even forced to collect their own straw to make bricks for the pharaoh's construction work. Does this not remind us of Li Ts'ui-lien, the Chinese daughter-in-law, who had to cook breakfast for the entire family with only two bowls of thin rice porridge, and to make tea for them with only boiling water and no tea leaves? If this stirred the pent-up bitterness in Ts'ui-lien to open revolt, how could the deep distress suppressed within those Hebrew slaves not have forced them into a desperate flight from Egypt? But making bricks without straw was not all. When a male child was born to a Hebrew mother, he was instantly put to death by the pharaoh's order. The unspoken bitterness of those murdered children must have joined with that of their elders, becoming a mighty cry reaching out to heaven.

The cry of their suffering reached God. To the startled Moses God said from the burning bush: "I have indeed seen the misery of my people in Egypt. I have heard their outcry against their slave-masters. I have taken heed of their sufferings, and have come down to rescue them from the power of Egypt" (Exod. 3:7–8). Thus began the great saga of the exodus.

The history of Israel was deeply affected by the culture shaped by the suffering of its people. The tragic fall of Jerusalem and the humiliating experience of the exile have already been mentioned. It was during the exile that the culture of suffering attained the zenith of tragic nobility filled with redemptive significance. I am referring of course to that great prophet-poet Second

Isaiah. His fourth and last of "the servant songs"[9] shakes our souls and moves our hearts in the presence of God who heard the cry of deep distress from the Hebrew captives and who will hear the cry of our pent-up bitterness from lands of political oppression:

> He [the servant] was despised and rejected by men;
> a man of sorrows, and acquainted with grief;
> and as one from whom men hide their faces. . . .
>
> Surely he has borne our griefs
> and carried our sorrows;
> yet we esteemed him stricken,
> smitten by God, and afflicted. . . .
>
> He was oppressed, and he was afflicted,
> yet he opened not his mouth;
> like a lamb that is led to the slaughter,
> and like a sheep that before its shearers is dumb,
> so he opened not his mouth.
>
> By oppression and judgment he was taken away;
> and as for his generation,
> who considered
> that he was cut off out of the land of the living,
> stricken for the transgression of my people? [Isa. 53:3–8, RSV].

We are not just listening to a poem. We are hearing the cry of one going through unbearable suffering. We are not just seeing words in beautiful verse, but staring at the soul consumed by deep bitterness. No matter who the servant was who inspired the prophet-poet to write these noble verses, we are absorbed into a culture of suffering bearing within it a tremendous force of redemption.

Surely this kind of culture cannot just disappear into thin air. It cannot dissipate into a mere struggle for existence. On the contrary, the redemptive force released by such a culture of suffering was to become concentrated and sublimated in one person a few centuries later. In Jesus of Nazareth that culture of suffering took the form of death on the cross and in life out of the tomb. Here suffering and bitterness are no longer endured with the spirit of revenge. What one hears is not a cry for vengeance. In Jesus suffering and bitterness become transformed into forgiveness, transubstantiated into love, and transfigured into life. In Jesus we encounter the suffering love of God—the forgiving, redeeming love of God. What a humbling and yet exciting experience for Christians and theologians in Asia to realize that in our culture of suffering the redeeming love of God can be also at work.

7

What Do Statistics Mean?

CRIME AGAINST HUMANITY

Amnesty International is a London-based human rights organization. Its tireless work of locating political prisoners, adopting them, documenting and publicizing their predicament, and securing their release won it the Nobel Prize in 1980. In 1975, for example, it adopted 2,015 new political prisoners.[1] In its 1980 annual report it stated that in December 1979 twenty-six thousand persons were held in prison camps in Vietnam; that two thousand persons had been arrested in Kabul, Afghanistan, in February 1980.[2] In 1981 it announced that it had the names of more than five hundred political prisoners in the Republic of Korea.[3] If all Asian countries could be taken into account, the numbers would be staggering. And if all political prisoners—better called "prisoners of conscience"—in the entire world could be counted, the numbers would be overwhelming.

Statistics are not just numbers. There are stories behind the numbers. Statistics have a soul. They live in the lives of men, women, and children who have lost their names and have been turned into mere numbers. They have a mountain of stories to tell, mostly tragic. They have an ocean of tears to shed, tears of pain and sadness. And they have desperate appeals to make, appeals for freedom, dignity, and love. Statistics on prisoners of conscience are a mobilization of shame,[4] of shameful crimes committed by human beings against other human beings.

Such statistics have to be decoded today. They deal with human beings. They tell us what we human beings are like. They are a proof of what we humans are capable of in terms of inhumanity. Such statistics tell the dark side of the story of humanity. That is why theologians should not disregard them. They should engage their theological minds in some hard reflection. There is theology in statistics, and a *living* theology at that.

There is the story of Charito Planas, director of the Philippine Chamber of Commerce.[5] Imelda Marcos, the first lady, and Charito Planas were campaigning against each other for a seat in the newly created National Assembly under President Marcos's martial law. Imelda Marcos arrived in one part of Manila in a black limousine accompanied by scores of security agents. She told her subdued audience that she could bring their needs to the president and have them fulfilled. In another part of the city Charito Planas was standing on top of an oil drum, holding up an enlarged photograph of Imelda Marcos wearing a diamond tiara. She said to the excited crowd: "This crown is worth 10 million pesos. Do you know what you can do with 10 million pesos? We could build a thousand houses for the poor." She was "taken care of" soon thereafter:

> On October 3, 1973, at 10:00 P.M. she was at home, resting in her room. There was a loud knock on her bedroom door. "This is a raid. We are raiding your house."
>
> Everyone at Charito's home was placed under armed guard in the living room. The police went from room to room conducting a search. By midnight another contingent of soldiers arrived, bringing their number to over a hundred. . . .
>
> Charito was taken to an overcrowded prison where she was fingerprinted a dozen times. This was a temporary holding center that contained both political prisoners and criminals. That night she slept on the floor.
>
> The following day she was moved to Camp Crame . . . . After several days she was transferred to Ipil Reception Center at Fort Bonifacio, a camp for political prisoners. . . .
>
> But Charito did not remain in Ipil Reception Center long. One evening she was told to report to office headquarters.
>
> "Bring all your things with you."
>
> "Why? What do you want?"
>
> "Never mind. Just get everything."
>
> She took some clothes and a radio which had been brought for her. Then they blindfolded her.
>
> "I felt like a thing—a thing just taken and placed somewhere. It was dehumanizing. If you are a human being, at least you're told where you're going. What's the use of not telling you? So the very moment I was blindfolded I was like a thing, something less than human."

The story of Charito Planas is the story of a crime against humanity. And there are as many such stories as there are political prisoners. First of all, criminals dressed up as state authorities come to raid your house in the middle of the night. It is a criminal act, fittingly executed under cover of darkness. But there is another reason why they prefer to pounce on you after darkness has ended a busy day. At night you are off guard. During the day when you are at work in a factory, in an office, at school, you have to look your best, all geared up to do your job well. When at last the day is over, you come home to rest, to relax, to revitalize your humanity. That is what home is for. State criminals know that. So they come for you at night, taking you by surprise, putting your humanity under their control.

The next step is to destroy your home. They search it, empty your cupboards, pull out drawers, scattering your clothes, books, and other belongings on the floor. They turn your home into a chaos no longer recognizable as your home. This is another assault on your humanity, for what is humanity if it has no home, if it does not belong somewhere? Searching your home and destroying it is done to let you know that you are now a nonperson. You can only stand by in helplessness.

The criminals go further. They blindfold you and do not tell you where you are being taken. You are blindfolded. You are shut out from the world. You have lost not only your home but also the world. They are trying to destroy your identity. This is why those state criminals do not tell you where they are taking you. You have lost the right to know where you are. You have become a mere plaything in their hands. This is exactly what Charito Planas felt. And it must be the feeling of thousands and thousands of other political prisoners.

The state authorities have assaulted your humanity. It is a blatant crime against your humanity and a blasphemous crime against God. Humanity is given by God. It comes from God and belongs to God. And it is this God who shows us what a full and rich humanity is in Jesus Christ. To use the language of the author of the fourth Gospel in the New Testament, "the Word became flesh and dwelt among us, full of grace and truth" (John 1:14). The author is saying that God is with humanity and God is with it to make it full of truth and grace, to make it true, rich, and beautiful. To use the expression of an earlier chapter, God *images* God's own self in us human beings.

For this reason state authorities have no claim over anyone's humanity. They did not give it and they cannot take it away—except by violence. That is what they want to do. They come armed with rifles and bayonets. They come to rob you of your humanity. And in doing so, they rob God of the humanity that belongs to God. The arrest of political prisoners does not entail simply a political struggle between the state and its citizens; it entails a crime against humanity and against God. Is there not, then, considerable theology to be done here?

There is a "doctrine of God" hidden in the statistics of political prisoners. We also encounter in those statistics the Jesus Christ we have been searching for in erudite volumes of traditional theologians. As we know, religious and political authorities joined forces to arrest Jesus, blindfold him, mock his humanity and turn him into a nonperson. An English doctor working in Chile was struck by the resemblance between Jesus and her fellow medical worker arrested at the time of the military coup. As she told it:

> Suddenly I saw for the first time the similarity between what I had been reading in my Bible and what I knew was happening to Jaime: the sudden and violent arrest, the insolent interrogators, the rough hands that tore away his clothes leaving him humiliated and vulnerable; then the blows and the laughter of the tormentors and finally the fixing spread-eagled to

> the bed for the shocks to break his spirit. I was appalled. Never had the passion of Christ, read and reread since childhood, moved me to more than a gesture of sadness or an act of contrition, but now I was filled with anguish and nausea. The vision of Christ still living and still being crucified amongst us took on clarity and meaning that was quite new to me, and I wept for Jaime and for Christ, knowing that they were one.[6]

Jaime and Christ are one! Traditional theology did not tell us that, and I do not believe it ever will. It will not permit identification of Christ and Jaime.

But our theology must be able to make such identification—and boldly. Did not Matthew remember Jesus as saying: "When I was hungry, you gave me food; when thirsty, you gave me drink; when I was a stranger you took me into your home" (Matt. 25:35)? Jesus is saying that theology begins in the life we live daily and in the world in which we struggle with other human beings to be human. This is *living* theology. It is this kind of living theology that we must image in Asia. It is this kind of living theology that we must look for in the Bible, in both the Old and New Testaments, and in church history. It is also this kind of living theology that we must search for in the histories of other faiths and in our own histories. Then we may know what to make of Jesus of Nazareth and where to find him.

THE RICH CONSUME THE POOR

> A 1973 United Nations report, *Multinational Corporations in World Development*, providing 1971 figures, indicates that the total foreign direct investment in the noncommunist countries (the market economies) amounted to $165 billion, with an estimated annual production valued at $330 billion. The U.S. share of this investment was $86 billion or 52%, compared to $59.4 billion in 1966. Over four-fifths of this total was owned by the United States, the United Kingdom, France, and the Federal Republic of Germany. (Total U.S. direct investments abroad climbed to $137.2 billion in 1976.)[7]

> Compare these statistics with the following:

> The United Nations Children's Fund (UNICEF) estimated in 1978 alone more than 12 million children under the age of five died of hunger. The International Labour Office estimated the number of destitute at 700 million in the early 1970s. World Bank estimates today puts them at 800 million. This suggests that almost 40% of the people in the South are surviving—but only barely surviving.[8]

How can these two sets of statistics make sense? How can they tally with each other? On the one hand there is extreme wealth amassed by transnational corporations. The investments they make in Asia and elsewhere are in the billions of dollars! On the other hand there is extreme poverty: 800 million persons barely surviving, representing more than 40 percent of the population in the southern hemisphere. What is this monster called a transnational corporation that is investing so much wealth in Asia but is making so many of our brothers and sisters destitute?

We may be surprised to hear that transnational corporations represent the best that science and technology have created. But it is true:

> They are a human social organism equipped with the best scientific mind, the most information, the greatest financial resources, the most efficient technology, and the most complex organization. . . . It is the most powerful, creative social corpus to emerge in human history.[9]

Such an organism ought to do a lot of good, not harm. It should be able to bring blessings, not curses. But a great deal of harm has been done to Third World countries where transnational corporations have moved in with massive capital. With their enormous power to organize and exploit, they have brought curses to those countries. Transnational corporations must be monsters in disguise, bent on greed and gain at the cost of the blood and life of the human beings they touch and use. This at least we must know about them, although the monster is elusive in nature and not always plainly visible.

Why has this organism, created out of the best in science and technology, turned into a terrible monster living from the sweat and blood of human beings? The reason seems to be that it is an organism without a soul. It is a human organism, but it has no human heart. It is a social organism, but it has no social conscience. It is an organism that has no feelings for human misery. It shows no emotion at the sight of the millions of destitute persons it has created.

There is story after story of how workers and their families suffer under this insatiable monster, which descends on them with its huge investments only to carry away the fruits of their back-breaking labor, leaving them with only a pittance for bare survival. Here, for example, is the testimony of a worker in Indonesia employed at Fairchild, a U.S. electronics company producing semiconductors:

> I started working at Fairchild in January 1978. They put me in the optical test section where I have to look through a microscope to test the chips before they are bonded. It took me two weeks to get used to using the microscope.
>
> When I first came, last year, they paid me Rp 390 a day ($US 0.80). After a three month "training" period they gave me Rp 450 a day. Now I get Rp 490. After the training period they set my quota at 15 trays a day. Now I have to test 25 trays a day. I think there are between 160 and 180 chips in each tray, so I test around 3,500 chips a day.

> I get up a 5:00 A.M. and take the bus to work. The shift starts at 6:00 A.M. and goes until 2:00 P.M. . . . We have a ten-minute tea break at 8:00 A.M. and a 15-minute lunch break at 9:15.
>
> After six months I became sick with red eyes [conjunctivitis]. I don't know why this happened. Other friends at work got sick too. The supervisor told me to clean my microscope so nobody else would get it. Then he gave me a two-week medical leave. While I was at home, my family all got red eyes too.
>
> I don't earn enough money to give my mother much, but I give her food money sometimes. I like to buy my brothers and sisters *basko* [noodle soup sold by street vendors]. It costs Rp 50 a bowl, so if I buy it for all of us, it costs my whole day's salary.[10]

"I don't earn enough money to give my mother much," says the worker. This is an understatement. The daily wage of one U.S. dollar, even by Indonesian standards, is a subsistence wage only. How can he buy his brothers and sisters *basko* that costs one-tenth of his daily wage?

Besides the low earnings, he and other workers get conjunctivitis and give it to other members of their families. The sanitary situation in factories run by transnational corporations is appalling. No measures are taken to protect workers from health problems. They are just tools for production. They are easily replaced. With an abundance of unemployed persons waiting in line for work, labor is cheap. Many Third World countries are a paradise of cheap labor for transnational corporations. And helped by corrupt authoritarian governments, they do not have to worry about strikes as they do at home.

Statistics are not just numbers, figures, and percentages. They are alive with human lives—lives of workers, day laborers, peasants in Asia and other parts of the Third World. They speak—loudly. They speak about the plight of workers who cannot earn enough to feed their parents, wives, and children. They weep—bitterly. They weep for humanity despoiled in exchange for a substandard wage. And they cry out for human dignity suppressed in order to give taskmasters from abroad huge profits to send back home. Into statistics is packed human misery. They burst with human tragedy. But you will not know this until you put together statistics and the human stories that make them possible.

Theologians must study statistics very assiduously. There is such a thing as the theology of statistics. The study of statistics is not a subject monopolized by schools of economics. It must enter theological classrooms. But we do not study them as do scientific statisticians. We are theological statisticians, because we study statistics not as pure economic data, but as human data, not as hard and cold numbers, but as figures throbbing with human sweat and blood. Statistics, in the hands of theologians, turn into stories that others live and tell with passion and in passion (suffering). The theology of statistics is a part of *living* theology.

PLOWSHARES AND SWORDS

Table 1

1981 Public Expenditure in Millions $US[11]

	Military	*Education*	*Health*
Bangladesh	118	160	28
India	3,498	3,360	1,360
Indonesia	1,642	845	668
Malaysia	607	950	272
Pakistan	990	390	120
Philippines	512	520	166
South Korea	2,876	1,240	120
Taiwan	1,809	940	603
Thailand	836	790	154

What do the statistics in Table 1 say to us? What do they mean? They speak to us in anguish. Their meaning is passion (suffering).

In most Asian countries military spending is disproportionately high in comparison with spending on education, health, and other social programs. Military preparedness is deemed more important than human preparedness. The development of military strength is more crucial than human development. Officialdom explains: Without national security how can there be personal security? If national borders are not safe, what is the use of excellent education and good health for the general population? If national sovereignty is not defended at any cost, how can there be human rights for the citizens? The world is involved in a fierce arms race. Might is right. This is how geopolitics works. Even nations in Asia, poor as they are, are deeply involved in world power politics. Does all this not justify high military spending? It is all for the sake of our citizens!

The world has become a giant marketplace for "death-merchants" to sell their military hardware, especially in the Third World. It is estimated that arms transfers worldwide totaled $20 billion (US) in 1980, 80 percent of which went to the Third World, with the Middle East the biggest and Asia the second biggest buyer. It is also true that the United States is the largest arms supplier, followed by the Soviet Union.[12] These two superpowers are the two super death-merchants. It is they who are to blame for our huge military expenditures. We live in their military shadows.

But this is only half of the picture. The fact is that military spending perpetuates poverty in Asia, depriving millions of adequate food, shelter, health, and education. In the case of India, for example, the cost of one submarine would give 200,000 villages drinking water; the cost of servicing 900 aircraft for one year has the market value of one million tons of wheat, which could feed one-fifth of India's population—that is, more than 100 million persons—for ten days; the cost of five MBT tanks would build a primary school in 12,500 villages.[13]

These statistics make one ponder. Geopolitics or not, human beings are starving because of the arms race. Power politics or not, children go uneducated. National security or not, hundreds of thousands of villagers have no safe drinking water. These are statistics of the people. They challenge the statistics of rulers. With individual life threatened, these statistics cry out, there is no national security. Geopolitics, they shout, makes a people's unbearable life even more unbearable. Power politics, they plead, adds insult to already injured humanity.

These statistics tell us that the ruled do not believe in their rulers. They tell us that what human beings want—badly and desperately—are not tanks, jet fighters, submarines, or nuclear arms, but food, clothing, shelter, literacy, and health. What they need is human dignity. This is their true security.

Then there is the fact of the militarization of government and political systems in many Asian countries. This is a scourge that causes endless suffering. With weapons paid for with tax money, and with soldiers and police trained with the revenues from domestic labor, rulers turn against the ruled. The government becomes militarized from top to bottom. The entire nation is politicized from north to south, from west to east. In matters that concern the individual politically and personally, whether it is the election of a president or policy on national defense, all citizens are expected to think the way those in power tell them to, even if it contradicts what they know to be true.

The Ministry of Truth in the Big Brother government in *Nineteen Eighty-Four*, the classic novel on totalitarianism by George Orwell, proclaims that "war is peace, freedom is slavery, and ignorance is strength."[14] It is of no use to shout and protest that the very reverse is the truth. It will only land one in prison and lead to liquidation. That was the fate of Winston Smith, a hard-working government clerk. This is what he had to learn:

> The Party told you to reject the evidence of your eyes and ears. It was their final, most essential command. His heart sank as he thought of the enormous power arrayed against him, the ease with which any Party intellectual would overthrow him in debate, the subtle arguments which he would not be able to understand, much less answer. And yet he was in the right! They were wrong and he was right. The *obvious*, the silly, and the true had got to be defended. Truisms are true, hold on to that! The solid world exists, its laws do not change. Stones are hard, water is wet, objects unsupported fall towards the earth's centre . . . he wrote [in his diary]: *Freedom is the freedom to say that two plus two make four. If that is granted, all else follows.*[15]

It was this freedom that proved to be his undoing. And how much he had to go through in the torture chamber and in the interrogation room! Finally he ended up "in the public dock, confessing everything, implicating everybody. He was walking down the white-tiled corridor, with the feeling of walking in sunlight, and an armed guard at his back. The long-hoped-for bullet was entering his brain."[16]

The innocent-looking statistics on military spending are not innocent at all. Behind them is hidden an autocratic ruler, a party chairman, a state executioner. This is what those statistics mean. They tell us that the police are just around the corner to get us. They warn us that secret agents are on our trail. They remind us that the struggle for democracy is a crime against the state. How one wishes such demonic statistics would disappear from our life, from our society!

But this is not just *our* wish. It is the wish that millions and millions of persons from ancient times to the present day have cherished against all odds. It is the hope of countless oppressed men, women, and children—a hope that never dies. And what a noble and sublime expression of that wish and hope we hear from the lips of Isaiah in ancient Israel! Living at a time when the nations were playing power politics to the hilt and rumors of war were rampant, the prophet was inspired to say:

> [God] shall judge between the nations,
> and shall decide for many peoples;
> and they shall beat their swords into plowshares,
> and their spears into pruning hooks;
> nation shall not lift up sword against nation,
> neither shall they learn war any more [Isa. 2:4, RSV].

Since the prophet uttered those inspired and inspiring words, a world without war has receded more and more from the realm of reality. Nations have learned more and more about the art of war. They have refined ploughshares into nuclear submarines and intercontinental ballistic missiles. And more and more prisons are built to house political dissidents and prisoners of conscience.

But Isaiah's dream is still valid. Its message is all the more urgent today, for the destiny of our world is threatened by the fifty-thousand nuclear warheads known to be deployed by aligned and nonaligned nations. Does this not tell us what *living* theology must do? One thing is certain. Theology cannot go on propagating theories of a just war. The fact of nuclear weapons that can destroy the earth many times over makes war, any war, unjustifiable. Nor can we allow theology to be used in support of a government that robs its people of the freedom to say that two and two make four. Ours must be a theology dedicated to the dream of Isaiah the prophet and to the emergence of a sane society where freedom is respected and made the basis of government and political systems. Our *living* theology must be a political theology.

8

Stones Cry Out

SILENCE OF THE UGLY STONE

Freedom allows one to say that stones are hard. It is as simple as that. But in a country gripped by a power-obsessed ruler who forbids it to be said, it takes courage to say such a simple thing. Stones are hard. Even 3-year-olds know it. But in a nation under an authoritarian regime it is not an easy matter to say openly something that is forbidden. Those who live in such a country have learned the wisdom of keeping silent. They turn themselves into silent stones. A Taiwanese poet has written these lines on an "Ugly Stone":

> Vegetation fights for every inch of land,
> Leaves crowd from height. . . .
>
> Buds blossom
> One after the other,
> Although a small hermitage garden,
> Vegetation is bursting too.
>
> At the corner sits the stone.
> Ye ugly stone which neither
> Lengthens nor expands;
> Never swept by storm
> Or meets the invitation of gong and drum.
>
> Could one guess that the silence
> Of the ugly stone is beyond
> Pleasure, anger, grief or joy?
> Lovely, tall as grey elephant dark
> At leisure and duty.

Ye one ugly stone,
With serious attitude,
Glory the small garden.[1]

The ugly stone! The silent stone! What are you doing in the hermitage garden? In the nation that has turned into a hermitage garden, products of the land and the factory are evidence of economic progress. And the flowers praise the virtues of those in power and dedicate their beauty to them. But this stone, so ugly and obstinately silent, sits there brooding.

The ugly stone neither lengthens nor expands. It does not change in compliance with those in power. In its silence it speaks. It maintains the truth that two and two are four. In its obstinate silence it thus speaks of freedom. It is not affected by changes in the weather. It retains the common sense that water is wet. And it does not move an inch to accept an invitation from higher authorities for a political breakfast. It knows where its place is. Its place is in the garden, speaking as loudly as it can in the hermitage nation by its silence and through its silence.

Could one guess, asks the poet, whether the ugly stone is in pleasure, in anger, in grief, or in joy? Yes, one can guess. The ugly stone is not pleased. Nor is it joyful. Otherwise it would not look ugly. It would look pleasant, if not beautiful. It would look acceptable, if not resplendent. But it looks ugly because it is in grief and anger. It grieves at the lack of freedom and is angry at the negligible progress toward democracy. But with its grief and anger it glories the hermitage garden. It keeps alive the truth that two and two make four. It is a bastion of sanity and common sense for the nation. It maintains human dignity for its inhabitants.

THE STONES WILL CRY OUT

But there comes a time when the language of silence, though powerful, will no longer communicate. It is taken by those in authority as an indication of weakness, as evidence of apathy, a sign of resignation. When that time comes, the passion concealed within the silent stone will burst out in shouting, the fire contained in it will blaze up, the anger and grief suppressed in it will burst into action. This is what happened to a large crowd that followed Jesus as he entered Jerusalem for a final showdown with the religious authorities.

It must have been an extraordinary event. Here is Jesus riding on a colt slowly but steadily moving toward the city. The hour has come! This is at last the time of deliverance from Roman colonial rule! This is going to be another exodus in the history of Israel! But why on a colt and not on a horse, like a general or a king? Those who were following Jesus, including his own disciples, must have been puzzled. They must have searched their memory of the scriptures for some clues. And they found some. They remembered what a prophet had said at the time of the exile in anticipation of a great exodus from the land of captivity:

Tell the daughter of Zion,
Behold, your deliverance has come.
His recompense comes with him;
he carries his reward before him [Isa. 62:11].

And the prophet Zechariah had proclaimed that wonderful message of a king coming, not on a horse, but on an ass:

Rejoice, rejoice, daughter of Zion,
Shout aloud, daughter of Jerusalem;
for see, your king is coming to you,
his cause won, his victory gained,
humble and mounted on an ass,
on a foal, the young of a she-ass [Zech. 9:9].

It is Matthew who left us a record of how the exciting scene of Jesus' entry into Jerusalem conjured up in his mind these passages from the prophets a few hundred years earlier and combined them in his own reconstruction of the story of Jesus' entry into Jerusalem:

Tell the daughter of Zion,
Behold, your king is coming to you,
humble, and mounted on an ass,
and on a colt, the foal of an ass [Matt. 21:5, RSV].

This may have been afterthought on Matthew's part. But the crowd with Jesus, his disciples included, did look to him for the fulfillment of a promise of a national messiah-king coming to reestablish the kingdom of Judah. They were to be disappointed. It might be that Peter's denial of Jesus was not simply out of cowardice, but out of disappointment—his hopes of national restoration shattered. It would also be too simplistic to conclude that Judas's betrayal of his master was motivated by love of money. Thirty silver coins (Matt. 26:15) were not very much. It could be that he was terribly disillusioned when Jesus did not seize the moment to rise in revolt against Rome. He was probably a Zealot. Perhaps Peter too.

What, then, about Jesus himself? From the records in the Gospels, one will never know what was in his mind. But there are some hints, very vague hints to be sure, here and there that Jesus was not altogether apathetic to a political solution. When he was warned that Herod Antipas was after his life, he said: "Go and tell that fox . . . " (Luke 13:32). These words could have been charged with political overtones. And there is the cryptic passage in Luke's Gospel (no parallel in the other Gospels) about the two swords. Just as they were about to leave the table of the last supper and go out to Gethsemane, Jesus said to the disciples: "Whoever has a purse had better take it with him, and his pack too; and if he has no sword, let him sell his cloak to buy one" (Luke

22:36). Was Jesus asking whether they were combat-ready? One may wonder. The disciples obviously took their master seriously. "Lord, Lord," they replied in excitement, "we have two swords here." To this Jesus' response was: "Enough, enough!" (22:38). Was this Jesus' approval of their preparedness or his consternation at their grossly misunderstanding his intentions? It is difficult to say.

Then there is the matter of Jesus' asking for a colt to ride on for his entry into Jerusalem. Were those words of the prophets quoted later by Matthew in Jesus' mind also? Was he going to ride on a colt as a sign of spiritual messiahship? But he must have known that others would interpret it politically. Then perhaps some political implications were not totally lacking in Jesus' decision to enter Jerusalem, the city of David, on a colt.

At any rate, Jesus' entry into Jerusalem stirred exhilaration among the crowds. "Many spread their garments on the road, and others spread leafy branches" (Mark 11:8, RSV; par. Matt. 21:8; Luke 19:36). What a royal welcome! They matched their deeds with their words and shouted:

> Hosanna! Blessings on him who comes in the name of the Lord; Blessings on the coming kingdom of our father David! Hosanna in the heavens! [Mark 11:10; par. Matt. 21:9; Luke 19:38].

This is a call for salvation. Hosanna! Save us! It is also a cry of jubilation, for the savior has come, riding on a colt. He comes in the name of their God to restore the "kingdom of our father David." As Matthew has it, Jesus is "the son of David," whereas for Luke he is "the king who comes in the name of the Lord." The earliest Christian community might have considered the Davidic kingdom to be God's kingdom still to come at the end of time. But to those following Jesus into Jerusalem in great excitement, the kingdom of David on their lips must have had a strong political note. Undoubtedly they were welcoming Jesus into the city of David as a political messiah.

Luke alone gives further clues about Jesus' entry into Jerusalem as perhaps a potentially explosive event. "Some Pharisees who were in the crowd said to him [Jesus], 'Master, reprimand your disciples'" (Luke 19:39). These must have been Jesus' enemies ordered by their religious authorities to watch his movements closely. They must have sensed a political danger that could undermine their uneasy truce with the Roman authorities. Jesus' words and deeds openly challenged and contradicted their orthodoxy. Political success for him would certainly end their religious privileges and status. The crowd must be stopped. And the only person who could do it was Jesus. That is why they wanted him to reduce "the whole company of his disciples" (19:37) to silence.

Jesus refused to do what his enemies asked him to do. He showed defiance to their impudent request when he retorted:

> I tell you, if my disciples keep silence, the very stones would cry out [Luke 19:40].

These were very strong words. Jesus must have pronounced them with determination. Did he realize the political implications of what he said? He must have. Even if he had not meant it to be political, how could he have failed to know it would give encouragement to the crowd already politically aroused? Indeed, "what history tells us is not that Jesus was apolitical but that he offered a new alternative to Zealotism. Yet his alternative also has political implications and repercussions."[2]

The masses have been silent for too long, both religiously and politically. They have had to bear the brunt of both political and religious oppression. On the one hand they are burdened with taxes imposed by the Roman colonial government. They have suffered humiliation at the hand of colonizers. But their own religious authorities, on the other hand, have not made their life any easier. There must have been a lot of pent-up bitterness in their intestines and in their hearts. It is Jesus who made their deep distress shout and cry out in the open.

Jesus used harsh terms to condemn the religious leaders. "Alas, alas for you," he said, "lawyers and Pharisees, hypocrites that you are! You shut the door of the kingdom of Heaven in people's faces; you do not enter yourselves, and when others are entering, you stop them" (Matt. 23:13). No one before Jesus had dared to challenge them like this, calling them hypocrites. His followers must have at first stared at him in disbelief, being afraid for him and for themselves also. But they must have come to hear in those daring words of Jesus their own distresss shouting at the top of its voice. How much they had longed for the day when their pent-up bitterness could be heard, but now Jesus is their anguish, speaking, crying out, and taking their religious masters to task. In Jesus they have their injustice done to them vindicated.

Jesus' words to the religious leaders are straight and sharp. He must have been fully conscious of standing on the side of the politically and religiously oppressed when he again said:

> Woe to you lawyers also! for you load people with burdens hard to bear, and you yourselves do not touch the burdens with one of your fingers [Luke 11:46; par. Matt. 23:4].

At last Jesus said what must be said. His hearers must have felt the centuries-old religious burden lifted from their shoulders. For the first time in their lives they felt religiously unencumbered. As if to confirm their feeling of liberation, Jesus gave them assurance: "My yoke is easy, and my burden is light" (Matt. 11:30). A new era of faith and religion has begun.

What happened on the religious scene also happened on the political stage. In welcoming Jesus to Jerusalem as king and messiah, the crowds let their political anguish cry out. Jesus riding on a colt embodied their political hope. In Jesus they saw their political humiliation gone, their political integrity restored, their political rights fulfilled. Jesus must have heard their deep distress in their cry and understood what it meant. No power on earth, even all the religious and political powers of that day combined, could suppress it anymore. If it was silenced and forced back into the bodies and souls of the people, then "these very stones will cry out"! The "groaning in travail" in the heart of the creation would erupt and engulf the world with its roar.

Jesus' words must have staggered his enemies. Confronted with such powerful words, they must have been reduced to silence. A dramatic change has now taken place in that explosive moment when the power of Jesus and the power of his enemies size each other up for confrontation. It is now for the people to be vocal and for the political and religious leaders to be silent. It is now the time for the people to shout out loud and for the leaders to keep dead silence. The hour has arrived for the pent-up bitterness of the humiliated to rise from the bottom of their hearts in a magnificent chorus venting its sorrows and shouting its hopes.

As to those who have held political and religious power over the people, they must listen to that passion cry and understand its implications. That is why Jesus refused to order his followers to be silent. He did precisely the opposite. He encouraged them and said resolutely: "If my disciples keep silence, the very stones would cry out!" If Jesus were with us in person today, he would certainly take the same stance. He was not apolitical. How, then, can there be an apolitical theology? How can there be an apolitical church? And how can there be an apolitical people and apolitical Christians?

IF THE LAND COULD SPEAK

What do we do to become a political people? What must we do to become political Christians? We do not have to *become* political; we are political already by reason of being members of society, of a nation, and of this political world. To become political Christians we do not have to join a political party, or, not content with it, form a "Christian" political party. As Christians and as citizens of a country, we are political already. Political theology, then, is not doctrines of church and state, not theological theories of politics and political systems. At least that is not the kind of political theology we should strive for in Asia. The life of Asian peoples is itself full of political stories. The task of political theology is to discover them, to penetrate into the woes and joys, despairs and hopes, behind those stories, and to encounter and experience the human soul possessed and cherished by God. Political theology is, then, both political and theological. In those stories of the people we come to know ourselves and the world politically. But at the same time we find ourselves in the presence of God, knowing better who our God is.

It is this kind of political theology that we have in a poem entitled "Sounds from the Valley" from the Kalinga people in the Philippines:

> If the land could speak,
> It would speak for us.
> It would say, like us, that the years
> Have forged the bond of life that ties us together
> It was our labour that made the land what she is.

And it was her yielding that gave us life.
We and the land are one!

But who would listen?
Will they listen,
Those invisible,
Who, from an unfeeling distance, claim
The land is theirs?
Because pieces of paper say so?
Because the pieces of paper are backed by men
Who speak threatening words;
Men who have power to shoot and kill,
Men who have power to take our men and our sons away?

If the land could speak,
It would speak for us!
For the land is us!
And we speak!
But who will listen?[3]

How could the land speak? It is speech-less. Like stone it has no power of speech. If the land could speak. . . . This must be an unrealistic wish.

Unlike stones, land has the power to produce food vital to human life. It is this productive power that makes the land valuable to human beings. Without land, there is no life, and there are no human beings. Land and human beings share a common life and destiny. "A bond of life" is forged between the land and those who work it and depend on it. Is there not in this simple language, in these matter-of-fact words, a profound theology of creation reminiscent of the second creation story in Genesis? There God made human beings from the dust of the ground. To use the language of this Kalinga poem, we can say that God made us from the land. Land and us, we and land—this bond of life is forged by God. We live in land and land lives in us. The Kalinga poet, I am sure, had no academic training in theology, any more than did the storyteller who left us that simple but magnificent story of the creation. And yet there is so much theology of creation in both writings.

There is something more. Persons and land not only share life together; they also share destiny together. "We and the land are one," says the Kalinga poet. The storyteller in Genesis said the same thing in a different way. In the story of the fall after the story of the creation, the storyteller says with much insight: "You are dust, and to dust you shall return." Again can we not use the word land and say: "You are land, and to land you shall return"? This is of course a statement about the natural process of life for the Kalinga peasant as well as for that storyteller. But it is also much more than that, again for that storyteller and for the Kalinga people. On the surface it tells us where our life will end at death. But our power of imaging shows us something beyond death. It enables us to see life, through death, disappear into land to live again!

Human beings and land become truly and thoroughly integrated to give life, to produce the power of life, in the continuing process of life. The land before you, the land on which you stand, is not just land. It teems with lives—the lives that have gone before us. And it is the land ready to receive us back and have us live in its womb. It is also ever prepared to have all the lives of all future generations return to its womb for the conception and birth of new lives.

All this, and perhaps more, is in that Kalinga poem and in the stories in the Christian Bible. It is a great pity that modern civilization strongly alienates us from the land. Buildings are built higher and higher to house us in midair, swaying between heaven and earth. Modern architecture makes us wonder where we belong. We do not belong to the sky, although we have learned to travel by air and to intrude into space. We are supposed to belong to the earth, but we live far above it, detached and separated from it. Perhaps this is one of the reasons why many of us today, especially those who live in cities, feel homeless.

Most of the food we eat, "civilized" food, is processed food. It is washed and cleaned mechanically. It is shredded into fine pieces by machines. It is immersed in chemical preservatives. Or it is frozen hard—hard as a rock. Every trace of the land in it is destroyed. The taste and smell of the land are removed from it. It is as though we eat vegetables grown in a laboratory, beef or pork produced in test tubes. Small wonder we do not feel "we and the land are one." That Kalinga poet must have been a farmer. And for that matter, our storyteller in the Bible could have been a farmer too; at least he must have lived very close to the land.

To take the land away from the Kalinga peasants amounts to taking life away from them. It is not only that the land yields enough for them to earn a living. It is not only that the land gives them a place to put up a shelter from the wind and rain. It is a matter of life! But those armed men who come from the state agencies cannot understand this. They are blind to the fact that the land trembles when the farmers tremble. They do not hear the land sob when the farmers sob. They do not see the land contorted in pain when the farmers are contorted in pain. All they know is that the farmers must sign the paper to part with their land. All they have is the power to make the farmers leave their land.

If the land could speak! But the land does speak. Did it not speak after Cain had murdered his brother Abel (Gen. 4:1–16)? God faced Cain with the question: "Where is your brother Abel?" And from him came the infamous answer: "I do not know. Am I my brother's keeper?" Cain underestimated the power of speech that the land had. More likely, he did not believe the land could speak. He was a tiller of the soil. He worked the land but he did not seem to develop a kinship with the land. How could he know then that the land could speak? God had to tell him: "Hark! Your brother's blood that has been shed is crying out to me from the ground!" Yes, God heard Abel's blood crying out from the land. Cain was totally exposed. He had to be punished for the crime of fratricide.

The land does speak. It does not just lie there waiting to be exploited and tortured. A Kalinga woman tells us so:

> The government had decided to build a dam in our mountain region. They began bringing in equipment to carry out a survey. They built temporary camps and erected tents to hold their equipment. The protest of we Kalingas was strong because we did not want the dam to be built.
>
> In our barrio we wondered what to do. We had written letters of protest to the President and the government departments, but we received no response. . . . It was decided that the whole community would dismantle the camp, and as a protest we would march with the equipment to the provincial barracks, forty kilometers away. . . .
>
> At dawn we approached the camp. There were several hundred of us—old men, young people, children, men, and women, and we took part in dismantling the tents holding the equipment. The engineering team were still asleep in their camp nearby.
>
> We began our march to the office of the provincial governor. We walked without stopping for lunch, and by early afternoon had covered the forty kilometers. . . .

The confrontation resulted in more pressures on the Kalingas to surrender their land for the building of the dam. But they persisted. "It is a stalemate situation now," says the Kalinga woman. "We are like prisoners in our community. We cannot travel on the roads where military check-points are placed, but we have our mountain trails and can visit each other's barrios."[4]

The land did speak. It spoke in the Kalingas' letters to the president. It spoke when they dismantled the camps and tents of the engineers. It spoke in their protest march. The Kalingas have not won. Not yet. But when they and their land cried out with one voice, dam construction did not proceed. At least a stalemate ensued. And the land is still with them. It is against intruders. It protects the Kalinga people from the soldiers who surround them and control the roads; it gives the Kalingas mountain trails so that they can visit each other's barrios.

SONG OF ARIRAN

The oppressed and humiliated have been speaking out of their suffering since the time of Abel, but theologians in Asia have just begun to hear them. Their groanings, their complaints, their sobs—in a word, their distress and anguish—were not in our theological textbooks. What we used to hear were the conquests of kings and emperors, the edicts of popes and decisions of cardinals, the great teachings of court theologians and church scholars. But we seldom had the chance to hear how ordinary persons lived and died. It was beyond our theological purview to dream about the land speaking for its dwellers and its dwellers struggling for the land, although it was right in the story of Abel's murder in the fourth chapter of Genesis. It was beyond our imagination to see that there was so much theology to be found in the marketplace, in the rural community, in the mountain village. But theology begins where God is. And God is there in the busy marketplace, in a humble village community, in a remote mountain region.

God is everywhere. God speaks out of everywhere. And God is at work everywhere. God was with the prisoners on their way to execution singing the "Song of Ariran," a Korean folksong that has not ceased to speak to oppressed Koreans since it was first sung about three hundred years ago:

Ariran, Ariran Arari O!
Crossing the hills of Ariran.
There are twelve hills of Ariran
And now I am crossing the last hill.

Many stars in the deep sky—
Many crimes in the life of man.
Ariran, Ariran Arari O!
Crossing the hills of Ariran.

Ariran is the mountain of sorrow
And the path to Ariran has no returning.
Ariran, Ariran Arari O!
Crossing the hills of Ariran.

Now I am an exile crossing the Yalu River
And the mountains and rivers of three thousand *li*
are also lost.
Ariran, Ariran, Arari O!
Crossing the hills of Ariran.[5]

You have to know the tune to be gripped by its profound pathos. You must sing it to catch the deep tragic sense of life these words try to convey. And if you know the story behind it, you cannot but be moved and shaken:

> Near Seoul is a hill called the Hill of Ariran. During the oppressive Li dynasty there was a giant solitary pine at the top of this hill, and this was the official place of execution for several hundred years. Tens of thousands of prisoners were hanged on a gnarled branch of that ancient tree, their bodies suspended over a cliff at the side. Some were bandits. Some were common criminals. Some were dissident scholars. Some were political and family enemies of the emperor. Many were poor farmers who had raised their fists against oppression. Many were rebel youths who had struggled against tyranny and injustice. The story is that one of those young men composed a song during his imprisonment, and as he trudged slowly up the Hill of Ariran, he sang this song. The people learned it, and after that whenever a man was condemned to die he sang this in farewell to his joys or sorrows. Every Korean prison echoes with these haunting notes, and no one dares deny a man's deathright to sing it at the end. . . . It is a song of death and not of life. But death is not defeat. Out of many deaths victory may be born.[6]

There is theology in the song of Ariran. Or rather there is theology in the hearts of those climbing the twelve hills of Ariran to meet their death, whether bandits, dissident scholars, or rebellious youths. The world of strife below the hills recedes into the past with every step you climb Ariran. Yes, there are many stars in the sky and many crimes in human life. And there are so many crimes of injustice in the land of the oppressor. Sorrow in your heart? Fear in your soul? Bitterness in your bowels? The mountain of Ariran is the mountain of sorrow. The trees, bushes, and stones must be singing the song of Ariran with you in deep sorrow. They echo your fear. They sing your sorrow. From the heart of the universe surges forth the suppressed groaning of anguish, turning into a mighty chorus of anger, and drifting away into the hearts of the generations yet unborn. Accompanied by this cosmic chorus that sobs with you and weeps with you, you reach the last hill. Then what? Death or life? Death! Your song of Ariran ceases. But also life! The song of Ariran has not ceased. It continues to be sung and sung until there will be no more injustice in the world. You live in that hope. God holds you in that hope. God gives you life to live in that hope.

If Jesus had known the song of Ariran, he would have sung it as he trudged along the road to Calvary. The followers would have sung it with him. If they would not, the stones would—the very stones Jesus said would cry out if his followers were silenced. And as Jesus reached the top of the hill of Golgotha, his enemies believed that he had reached his last hill. But the last hill it was not going to be. In fact it turned out to be the first hill of a new life, the life of resurrection! Because of this life of resurrection, millions and millions of persons since the tragic hill of the skull have been singing the song of life. The song of Ariran and the song of Golgotha! Do they not echo each other? Do they not call one to the other?

9

Birth of Freedom

A CONFESSION

The song of Ariran (chap. 8) is a song of freedom. How can this be true? It seems rather a song of bondage. It is sung by prisoners on their way to execution. But freedom is not just a matter of being freed from chains and shackles. It is a matter of the spirit. Your limbs may be incarcerated, but your spirit can be free. Your body may be confined to a prison cell, but your soul can soar out into the sky. Did Jesus not say: "Do not fear those who kill the body, but cannot kill the soul" (Matt. 10:28)? Freedom is born out of the spirit and the soul, which the powers of this world cannot kill.

Birth of freedom is birth of true humanity. It is the birth of God in us human beings. Whatever name we may give God, God is freedom. The idols we create—gods, to worship ourselves, to adore our own minds, to satisfy our greed for power—are unfree products of human narcissism. They prosper and decline with the fortune of those who create them, be it political, ideological, or religious. A narcissistic god is a god in bondage. It does not have freedom. It cannot give freedom.

But the birth of freedom in our spirit and in our soul makes us aware of God who is the power of freedom and who gives that power of freedom to us. It is the power that enables stones to cry out, makes the land speak, and empowers the silenced soul to break out in song. In Asia today we are witnessing the birth of this power of freedom in Asian humanity bound by centuries of fate not instituted by God but by emperors, kings, warlords, and landlords. It is a painful era. But it is also a glorious time. And there is much theology to do at this painful and glorious juncture of history in Asia.

If freedom is a matter of soul and spirit, it then must be a confession to the God who is freedom and who gives freedom. It is also a testimony to those who struggle for freedom to be born in them and who experience God near them and in them. Here is such a confession and a testimony. It is called "Potato"—the confession and testimony of a potato:

Ferociously
They pluck me out of the warmth of the earth
Root and all, saying
Here is the freedom we give you

Then they bake me
Boil me in oil
Dry me under the scorching sun
Cook me with rice
Served steaming hot in bowls

They eat my most nutritious parts
And feed pigs with my less edible leaves

All this
I used to endure
Secretly lamenting over my own fate
Ah, who has made me into a potato
Potato everyone so much desires

But it has to be different now
From today
I will not be silent any more
I will stand up to speak
Whether you want to hear or not
I will speak out as potato and for potato

This is what I will say loud and clear
Facing the vast fields and plains
Do not please deal with me in this way
I am innocent
I have not committed a crime![1]

This is a parable in poetry—a parable of the history of the suffering people of Taiwan, that potato-shaped island on the western rim of the Pacific Ocean, sandwiched between Japan and the Philippines, one hundred miles off the southeast coast of China.

The poem is a historical parable of Taiwan in modern times. In 1895 the island was ceded to Japan by the Ching government of China in the aftermath of the Sino-Japanese war. In its half-century of colonial rule, Japan developed and exploited Taiwan for its own industrial development at home and as the advance station of its military ambitions vis-à-vis Southeast Asia. With the defeat of Japan in World War II Taiwan came under the control of Nationalist China. But the tragic history of the people on this potato island did not end there. In 1949 the Nationalist government, defeated in the civil war with the communists, fled to Taiwan and has since made the island into a bastion of anticommunism and ruled its people with martial law. In all these changes, the Taiwanese were, like potatoes in the fields, plucked from the warmth and security of their life and told by their rulers, whether Japanese or Chinese: "Here is the freedom we give you."

But freedom cannot be given. It has to be won. Freedom given by those who have the power of life and death over you is not freedom. It is slavery. It is oppression. It is not *your* freedom; in fact it is the freedom of your master to "bake you, boil you, and cook you" and have you served up steaming hot on their lavish dinner table. Japan made Taiwan into a prosperous colony for Japanese needs. The Nationalist government created "an economic miracle" out of the hard labor of the people and the rich resources of the island, perpetuating its one-party rule in the name of the recovery of China—a dream the rulers, though no longer believing it themselves, use in order to hold onto their power and privileges. During all this time the potato people, the Taiwanese, who have a legitimate claim over the potato-shaped island as their ancestral home, endured and lamented their fate, as if saying, "Who has made us into potatoes—potatoes that every robber regime so much desires!"

Then came the rumor that Richard Nixon, the president of the United States, known for his staunch stance against communism throughout his political career, was making plans to visit Peking in early 1972. The rumor shook the island, from the rulers on top down to ordinary citizens at the bottom. The outcry of betrayal by the longtime ally, faithful friend, and comrade-in-arms—the United States—was all that could be heard from government officials, newspapers, and party functionaries.

The potato citizens could not endure it any longer. They decided that "they will not be silent anymore, that they will speak out for themselves," and not let government and party officials continue speaking for them. The first to speak out was the Presbyterian Church of Taiwan. On December 30, 1971, it issued a "Public Statement on our National Fate," saying among other things:

> We, the people on Taiwan, love this island . . . We note with concern that President Nixon will soon visit the Chinese mainland. Some member countries of the United Nations are advocating the transfer of Taiwan to mainland rule, while others insist on direct negotiation between Taipei and Peiping [Peking], which means substantially the same betrayal of the people on Taiwan.
>
> We oppose any powerful nation disregarding the rights and wishes of fifteen million people and making unilateral decisions to their own advantage, because God has ordained and the United Nations Charter has affirmed that every people has the right to determine its own destiny.

The potato has spoken! The long silence is broken. The seed of freedom and democracy sown in the hearts and minds of the people is to germinate and grow, developing into an exciting and tragic struggle for the right of self-determination of the people of Taiwan.

Political theology developed by some Christians of Taiwan has its roots in this historical situation. It is a theology born out of the history of the people of Taiwan. It is a theology trying to respond to God's redeeming love at work not only in ancient Israel, not only in the countries in the West deeply influenced by the Christian faith, but in Taiwan where the destiny of the people lies at the mercy of authoritarian regimes and foreign powers. The movement of "Formosan [Taiwanese] Christians for Self-Determination," formed in March 1973 in Washington, D.C., was a response to the "Public Statement on our National Fate" and to the turn of history setting Taiwan on an uncertain course toward its future.

In the editorial of the first issue of *Self-Determination* published by the same group, it was said:

> We Taiwanese, fifteen million of us, have an appeal to make. We have a cause to fight for. We have a claim to make. And we have a dream to dream. We appeal to the community of nations to respect our integrity and dignity as human beings. We claim that we Taiwanese are entitled to determine for ourselves our own future and destiny just as any other group of people. We call upon all Taiwanese to fight for this right of self-determination. And we dream of the day when Taiwan will play a responsible part as a nation-state in the world community of nations and peoples.
>
> This, in essence, is what Formosan Christians for Self-Determination stands for. As Christians, as well as Taiwanese, we believe that the above claim is an inalienable part of our faith in God who created human beings in God's image. Taiwanese, no less than men and women of other nationalities, are created by God for freedom, justice, and equality. It is in our effort to manifest these divinely given qualities that we become human.[2]

The spirit of freedom is nurtured in the womb of history. The yearning for justice is inherent in the human soul. Without a longing for equality, human community becomes disfigured by the struggle for sheer power and gain. These are not just political statements. They are theological convictions derived from the creation of human beings in God's image. Political theology was born with the creation. Taiwan is of course part of that creation. That is why self-determination becomes the core of political theology for the people of Taiwan.

I HAVE NOT COMMITTED A CRIME

The poem by the Taiwanese poet is not only a historical parable. It has proved to be a prophetic parable. The poem is about the past of Taiwan. But it is also about its future. The future it predicted turned out to be as gloomy as the dark sky. But it also points to a lonely star barely visible in the sky shimmering with all the power it can muster. "This is what I will say loud and clear," the poet summons all his courage and declares: "I am innocent! I have not committed a crime!"

A storm was brewing on Taiwan. Individuals and groups spoke out more and more for freedom and democracy. Then there was another rumor—the rumor that President Carter's government was proceeding with normalizing Sino-American relationships. The rumor swept across the island like a hurricane. Again the government took shelter in cries of betrayal, invoking the wrath of heaven on the Carter administration in the name of faithfulness and fidelity in human conduct as taught in Confucian ethics.

In the midst of all this fury and outcry, it was again the Presbyterian Church in Taiwan that spoke out. It made public on August 16, 1977, "A Declaration on Human Rights." The declaration reads in part:

> Our church confesses that Jesus Christ is Lord of all humankind and believes that human rights and a land in which each one of us has a stake are gifts bestowed by God. Therefore we make this declaration, set in the context of the present crisis threatening the 17 million people of Taiwan. . . .
>
> As we face the possibility of an invasion by Communist China, we hold firmly to our faith and to the principles underlying the United Nations Declaration of Human Rights. We insist that the future of Taiwan shall be determined by the 17 million people who live there. We appeal to the countries concerned—especially to the people and the government of the United States of America—and to Christian churches throughout the world to take effective steps to support our cause.

The dramatic changes in Sino-American relationships hastened the pace of the political theology being fashioned by Taiwanese Christians in Taiwan and elsewhere. The declaration concluded with an urgent plea to the Nationalist government, urging it "to face reality and to take effective measures whereby Taiwan may become a new and independent country."

A bomb exploded! The word "independence" had long been a political taboo in Taiwan. It undermined the claim of the government to sovereignty over the whole of China. It challenged the legitimacy of those in power, who imposed themselves on the people of Taiwan by force. The repercussions of the declaration were not hard to predict. It brought down the wrath of the government on the Presbyterian Church. It eventually led to the trial and imprisonment of some church leaders later when an occasion presented itself—the International Human Rights Day Rally on December 10, 1979, the occasion used by the government to crush fledgling democratic movements and send some young and able political opposition leaders to prison.

But the declaration spoke what was in the minds of most of the people of Taiwan. It broke the political stalemate that made it difficult for movements in favor of political democratization in Taiwan to come out into the open. It also found a strong echo in the editorial of the December 1977 issue of *Self-Determination* under the title "From Self-Determination to Self-Government":

> Self-determination as a means by which political power of the people is exercised is essentially democratic in nature. It is one of the most elementary conditions for forming a democratic form of government. Democracy which is not built on the people's right of self-determination is a wolf in disguise of a sheep. It is autocracy and not democracy. . . .
>
> In the case of Taiwan, self-determination of the people must be translated into a self-government by the people and a self-government for the people. It is common knowledge that the Nationalist government in Taiwan is a government by the Nationalist Party and a government for the Nationalist Party. It is a Party's government and not the government of the 17 million people. . . . The Nationalist government treats the 17 million people under its control as if they were ignorant children who can be contented and happy with candies and lollipops, leaving important family decisions affecting their future with their elders.
>
> All this must change if Taiwan and its people are to survive. . . . A Taiwan fortified with the will and determination of the 17 million people will prove inviolable. But a Taiwan governed by a Party living in the dream-world of the lost past will not stand the eventual abolition of the defense treaty with the United States, not to say invasion from the other side of the Straits.
>
> Mencius once said to King Hsuan: "When all your immediate ministers say that a man is worthy, it is not sufficient. When all your great officers say so, it is not sufficient. When all your people say so, look into the case, and if you find him to be worthy, then employ him. When all your immediate ministers say that a man is no good, do not listen to them. When all your great officers say so, do not listen to them. When all your people say so, look into the case, and if you find him to be no good, then dismiss him. . . . "
>
> The overwhelming majority of the people in Taiwan either believe firmly in silence or say with a timid voice that the Nationalist government must face reality and that Taiwan must become a new and independent country. It is this voice of the people that must be listened to, and not that of great officers and immediate ministers. On this voice of the people depends the political future of Taiwan and the political destiny of its 17 million people.[3]

The issue was clear. The government and the people were joined in a battle for self-determination and self-government.

Then came that fateful day—the day on which the human rights rally was held, in December 1979, in the southern city of Kaohsiung. It was planned as a peaceful rally to be addressed by prominent dissident politicians. More than thirty thousand persons were waiting eagerly to hear the speeches. But the government too was ready. It plotted in advance to turn the rally to its gain. Riot police were mobilized. They provoked the crowd and turned the rally into a brawl. The blame for it was firmly laid on the shoulders of the opposition leaders. They were arrested, tried on charges of sedition, and sentenced to long-term imprisonment. This seems the end. Another chapter in the tragic history of Taiwan is closed. The general population seems to have lapsed back into silence again.

A dark cloud has descended on the political future of the citizens of Taiwan. They may sigh and fret in their hearts, but outwardly they behave as if nothing has happened. How is one to describe the gloom that has set in in the depths of their souls? A Taiwanese folksong, "Flower on a Rainy Night," seems to do it best:

> Flower on a rainy night
> Flower on a rainy night
> Fell on the ground in the wind and rain
> Out of everyone's sight.
> It sighs day and night
> It has fallen not to rise again.
>
> Flower on the ground
> Flower on the ground
> Who pays attention to it?
> Merciless wind and rain destroy its future
> The flower is withered, withered
> What can it do?
>
> Merciless rain, merciless rain
> It has no concern for our future
> Is not mindful of our frailty
> Covering our destiny with darkness
> Causing us to fall from the branch
> Out of everyone's sight.
>
> Rain-drops, rain-drops
> You lead us into the pool of suffering
> Not mindful of our frailty
> Covering our destiny with darkness
> Causing us to fall from the branch
> Out of everyone's sight.[4]

If this Taiwanese folksong is not equal to the hymn of the exiled Jews in Babylon (Ps. 137) in its spiritual depth, it is at least equal to it in its profound pathos, in its untold agony of the spirit, and in its passionate plea to the world of nations and peoples.

What we hear in this folksong is the voice of the innocent. It is the voice of that potato, plucked out, baked, boiled, and cooked, but which was finally able to declare: "I am innocent! I have not committed a crime!" And this is what the world was to hear from the political leaders arrested during the human rights day rally and tried in the martial law court. Lin Yi-Hsiung, whose mother and twin daughters were, after his arrest, mercilessly murdered, wrote from prison: "After questioning me for about ten days, they wrote down a statement. In this statement they said that I went onto the platform at Kaohsiung and made a speech to incite the crowd. This is ridiculous! As far as I remember, I didn't say a word. There should be tapes, and they can prove it."[5] There were complete tapes of the rally. But at the trial the military judge brushed aside the request of the defense lawyers to have the tapes played.

The court was unable to prove that Li and the other defendants were guilty. But they were declared guilty of sedition anyway. In the words of the presiding judge: "We [judges and prosecutors] have to be responsible to several quarters—the pressure is very heavy."[6] He must have said this during a brief moment when his conscience pricked him. He must have said it just to himself, not to be heard by others. No, they are not guilty! The presiding judge knows it. The prosecutor knows it. Still they have to be declared guilty. Yes, freedom has to be *won*; it is not handed out to you by those in power. It has to be born in the hearts of the people. It cannot be manufactured in the test tubes of a pseudodemocracy.

THERE IS A TOMORROW

The struggle for freedom has to begin all over again. Freedom can be tried in a military court. It can be declared guilty of attempting to overthrow the government. And it can be imprisoned for months and years. But it will never die. It will be born again and again, making its cry heard and repeating its claim to the right of existence. There is always a tomorrow for freedom. A poem, "Sleep, My Child," written by a Taiwanese girl in a senior elementary school, seems to imply such a tomorrow for freedom:

> To bed now, my child!
> It is already very late.
> Tomorrow, we still have work to do,
> Tomorrow, we still have to go to school.
>
> Child! Why are you not yet asleep?
> I know:
> You still have so much to say.
> I know:
> You still have many things you want to do.

But,
Tomorrow . . . .
I know when you all grow up,
You will surely know what it is that I want to say.
Sleep then, my child![7]

Tomorrow! What kind of tomorrow would that be in the heart of a small child? What dreams could be contained in the tomorrow of an innocent girl?

Small or big, tomorrow is tomorrow. It is a new day different from yesterday. For the children whose yesterday quickly becomes a distant memory, tomorrow is all they have. It seems so slow in coming. It seems to crawl at a snail's pace. If only it were possible to order it to come faster! If only it were possible to run to it! That is why the child in this young girl's poem does not want to go to sleep, although it is already very late, although it is long past bedtime. The child wants to stay up until tomorrow arrives.

There is a tomorrow. There must be a tomorrow. The child believes in it. It is not just a tomorrow repeating yesterday. The tomorrow in the child's dream must be a new tomorrow. There will be new friends to meet, new things to learn, new songs to sing. There will also be new frustrations, new annoyances, new difficulties. Tomorrow is always a challenge. Tomorrow will add a little height to that child, a little more weight, a little more self-awareness, and a little more self-confidence. That is why the child is impatient with its slow arrival. Perhaps this impatience of the child with tomorrow is the impatience of waiting for freedom to arrive. A child does not know what freedom is, what its definition is. But it knows freedom by instinct and by nature. Even a child is aware that unfreedom is against human instinct and contradictory to human nature. Yes, it is freedom that the child in the poem is really waiting for—it is freedom that tomorrow will bring! That is why the child refuses to go to bed. That is why it tries very hard not to be overtaken by sleep.

But what the child does not know in its innocent mind is that there is a lot of work to be done between today and tomorrow. A tomorrow laden with dreams and possibilities does not come of itself. The tomorrow that comes of itself is not any different from yesterday. It does not bring surprises. It has no freedom to offer. That is why the mother has to tell the child: "Tomorrow, you still have work to do. Tomorrow, you still have to go to school." There is indeed a lot to do before tomorrow arrives. There are failures of yesterday to be mended. There are frustrations of the past to be overcome. There are also the chagrins of the day before yesterday to allay. At the same time there are new lessons to learn. New strength must be acquired. Wisdom must be deepened, visions reshaped, and commitment renewed. Then tomorrow will come. And it will be a *new* tomorrow.

The child must know this. But the mother senses something else in her child who is determined to sit up until tomorrow arrives. She senses there must be a reason why her child wants tomorrow so badly. Waiting for a new doll? Expecting her father to come home from a trip? Looking forward to the visit of her grandparents? Maybe. But there may be something more. For the mother knows her child "has so much to say and has many things she wants to do." What is it?

Although the child cannot say it and explain it, it must be something her mother cherishes in her heart, something she herself longs to have badly. So, urging her child to go to bed, she says: "When you grow up, you will surely know what it is that I want to say." What is this that the mother expects her child to know when grown up? It must be freedom—the freedom to decide the future of Taiwan and the destiny of the people of Taiwan, not by the superpowers, not by those who rule them, but by themselves. As long as such a dream exists in the hearts of the people, in the innocent souls of children, then there will be a tomorrow for Taiwan, there will be a future for its people.

To make that dream real, there is a lot of work to do between today and tomorrow. The child must go to bed and wake up refreshed for the work waiting to be done before tomorrow arrives. The child has to grow. Those in prison unjustly sentenced on charges of sedition must be supported. Efforts toward democratization must continue. And what is in the mind and heart of the people must be heard both inside and outside Taiwan.

There were many, many tomorrows in the life of the people of Israel enslaved in Egypt. Standing in front of the pharaoh who refused to let the Israelites go, Moses said: "Tomorrow this sign shall appear. . . . " When tomorrow came, the pharaoh's house was infested with swarms of flies and the country was threatened with ruin by them (Exod. 8:23); all the herds of Egypt died (9:5); locusts devoured all the vegetation and all the fruits of the trees (10:15). Eventually the tomorrow for the people in bondage came. The Israelites left Egypt.

Jesus also spoke about tomorrow. He was warned that Herod the king was seeking to kill him. But he replied: "Go and tell that fox, 'Listen, today and tomorrow I shall be casting out devils and working cures; on the third day I reach my goal' " (Luke 13:32). Jesus' days are fully occupied. He cures sickness in body and in spirit. He brings the good news of God's love to the people. These days of his are full of dangers. The cross is never far away. But there is a tomorrow, a glorious tomorrow. On the third day he will rise from the dead! Jesus' tomorrow is his resurrection.

With such a tomorrow before him, Jesus was remembered as saying to the careworn persons who were always driven back to repeat a dismal yesterday: "Do not be anxious about tomorrow; tomorrow will look after itself. Each day has troubles enough of its own" (Matt. 6:34). Jesus was not saying that tomorrow will arrive without effort on our part. "Each day has enough troubles of its own," he said. But there will be a tomorrow, different from yesterday. This tomorrow is the tomorrow of resurrection, of a new life. It is the tomorrow God will give you. With such assurance Jesus tells his worried listeners not to be anxious about tomorrow.

Our theology must not be a theology of yesterday. It must be a theology of today, and especially a theology of tomorrow. Political theology in particular must be a theology of tomorrow. We do not see our wrongs of yesterday vindicated today. We cannot have our dreams of freedom and justice realized in the immediate future. But all sorrows felt, all tears shed, all blood spilt, and all dreams shattered will add up to a tomorrow that God will give. What kind of tomorrow, we cannot predict. We can see it only dimly. But it is going to be our tomorrow because it is God's tomorrow. Our theology must be a commitment to that tomorrow of ours because it is God's tomorrow.

10

Passion of the Womb

NO HALF-HEARTED LOVE

The word "passion" has a twofold meaning. On the one hand passion is strong love. Half-hearted love is not passion. It is love with only half your heart. But, is heart still heart when it is halved? Is a halved heart, a heart cut in two, not a dead heart? How, then, can a dead heart love? Half-hearted love is not true love. Certainly not. Love and half-heartedness have nothing to do with each other. Half-hearted love is an adulteration, a caricature, a desecration of true love.

If love is love, it must be full-hearted love. Love with a heart not severed in two is love in the true sense. A full heart is a living heart. Only a heart that lives can love. Only a heart that pulsates with life is capable of loving. You can love someone truly only when your heart is full, living, and pulsating. You can be truly loved only by someone whose heart is beating in full and exciting rhythms.

If this is true of our love for each other, it ought to be even more true of our love for God. Let us recall the Shema in Deuteronomy, to which we referred earlier. The great confession, which was the foundation of faith for the people of ancient Israel, says at the beginning: "You shall love the Lord your God with all your heart, and with all your soul, and with all your might" (Deut. 6:5, RSV). "All" is the crucial word here. It is *all* your soul and heart and might that you must put into loving God. Only part of your heart, soul, and might will not do. This "all" has the same meaning as the word "full." The Shema confession can also, then, be said in this way: "You shall love the Lord your God with your full heart, with your full soul, and with your full might." Loving God must be a full-hearted act. Believing in God must be a full-souled act.

Jesus, too, talked about full-hearted love. And he did not just talk about it. His was a life and a ministry of full-hearted love. This is why curing a seriously ill person was more important to him than observing the time-honored Sabbath law. It is this kind of full-hearted love that he tried to impart to his disciples.

An example would be the story of Jesus having breakfast with his disciples by the sea of Tiberias after the resurrection (John 21). It must have been a sober occasion after all that had happened not long before in Jerusalem: the last supper, Jesus' arrest, the denial by Peter and the disciples' desertion of Jesus, the crucifixion. . . . All this made the morning air they breathed by the seaside heavy. Their hearts must have been heavy, too.

It was Jesus who broke the pensive silence. What a relief it must have been for the disciples. If only Jesus would speak to them, they must have been saying over and over in their hearts. Jesus could give them a harsh rebuke. He might heap angry reproofs on them. They deserved all this, they thought to themselves. It would be better for Jesus to get it over with. But this was not what Jesus did. He said quietly but firmly, punctuating each and every word with love: "Simon, son of John, do you love me more than all else?" (21:15). Here is the foundation of the faith that came to be centered in Jesus. That faith can be expressed in the manner of the Shema: "You shall love your Lord the Savior with all your heart, with all your soul, and with all your might." That faith was born in the hearts and souls of those disciples who had breakfast with the risen Jesus in the quiet hours of the morning by the sea of Tiberias.

But passion has another meaning. It also means suffering. Love and suffering. How can they be together in one word, "passion"? Are they not mutually exclusive? No, and it is not by accident that love and suffering are joined together in passion. Passion as full-hearted love is not self-contained. It does not and cannot remain within itself. Self-love is not passion as full-hearted love. Passion is full-hearted love because it goes out of itself and enters into others. There passion as love becomes suffering, for in the others you encounter sickness and death. In them you are faced with poverty and oppression. And in them you perceive the struggle of the soul in a world of transience and finitude. In others you do not enter a paradise but a sea of bitterness.

Passion as love for others becomes passion as suffering for them. If no transformation of love into suffering takes place, then your love for others is not genuine. It is not full-hearted love but half-hearted love. The distance between love and suffering is very short indeed. Parents love their children and suffer for them. Children also love their parents and suffer for them. This, I believe, must be the basis of filial piety—a code of ethics that sustained life in China and elsewhere in Asia for thousands of years. It has been misused and abused abundantly both by parents and by children. The claim for each other on the basis of duty, and not on the basis of passion as love and suffering, corrupted filial piety and created many a family tragedy. Filial piety without passion becomes a chain, a burden, to be discarded as soon as possible.

But for life to go on, passion must be a suffering love. In the world of adversity passion as love capable of suffering has to find a place. The more tragic life is, the more loving and suffering passion must become. The more bitter an experience turns out to be, the more passion must struggle to be faithful to its ideal. This is what the mother is trying to tell us in these lines:

Amidst poverty, you popped out:
Cruel yet loving.
Parasite!
You have dimmed my hopes
Of material comfort,
Brought further toil
And disillusionment.

You whine in vain,
Mama's nipple, dried by us,
Unreplenished through
Malnutrition.

But when your unworried smile
Shines, fresh and untouched,
My hatred for you
Is engulfed by inflamed love.

In times of utter dejection
When the walls appear like slashed ash
And the leaden mood grows upon me
I turn,
And will turn to you,
Poor creature,
Cruel yet loving.[1]

What a heartrending cry from a poverty-stricken mother! But what a light of sublime love shines through her!

The birth of the child was unplanned and unwanted. It would only make an already difficult life even more difficult. The mother was totally in dismay. The extent of her plight is tragically expressed: "Mama's nipple, dried by us, unreplenished through malnutrition." A grim picture of a thin and dejected mother! Who can blame her for hating her newborn child! Who cannot understand if she wants to give it away? There are hundreds and thousands of such mothers in Asia. Extreme poverty seems to turn the natural love of a mother for her child into unnatural hate for it. This is a dreadful thing about poverty. It deprives you of your dignity. It even affects your nature as a human being.

But does a mother really hate her newborn child? It must be her fate and not the child that she hates. Fate, not her child, has been cruel to her. The world, not her child, has been hostile to her. Society, not her child, has been oppressive. The child is the victim of that same fate. The child, too, suffers from a hostile world and oppressive society, as does the mother. Such thoughts must be turning round and round in that mother's heart—the mother exhausted, confused, helpless.

Then the child in her arms moves. She looks at it and sees something entirely different from the cruel fate, the oppressive society, the hostile world:

> But, when your unworried smile
> Shines, fresh and untouched,
> My hatred for you
> Is engulfed by inflamed love.

An unworried child smiling in the arms of a worried mother. Does this picture not touch our hearts? It has touched the mother. And a miracle happens. Her hatred for the child becomes engulfed by inflamed love!

This is what passion as love and suffering is. The mother's heart engulfed by inflamed love for the child is a passionate heart—a heart that loves and suffers. The inflamed love of the mother is full-hearted love. Her heart is capable of loving and suffering. And how well the mother expresses all this, simply but profoundly: "poor creature, cruel yet loving." She says it all. There is nothing to be added. She puts all her passion into saying, "poor creature." All her heart goes out to the child, willing to do whatever she can to shelter it from harm. Then to the poor creature in her arms she says: you are "cruel and loving."

If one is cruel, then not loving; if one is loving, then not cruel. This is how we normally understand these concepts. But the strange thing is that in passion—love that suffers—being cruel and being loving transform each other into a kind of "love at any cost." Being cruel ceases to mean cruel words, cruel deeds, cruel nature. In true passion being cruel becomes a quality, a call, a cry, to love and to be loved even if the whole world crumbles. That mother cannot but love the "poor creature" in her arms—the creature that is "cruel and loving." Passion in her has reached its full height and depth.

Passion such as this mother's helps us to fathom the passion of God as both loving and suffering. Is this not what the cross is all about? Jesus on the cross is God in loving the world and suffering for it. In Jesus nailed to the cross God is saying to us: "Poor creatures, cruel and loving!" The world that brought Jesus to the cross must be a cruel world. We who have forced the cross on Jesus must be cruel human beings. And yet God loves us—all the way to the cross. Does the cross not tell us that God loves us in spite of everything? Does it not say to us that God cannot help loving us? "Father, forgive them," Jesus said on the cross. How much passion there is in these words!

A VOLCANO OF PASSION

How is it that a mother is capable of such passion? A father is also capable of it, but a mother seems to be more capable of it. The kind of passion a mother shows makes us feel the passion of God more closely, vividly, and personally. Is it because of the intense passion—loving and suffering—that the mother undergoes at the birth of her child? And is it that the passion shown in the birth of a child gives us a glimpse into the passion of God giving birth to creation?

Let us listen to what a mother tells us about how she went through the birth of her first child:

As a volcano when exploding
The womb extrudes its burning lava.
Who else could bear the labours?
Two lives cultivated the nature
Of the newborn child. . . .

The longing for death occurred
Suddenly she remembered
Mother had said before
"Marriage is to be bearable."

Like a volcano just before bursting
The womb was forced to extrude lava
At the extreme point of pain, she has to
cooperate with the womb
To bear the pain
To bear the burning
To bear the longest moment.

The volcano burst at last.
At the moment of exhaustion she realized
"Marriage is to be bearable."
The new mother called in her heart Mother!
Grateful tears fall from her eyelashes
She greeted the dawn with tears.[2]

This is a poetic expression of a real experience. Perhaps poetry with its short, tight verses, not prose with its long, loose sentences, is a fitting means for treating such an extraordinary event as childbirth. Prose is too wordy. But childbirth is not a wordy affair. It is filled with cries, short but urgent words of encouragement, silent tears, and then finally loud exclamations—exclamation of relief from the mother and exclamation of the newborn baby announcing its arrival. Can anything else except poetry be equal to the task of picturing all this?

For the mother childbirth is something like a volcano of passion—a volcano filled with passion ready to explode. The mother's womb is that volcano. That is where two lives—the mother's and the father's—are joined in beginning a new life. The father is with the mother in spirit all the time, but all the labor and pain are the mother's alone. From the moment a new life begins in her womb, a direct bond is created between the mother and the new life in her womb. It is a blood-relationship. It is a flesh-relationship. Through that vital umbilical cord the mother and the new life are directly and inseparably bound together.

The womb is the home of that new life. It is the entire world the new life has. It is where a creative power is at work to bring that new life to parturition. When the new life moves and kicks, the mother feels her own vitality. She knows the new life lives because she lives. And she knows she lives because the new life in her womb lives.

Then the day arrives when the mother's womb can no longer hold the new life that has outgrown it. That is the day when the mother's womb erupts like a volcano. An extreme pain of separation begins—the pain of the flesh of her flesh tearing away from her, the pain of the life of her life forcing its way out of her. "The longing for death" takes hold of her. Why a longing for death at the moment when life shows its most powerful vitality? It is because of the pain, the suffering. How could she expect that that life she has nourished with all her love would give her so much pain? But she has to know, and now she does know, passion is both love and suffering; it is both joy and pain. She has "to bear the pain, the burning, the longest moment."

This volcano of passion that a mother goes through at childbirth is not merely a physical passion. It must be a deeply spiritual passion also. If not, then why do "grateful tears fall from the mother's eyelashes" when her child is born? Why does she "greet the dawn with tears"? Is it because the ordeal is over? Is it because the pain is gone? It must be all this. But is there not something more? Even though most mothers may not be able to explain it, the tears must be tears of joy at having participated in the creation of life, tears of deep awe at being able to be co-creators of life with God. What an awesome thought it is! And what a revelatory experience it ought to be! The mother can only greet the new dawn with tears, holding in her arms the life that her womb has helped to create. We then begin to understand why that poverty-stricken mother is holding her "poor creature" close to her breast in infinite passion, engulfing it with her inflamed love.

We have barely begun to explore theologically the volcano of passion that a mother experiences at childbirth. Maybe this is the reason why our theology has been without much passion. We have not experienced much passion exploding like a volcano in our theology. It is all very orderly, the way we conduct the business of theology. And there is a certain logic that tells us how to do theology. It tells us that because God is transcendent, we must be very wary about trying to find God in created beings. An immanent God will incur the wrath of the transcendent God. Inasmuch as revelation must come from above us, from somewhere entirely out of our experience, we should not seek it in the world drowned in cries and noises that have no revelatory value. But this is the only world we know and ours is the only humanity we have. This is the only world through which God can say something to us. And ours is the only humanity at God's disposal if God wants to do something with *us* and for *us*.

God does not just deal with this world, but deals with it passionately, loving it and suffering for it. "God loved the world so much that he gave his only son to it" (John 3:16). But this is not logic. This is passion. How else would God be willing to part with God's own son for the sake of us? Nor is this a result of reasoning. It is a risk. And passion always involves risk, does it not? But only in risking will there be new discoveries and exciting experiences. Only when God had taken the risk of giving God's own son to us did God find us again and we God. God finds us still capable of passion—capable of loving and suffering. And in the passion of a mother at childbirth do we not see God's passion for the life that belongs ultimately to God? The passion of God and the passion of a mother, loving and suffering—do they not tell us where our theology should start? It should start from us human beings, human beings in union with God. It also shows us it should start from God, God in union with human beings.

What governs us in theology must be first passion and then logic; we should theologize first with the heart and only then with the brain. Passion brings God and human beings together. The heart makes us realize that God and human beings are joined together in loving and suffering. This passion and this heart must be the passion and heart of theology also.

THE FEMALE DIMENSION OF GOD'S IMAGE

Why is it that theology has been less than passionate? Why has it gone on for so long without much passion? Why has it not been able to find in the experience of passion, such as that of a mother giving birth to a child, a theology telling us some important things about God and about us human beings? And why has it been half-hearted about the passion—the love and suffering—we see and experience around us? One of the reasons seems to be this: theology has overlooked the female dimension of God's image. As mentioned in the liturgy of worship used in an Asian women's workshop:

> Loving God. . . .
> We know that in many of our sisters and brothers
> Your image has been scarred and tarnished,
> They have been drained by exploitation;
> Your image has been destroyed
> By people subjugating one another;
> The female part of your image
> Has been conveniently forgotten;
> But you meant your creation to be good,
> Your image to be whole.[3]

"The female part of God's image" has been suppressed and then forgotten by society, and even by the Christian church and theology!

Human society has become dominantly patriarchal, although anthropologists know of matriarchal societies. It was perhaps the frequent confinement of the female for childbearing and the responsibility for nursing on the one hand, and on the other the necessity to provide for the family on the part of the male, that contributed to the development of patriarchal society.

But there was no reason for theology to follow the patriarchal bias of society and tradition, if it had taken seriously the stories of the creation of humankind in the Old Testament. And again it is that simple but insightful storyteller who had some profound things to say about our concern here. In that storyteller's account, Adam said to Eve when God brought her to him:

> Now this, at last—
> bone from my bones,
> flesh from my flesh!—
> this shall be called woman,
> for from man was this taken [Gen. 2:23].

Does this not say woman is a part of man? If she is taken from him, is she not dependent on him? Does he not have control over her? Is this not clear evidence that human society was ordained to be patriarchal?

This is what traditional theology has taught. But this joyful exclamation of Adam is followed by something else in the story: "That is why a man leaves his father and mother and is united to his wife" (2:24). Does this not surprise us? What human beings have been doing not only in the East but also in the West is largely the opposite of what is said here. Our marriage tradition has been that of having a *woman* leave her father and mother to become united with her husband.

But what about this matter of "woman being taken from man"? We have been listening to male exegetes on this long enough and we know their answer. Let us for once listen to a woman exegete, Phyllis Tribble, and see what she has to say.[4] The declaration of love between woman and man is translated as follows:

> This, finally, bone of my bones
> and flesh of my flesh.
> This shall be called *'issa* [woman]
> because from *'is* [man] was differentiated this.

Mark the last line! The new creature is to be called woman "because from man was differentiated this"! You may disagree with the translation "differentiated," preferring "taken from" (from the verb *lqh*), but obviously "woman" (*'issa*) and "man" (*'is*) in the poem are meant to explain the names and do not imply subordination of one party to the other.

This is not the whole story, however. The storyteller tells us that "God built up the rib, which God had taken out of the man" (2:22). How is this to be understood? Here is a fresh interpretation:

> The Hebrew verb "build" (*bnh*) indicates considerable labour to produce solid results. Hence, woman is no weak, dainty, ephemeral creature. No opposite sex, no second sex, no derived sex—in short, no "Adam's rib." Instead woman is the culmination of creation, fulfilling humanity in

> sexuality. Equal in creation with the man, she is, at this point, elevated in emphasis by the design of the story.[5]

Is this a forced interpretation? Forced or not, it brings out a dimension deeply embedded in God's intention for woman and man to become one flesh, to form a unity of souls, hearts, bodies, as caring, loving, and equal partners.

It does not much surprise us if our storyteller had this uncanny insight into God's creation. But it does surprise us when we find that there seems to exist a similar concern in the story of the creation from the priestly circles much later. In the priestly version God says: "Let us make humankind (*'adam*) in our image and likeness" (Gen. 1:26). But it must have at once been felt that this did not quite convey what was intended. So with breathless speed, hardly pausing at the end of the sentence, it was added: "So God created man [*'adam*, humankind] in his own image . . . ; male and female he created them" (1:27).

This last sentence is not an afterthought. It is an expansion of the sentence that preceded it. It is an explanation of the word "humankind" (*'adam*) in the previous statement. What the priestly writers wanted to say must be that *'adam* is not just male; *'adam* is humankind; it is male *and* female. All this is very exciting, is it not? We must read the Bible with our eyes open, our mind alert, and our heart warm and tender. Theology too must be done this way. Even those priests in the land of exile, preoccupied with their national tragedy, were capable of doing theology with wide-opened eyes, alert minds, and warm, tender hearts when it came to giving an account of God's creation of humankind. If they were able to do this in those ancient days, why not we today?

At any rate, *'adam* is not *'adam* if it is male only. Humankind is not humankind if it is male alone. For *'adam* to be *'adam* there must be female as well as male. It is male *and* female that make *'adam 'adam*, and it is they together that make humankind to be humankind. This is common sense. This is a straightforward fact. Even the priests in those times saw it. Why not theologians today? Theology has curiously and deplorably suppressed and overlooked the female part of God's image. It has been insensitive to the fact that without that part, that dimension, what it says about God, Jesus Christ, humanity, the church, and the world is seriously one-sided and truncated. God in theology with only the male part of God's image and without its female counterpart appears autocratic, domineering, and unapproachable, like the father in a patriarchal family, the emperor in a feudal society, or the dictator in a totalitarian country. Even Jesus Christ is worshiped and adored as priest and king with stress on power and glory. And the church has, of course, been a predominately male-dominated institution. Women are excluded from the priesthood, which surrounds itself with sacramental aura and protects itself from the female part of God's image. Theology has done immense injustice to God's creation by suppressing and then forgetting the female part of God's image in *'adam*, humankind.

But the Bible itself shows us how passionate theology can become, and how full-hearted it can be, when the female part of God's image enters God's saving activity in the world. I am of course referring to Mary's Magnificat (Luke 1:46–55).

Carrying the seed of the savior in her womb, Mary becomes consumed with passion for God. "My soul magnifies the Lord, and my spirit rejoices in God my Savior" (Luke 1:46–47). This is a cry from her womb. Her theology does not begin in her head. It begins in her womb. How can it not be a powerfully passionate theology? Her soul and her spirit have to shout in praise of God.

But her passionate theology does not remain within her womb. It is not a self-gratifying kind of theology. It is a theology that begins in her womb but is thrust out from there to enter God's creation—the creation full of corruption, injustice, and misery. It is here that Mary's theology of the womb reaches its best. For it turns into a political theology. And it is a passionate political theology. This is what Mary cries out from her *theo*-logical womb—the womb filled by the spirit of God:

> . . . the arrogant of heart and mind God has put to rout,
> God has brought down monarchs from their thrones,
> but the humble have been lifted high.
> The hungry God has satisfied with good things,
> the rich sent empty away.

Is this not political theology at its best? It did not come from Joseph her husband. It was not said by Zechariah, the priest and husband of her cousin Elizabeth. It was said by Mary in whose womb the savior was in the making, where the passion of God—loving and suffering—was taking form in a human person. This theology of the womb must be the foundation of all theology—theology of politics, theology of history, theology of cultures—theology of God's saving love for all human beings, all created in God's own image.

PART THREE
COMMUNION

11

A Cloud of Witnesses

LIFE IS COMMUNITY

Human beings are social beings. This is not a new insight; it was recognized by ancient sages. It has been the experience of all human beings since the creation. We have just seen how God, in the priestly account, created humankind in God's image; "male and female he created them" (Gen. 1:27). The earlier storyteller has also told us that male and female are to "become one flesh" (2:24). They are created to be different but equal. They are made to be independent but also interdependent. In this way their "differentiation returns to wholeness; from two comes the one flesh of communion."[1] Humankind is a communion of male and female, a community of human persons. To use the words of the author of the letter to the Hebrews, "we are surrounded by so great a cloud of witnesses" (Heb. 12:1).

Life is communion and develops into community. Life has a history, and that history takes place in community. Life expresses itself in culture, and that culture is formed in community. Life engages in social and political activities, and those social and political activities take place in community. From the dawn of humanity, life actualizes itself in religion, and religion is a community affair par excellence. Without community, life becomes rootless, homeless, anchorless.

Civilization is built by human community. In turn human community is strengthened by civilization it has brought into existence. But modern civilization is denying the community that has built it. It is not just denying it; it threatens to destroy it with nuclear weapons. The human community that created the civilization of atomic power is facing the danger of being destroyed by it. No wonder J. R. Oppenheimer, the physicist who headed the group of scientists who detonated the first atom bomb, had a terrible premonition of the god of death destroying the world. But it is no longer just a premonition. The world, in possession of at least fifty thousand known nuclear warheads, is actually in the clutch of a death-god. These nuclear warheads, if fired, would obliterate the entire earth, not simply the communities that human beings have built with labor and pain for thousands of years. What, then, could be more urgent today than to bring all our resources, including theological resources, to protect the human community from nuclear destruction? At stake is life, human life of course, but also all other forms of life created by God.

How crucial community is for humankind! A community is not just a place that can be identified by street names or village signposts. It is not merely an open square or a town hall where meetings are held on certain occasions. It is not a space to which numbers are assigned and houses and shopping centers built. Community is *persons*—engaged in the business of living and dying, believing and hoping, searching for meaning in this world and beyond it. Community is a matter of the spirit. It has to do with the future, and it has to do with faith that transcends the limitations of the present.

This must be the reason why the author of the letter to the Hebrews talks so much about persons in chapter 11, that great chapter on faith. We are told that "the world was created by the word of God" (11:3). Perhaps this could be put differently: "the great cosmic community that is the entire creation was created by the word of God," or "the human community was created by the word of God," or "persons are created by the word of God."

It must have been persons who were uppermost in the author's mind, for what follows are not accounts of how the world came to be filled with nations and governments, or how the human community created by God was made memorable by the rise and fall of great empires and dynasties. We find no such historiography in that chapter. Instead we are shown biographies of persons who kept their faith in God. Chapter 11, then, is a biography of faith—faith that experiences God's presence in the world dominated by demonic forces, faith that brings hope to those in despair, faith that beckons to the future when life seems to be slipping back into the past. That chapter is a tribute to the persons of faith who made community possible and real.

The array of the names mentioned is impressive. It begins with Abel, Enoch, Noah, followed by Abraham, Sarah, all the way down to Gideon, Samson, David, and Samuel. The author must have had to leave out many other names that he would have preferred to include. Nor did he forget women. Sarah is mentioned by name. Rahab, the heroine in the battle of Jericho, is mentioned too, as also the women who "received back their dead raised to life" (11:35). And there were countless other persons—their names unknown—who "were tortured to death, faced jeers, floggings, and prison bars" and those who were "in poverty, distress, and misery" (11:35-38). The history of the community in which the letter to the Hebrews was written is the history of persons, the record of how they kept their faith and fought for it. Persons are the center of that history.

This is a marvelous piece of theology, a theological exercise on faith—an exercise bearing on persons in the history of Israel. Persons make theology possible. It is within a community of persons that theology has its home. Humankind—male and female—was created in God's image, and was ordained to be community. Theology, then, has to focus on persons in community—persons created in God's image. Reflecting on this image of God, theology can then reflect on God.

Theology must take place in the church. This is what the author of the letter to the Hebrews did. In writing about faith in God, the author began thinking about persons in the history of Israel and persons in the community formed in the name of Jesus Christ. The church is not just structure, institution, or hierarchy. Nor is the church made up of ritual and liturgy alone. Nor does one understand the church if one understands only teachings and doctrines developed by learned theologians. To know the church, we must know persons who compose the church. To understand the faith of the church, we must understand the faith of believers who constitute the church.

TWO-THIRDS OF THE WORLD POPULATION

Table 2

Religious and Nonreligious Beliefs Worldwide (1980)[2]

Belief	*Adherents (millions)*		*Percentage of world population*	
Religious				
Christian	1,433		32.8	
Catholic		809		18.5
Protestant		345		7.9
Orthodox		124		2.8
Other		155		3.5
Non-Christian	2,030		46.4	
Islamic		723		16.6
Hindu		583		13.4
Buddhist		274		6.3
Confucianist		167		3.9
Tribal and Shamanist		103		2.4
"New religions"		96		2.2
Shinto		38		0.9
Taoist		25		0.6
Jewish		17		0.4
Other		4		0.1
Nonreligious and atheistic	911		20.8	
World population	4,374		100.0	

The figures tabulated in Table 2 show that only one-third of the world population is Christian—all Christian confessions, sects, and traditions taken together. The other two-thirds are Hindus, Muslims, animists, atheists. But they are human beings just as much as are Christians. They are within God's creation. But they have not been within Christian theology except as a kind of anomaly. Traditional theology has not thought of them as communities and persons in whom God was at work—two-thirds of the world population!

But they have been the object of heated debate, serious concern, and militant action in terms of Christian mission and missiology. They are missio-logical objects of Christian concern, not theo-logical subjects of dogmatics. They can only be mission-ized, not theo-logized. They do not acquire theo-logical meaning until they are mission-ized. God-meaning is not inherent in them, at least not positive God-meaning. God-meaning has to be given to them, grafted onto them.

To my mind, missiology has betrayed theology. It has chosen to ignore the theological meaning of two-thirds of the world population—persons created in God's image and likeness no less than are Christians. Mission efforts of the churches have blinded the theological mind of Christians and theologians. The missionizing thrust of the churches has paralyzed the theological sensitivity of Christians and theologians.

It is time for Christian theology in Asia to stand on its own feet, not undermined by missiology. Missiology must be derived from a theology that takes the other two-thirds of the world population just as seriously as the Christian one-third. Missiology as an independent department of Christian thought has to be abolished. Missiology in hand with theology can then take its part in discerning God's mission to redeem, renew, and re-create the whole of the old creation.

There is particular urgency for renewed theologico-missiological efforts in Asia. In Asia there are over 700 million Muslims, over 500 million Hindus, over 200 million Buddhists, 38 million Shintoists, 25 million Taoists. Seven hundred million Muslims must have at least 700 million stories to tell. Five hundred million Hindus must have at least 500 million stories to tell. We may listen for a lifetime but we shall never finish hearing all those stories. They are stories of all kinds—stories of misery and pain, stories of joy and hope, stories of human cruelty and forgiveness, stories of meeting with God who gives hope and life when human beings are threatened by despair and death. These are human stories in which God is involved.

Human beings—whether Christian or not—have stories to tell. In those stories we meet others, share the secrets of their hearts, and catch glimpses of their visions of the future. And in those stories we may encounter ourselves, realize better the secrets of our hearts, and come to refocus our vision of the future. We may also in those stories encounter God, catch a glimpse of God's secrets for humankind, and experience wonder at God's vision for the future of creation.

And there must be as many stories as there are Christians—stories of God's forgiving love, stories of undeserved grace, stories of souls in agony and spirits in pain, stories of the uncertainty of life and the assurance of faith. In such stories persons outside the Christian community may come to realize that God's forgiving love is not only for Christians but also for them. In them they may see their own soul in agony and their own spirit in pain, their own uncertain lives, and their need for the assurance of faith. And in these Christian stories they may meet the God who is also their God, get a glimpse of God's secrets for their own humanity, and realize they are also part of God's vision for the future of creation.

But stories of Christians and stories told by persons of other faiths are not just parallel stories designed for each other to read, learn from, and admire. These stories come together, penetrate each other, and become integrated into the same stories. This has been happening in Asia and elsewhere today. If Christians struggle for human rights, others too are involved in the struggle. If Christians yearn and strive for freedom and democracy, others do the same. When a workers' union is organized to protect workers' rights, in it are to be found Christians and others. When persons mobilize themselves for peace, it is a mobilization of Christians, members of other faiths, and even those who call themselves atheists. Barriers between Christians and persons of other faiths have been dismantled.

Why has this happened? Why is it that Christian stories and stories of persons outside Christianity can be written as the same stories? Because the world has been rebuilt into a global city by modern science and technology. We live closer to each other. The same dangers—the danger of nuclear war, for example—affect all human beings. The poverty that forces two-thirds of the human race to go to bed hungry is a situation common to Hindus, Muslims, and Christians. When an authoritarian government declares martial law, all citizens, Confucianist or not, suffer the same deprivation of freedom and human rights.

Christians and men and women of other faiths mingle behind prison bars. Peace marchers, regardless of sex, color, or creed, lock arms together and shout with one voice: "Peace, Not War!" In slums and deprived villages Buddhists, Christians, and ancestor worshipers work together to install a pipeline to make water available—water for washing, cooking, and drinking, water that restores human dignity to all.

But these stories are not merely about food, water, freedom, peace, or human rights. They are stories of persons created in God's image—persons in whom God imaged God's own self. What are the stories they tell? They are stories of the spirit, of the soul, of humanity, and also of God. The following story of an impoverished estate worker in Sri Lanka is a story of the soul, of the spirit. It is a story of persons in physical and spiritual agony and pain. It is a plea from the depth of the heart of an estate worker:

Gracious Mother we call to thee,
Look in mercy on our distress.
All these hill-land homes it grips
The demon of poverty and grief.

Many without homes dwell on the streets.
There's not much left, life's ebbing out.
O Goddess, who grantest all requests,
This much alone we ask of thee:
Give them just one small spark of joy
To lighten however dimly darkened lives.

Not long ago, they tell of thee,
A child cried "mother" in its hunger;
Your name you heard, that cry you answered
And fed that child, O Divine Mother.
Hearest thou not this pitiful crying
Echoing through these valleys and hills?
Babies sucking at breasts without milk.
Thousands of little ones calling thy name.
Come now as their mother and save them
At thy feet we humbly pray.[3]

What an earnest plea! It is the plea of an empty stomach. It is the supplication of a starving child. It is the prayer of emaciated humanity. When a hungry stomach calls to "Divine Mother," when an impoverished person pleads with the "gracious goddess," is it not a call and a plea from the spirit? Will not that plea reach God? Many psalms in the Old Testament are pleas made to God by those in distress. Psalm 107 says of them:

Some lost their way in desert wastes;
  they found no road to a city to live in;
hungry and thirsty,
  their spirit sank within them.
So they cried to the Lord in their trouble,
  and he rescued them from their distress. . . .

Some sat in darkness, dark as death,
  prisoners bound fast in iron,
because they had rebelled against God's commands
  and flouted the purpose of the Most High.
Their spirit was subdued by hard labor;
  they stumbled and fell with none to help them.
So they cried to the Lord in their trouble,
  and he saved them from their distress. . . .

Others there are who go to sea in ships
  and make their living on the wide waters. . . .
The storm-wind rose
  and lifted the waves high.

Carried up to heaven, plunged down to the depths,
tossed to and fro in peril,
they reeled and staggered like drunken men,
and their seamanship was all in vain.
So they cried to the Lord in their trouble,
and he brought them out of their distress.

Wanderers in the desert, prisoners bound in chains, sailors at the peril of high seas, and many, many others, make such prayers. They do not have to be Christians.

These are stories of the people. The psalmist tells of them with exciting rhythms: wanderers, prisoners, sailors in trouble; they cry out to God; God hears them and rescues them. Is this not the story of the Sri Lankan estate worker? Thousands of babies call to "divine mother" out of their grief and hunger. When rescue comes, it comes from God—God who rescued the wanderer, the prisoner, and the sailor. The story told by the psalmist and the story told by the Sri Lankan estate worker are the same story.

ONCE I WAS BLIND; NOW I CAN SEE

There are many stories in the church, in the communion of Christian believers. Theology ought to be interested in those stories. It must try to fathom God's saving love in them. It must meet God in them. But there is a danger we must be aware of. Traditional theologians have a built-in tendency to turn Christian stories into theological principles and axioms. They have a way of transforming vivid, unpolished, but exciting stories into orderly theses and antitheses. And they have such a strong power of systematization that stories are bound to get systematized out of all recognition; they become doctrines, dogmas, and canons of the church. We Asian theologians must resist with all our might any such tendency to make God transparent in principles and theses. We must decline the use of theological power to systematize two-thirds of the world population out of direct relationship with God even if, in so resisting, we as Asians have to be uncharacteristically impolite.

For us Asian Christians and theologians, there are also many, many stories to listen to among persons outside the Christian community. We must reject as bad the advice of traditional theology not to listen to them. Theology has to be done in the church; this we wholeheartedly agree with. But we have become aware that in addition there are also stories of persons outside the church—fascinating, heartrending, and inspiring stories. They invite us, beckon to us, and challenge us. We realize that the perimeter of theology has broadened, and the plot of theology has thickened. This is a totally new theological venture.

But in fact it is not a new theological venture. It was explored by Jesus, to the delight and joy of the people and to the dismay and wrath of the religious authorities of his day. The story of Jesus healing a person born blind, this story alone, will show how Jesus pursued this kind of theological venture wholeheartedly and in grand style. It is told by the author of the fourth Gospel, in a most vivid and fascinating way (John 9).

This is a drama of life in many acts. Yes, it is a drama. It is told in such fine detail and with such skill that all characters in it are alive, distinct, and compelling—each in their own way. Here John, the theologian who began his gospel with the ethereal statement "In the beginning was the Word" (John 1:1, RSV), becomes a delightful theologian-storyteller!

Jesus' disciples opened the drama. They pointed to a blind man and called to Jesus, "Rabbi." It may be that they were just trying to be clever. They called Jesus "Rabbi—teacher." They were pupils, capable of asking deep questions. "Rabbi, who sinned, this man or his parents? Why was he born blind?" (9:2). It might be that they were thinking of the proverb Jeremiah the prophet quoted: "The fathers have eaten sour grapes and the children's teeth are set on edge" (Jer. 31:29). It is a matter of karma! If the question had been asked by a Buddhist disciple, it would have sounded something like: "O great Teacher, Enlightened One, whose karma is this? This man's or his parents'?"

A man born with the karma of blindness! The question on the lips of a Buddhist monk would be a profound question. Asia has been in the powerful grip of karma from ancient times to this day. Asians have had to face the karma of human disasters and natural calamities from one generation to the next. It is Buddhism that mobilized the physical and spiritual resources of Asians to combat karma. Its great teacher was Gautama the Buddha. But the same question on the lips of Jesus' disciples would have sounded contrived. At most it could have been out of pity that they asked the question. And by relating blindness to sin, no matter whose sin, they turned the blind man into an object of theological debate and philosophical speculation.

But Jesus is not an academic teacher. He is not a rabbi who teaches from theological textbooks that disease is a result of sin. He categorically rejected the relationship between sin and blindness. He said to them: "It is not that this man or his parents sinned. He was born blind so that God's power might be displayed in curing him" (9:3). No question of karma is involved. This man was born blind and is blind. This is all that matters. And Jesus healed the blind man. It happened to be on the Sabbath day (9:16). By breaking the Sabbath, Jesus broke also the karma under which people had suffered for centuries—karma of the Sabbath. This was a liberation for the people, but for the religious authorities it was blasphemous. This was not the only time Jesus broke the Sabbath. He did it again and again. He was determined to break that karma.

But the curing of the blind man was not the end of the drama. It gave the drama new life. The fact that Jesus could heal blindness caused a great sensation among the people. But the fact that he did it on the Sabbath intensified the irritation of the religious authorities. They were determined to prove that Jesus was a fake, an imposter.

The drama quickly shifts to interrogation scenes. The pompous religious leaders now occupy the center of the stage. They had the man brought in and asked him what happened to him. The poor man must have been in total confusion. For the first time in his life he could see. He had so much to see and understand. A new life had just begun. He must have been full of wonder and excitement. Everyone should have been happy with him and for him. But here he was and those important dignitaries were asking him in menacing tones how he had been cured. What was the problem? What could he say? It was all so simple and straightforward. No question was asked of him by the man who had healed him, and he did not even know his name. All he knew was "he spread a paste on my eyes; then I washed, and now I can see" (9:16).

But the interrogators could not accept this statement of fact. It was possible that the man had not been born blind. He could have been lying, collaborating with that imposter. They had to have other witnesses. The man's parents were called in to testify that their son had not been born blind. The poor parents! They probably did not understand what was happening. But they were such simple folk that they could only say what they knew. They could not lie. Yes, the man was their son. And yes, he had been born blind. No power on earth could change these facts, not even the intimidating leaders of their religion. But as to how their son was cured, they said, "Ask him; he is of age; he will speak for himself" (9:21).

Those religious interrogators bent on proving Jesus to be a fake must have been exasperated. Attention was shifted back to the cured man again. As a last resort they invoked God's name and demanded: "Speak the truth before God. We know that this fellow is a sinner" (9:24). He then answered them: "Whether or not he is a sinner, I do not know. All I know is this: once I was blind, now I can see" (9:25). A great confession this! He can now see many things. He can see physically. But he can also see who has the truth. It is that man outside the religious establishment who has the truth. And those important leaders with all their religious authority behind them are wrong, totally wrong. They do not have the truth.

That confession must have made him bold. His realization of who was on the side of truth must have given him courage. When they denounced Jesus, saying, "as for this fellow, we do not know where he comes from" (9:29), the man could no longer contain himself. Although he knew little about the one who had cured him and probably had not even had a chance to take a good look at him, he knew he had opened his eyes. That is all there needs to be known. And this one important thing alone tells him who Jesus is, and where he comes from. He becomes eloquent: "Here is a man who has opened my eyes, yet you do not know where he comes from! It is common knowledge that God does not listen to sinners; God listens to anyone who is devout and obeys his will. . . . If that man had not come from God, he could have done nothing" (9:30–32). For saying this truth, the truth of what actually happened to him, he was expelled from the synagogue (9:34).

Does this story not show us there are witnesses to the truth not only inside a particular religious community but also outside it? A religious community, like the synagogue in the story, often insulates itself from truths residing in the world outside. The community defines the truth and protects it from a cloud of witnesses beyond its borders. It shuns others and goes to great lengths to prove that they are wrong. This is a disservice to the truth, to say the least. And more seriously, God's thoughts in relation to the whole of humanity are misinterpreted and God's ways in the whole of God's creation are misrepresented. This is a serious offense against the truth.

Theology in Asia must be a theology of the church. But it must also be a theology of Asia. It ought to listen to a cloud of witnesses within the church. But to a cloud of witnesses out in the world of Asia it must also listen. Listen we must to the stories of the inhabitants of the vast continent of Asia—listen with our hearts, our souls, and our might. Then we may be able to say in our theology, as that man cured of blindness by Jesus did, "All I know is this: once I was blind, now I can see." Theology is not debate. It is not argumentation. It is not reasoning. Theology is confession. It is a witness to the truth wherever it manifests itself.

12

Communion of Compassion

THE SPIDER THREAD

Akitagawa Lyunosuke (1892–1927) was one of the most sensitive, passionate, and deeply spiritual writers in the modern literary world of Japan. He wrote in prose, but with the magnificence of epic poetry. "The Spider Thread," one of his very short pieces, echoes the tragedies of human community within the world of the compassionate Buddha. It reads in part:

> It happened on a certain day. Unaccompanied, Shākyamuni Buddha was walking along the edge of a lotus pond in Paradise. Lotus flowers in the pond were all as white as pearls, filling the air with their fragrance. It was morning in Paradise.
>
> Skākyamuni Buddha paused. And through the lotus leaves covering the surface of the water he happened to see the world below. Underneath Paradise was Hell. . . .
>
> He caught sight of a man called Kandata squirming with other sinners in Hell. This man Kandata was a bandit who had committed murder, arson, and many other crimes. But he did at least one good thing. Once as he was going through dense forests, he saw a small spider creeping on the roadside. No sooner had he seen the spider than he lifted his leg intending to stamp it. But a thought came to his mind: "No, no. Small though it is, it must be endowed with a life. It is a pity to take that life." Thinking thus, he eventually spared the spider.
>
> As Shākyamuni Buddha was watching Hell, he remembered how Kandata spared a spider its life and began to ponder how he could rescue that man from Hell as a reward for the good deed he had done. As Shākyamuni Buddha looked around, he saw, to his delight, a spider making a web with its beautiful silvery thread on a lotus leaf. He picked up the spider thread with his hand and let it down to Hell through the pearl-like lotus flowers.
>
> At the bottom of Hell was this Kandata swimming and sinking with

other sinners in the pond of blood. It was pitch dark. The only thing that could be seen was a mountain of needles shining in darkness. What a desperate place! It was also as quiet as a tomb. Only sinners sighing weakly could be heard. . . . Even a bandit such as Kandata, almost choking in that pond of blood, could only wriggle like a frog about to die.

One day Kandata happened to raise his head and look at the sky above the pond of blood. And what a sight he saw! A silvery spider thread shining faintly moving towards him from heaven far, far away! As soon as Kandata saw it, he clapped his hands in joy. "If I take hold of it and climb up, I might be able to get out of Hell. And if I am lucky, I may even get to Paradise. . . ."

Thinking thus to himself, he grasped the spider thread with both hands as firmly as he could and started to climb upwards with might and main. . . . But hundreds of thousands of miles lie between Hell and Paradise, a distance not easy to cover however hard one might try. After a while Kandata felt tired and could not go any further. He had to rest, dangling from the middle of the thread. While resting, he looked down far below him.

Thanks to his effort, the pond of blood had disappeared in the darkness below. That frightful mountain of needles too was now only vaguely glistening in the distance far below him. His hands holding on to the spider thread, Kandata smiled and let words come out of his mouth for the first time in years: "I have done it! I have done it!" But as he cast a casual look over his shoulder, what a sight he saw! Countless sinners were climbing upwards with all their might from the bottom end of the spider thread like a parade of ants. Kandata was completely taken aback and for a while was only able to move his eyes, with his mouth wide open like a fool. This fragile thread could break with his own weight alone. How could it stand the weight of so many people? "Should it break, I would tumble down back to Hell despite all the pains it took me to get up this far." As he was in total panic, those sinners, hundreds and thousands of them, continued to climb that thin fragile spider thread, weakly shining in the dark. If nothing were done, the thread would break from the middle and send him falling down.

Kandata shouted at the top of his voice: "Hey, you sinners! This spider thread is mine. Whose permission did you have to get up here? Get down! Get down!"

Then all of a sudden, the spider thread, nothing wrong with it until this moment, broke with a sound right where Kandata was dangling, sending him like a top all the way down to the darkness below in the flash of a second. . . .

Shākyamuni Buddha was watching everything from the edge of the lotus pond in Paradise. Seeing Kandata sink into the pond of blood, he was very sad and resumed his walk.[1]

This is a parable—told with infinite sadness and profound emotion. Is this not a parable of the world in which we live? Is it not a parable that illuminates a tragedy of human community?

SUFFERING COMMUNITY

Buddhist faith began with Gautama the Buddha who perceived that life is in the bondage of suffering. Encounter with suffering shocked him into pursuit of enlightenment. "This, monks," he is remembered to have preached after he was awakened to the truth of life, "is the Noble Truth of Suffering *(dukkha)*":

> Birth is suffering, old age is suffering, illness is suffering, death is suffering; grief, lamentation, pain, affliction, and despair are suffering; and to be united with what is unloved, to be separated from what is loved is suffering; not to obtain what is longed for is suffering.[2]

There is a lot of common sense in this truth of the enlightened Buddha. This is our daily experience. It is what we go through in life. But it is so common that we tend not to see it. Or it is so unpleasant that we would rather forget about it. However, to be enlightened is not to avoid it but to stare it in the face and do something about it. And this is what the Buddha himself set out to do and what Buddhists face, often with remarkable zeal. Buddhism, then, has come to be looked upon, particularly by Christians, as a passive faith and a world-denying religion.

But it is not only Buddhism that is capable of the insight into life and world as suffering. Suffering too is very close to the heart of biblical faith. The name of Job at once comes to mind. Job's suffering was very great—his sons and daughters perished in one day, he lost all his possessions, and was himself afflicted with sores from head to foot. He poured his heart out in extreme pain:

> Perish the day when I was born
> and the night which said, "A man is conceived"!
> May that day turn to darkness; may God above not look for it,
> nor light of dawn shine in it.
> May blackness sully it, and murk and gloom,
> could smother that day, swift darkness eclipse its sun.
> Blind darkness swallow up that night;
> count it not among the days of the year,
> reckon it not in the cycle of the months.
> That night, may it be barren for ever,
> no cry of joy be heard in it [Job 3:3–7].

These words must have come out of Job's intestines, lungs, and heart. They are words of his anguish. They are not just complaints. They are a curse, cursing the day he was born. The extreme anguish resulting from suffering makes even a devout person such as Job capable of bursting into curses. The Buddha saw life in suffering, and he tried to control it instead of cursing it.

Suffering is also very much in evidence in the New Testament. That touching account of Lazarus's death in John's Gospel (chap. 11) shows us the deeply human side of the community around Jesus and even of Jesus himself. When Jesus arrived at the scene of mourning, both Martha and Mary, Lazarus's sisters, hardly able to control their sorrow, said to him: "O sir, if you had only been here my brother would not have died" (11:21, 32). There is so much anguish in these words! These are not words of accusation but of helplessness. Confronted with death, one has such an intense feeling of hollowness and helplessness. Death silences our hopes and dreams. It stops our time and devours our future. It stops and silences life itself. Death allows only one kind of language—the language of weeping. In that language we hear our own extreme sorrow and anguish, but we also hear the sardonic laughter of death, see its cruel smile, and shudder at its power over life.

When Jesus arrived, it was this language of weeping that he heard. Jesus must have been deeply affected by it. "When Jesus saw her [Mary] weeping and the Jews her companions weeping, he sighed heavily and was deeply moved" (11:33). I wish there had been cameras in those days to take a picture of Jesus "sighing heavily and being moved deeply." It would have shown a most human face. I have yet to see a painting of the heavily sighing and deeply moved Jesus in the company of the weeping Mary and her friends.

Up to this point Jesus had not joined in the language of weeping, although it was all he could hear around him. Was he thinking that Lazarus was not yet dead? Was he hoping that he was still alive? Or was he still not able to reconcile himself to the death of his dear friend? There is a saying in Taiwan that one does not cry until one sees the coffin. Was this perhaps also true with Jesus? Suffering, especially the suffering of death, raises in one a strong desire to reject what can be true. One refuses to accept it as a *fait accompli*. Was this the case with Jesus also? Perhaps. For Jesus asked them: "Where have you laid him?" He received the answer: "Come and see, sir." Then, only then, "Jesus wept" (11:35). Of course those who answered Jesus meant that Lazarus was already put away in a tomb. This must be how Jesus understood the answer. Lazarus is dead! That fact came home to Jesus. It struck him hard. He wept. He joined with the others in the language of weeping before this deadly enemy called death.

Again I have not seen a painting of Jesus weeping in the midst of the persons deeply gripped by the death of Lazarus. Is this profoundly human face of Jesus impossible to capture on a canvas? Is it beyond the power and skill of an artist to reproduce? I do not know. But in paintings of Jesus praying in Gethsemane, I have not seen a weeping Jesus either. Luke, the author of the fourth Gospel, tells us that Jesus "in anguish of spirit prayed the more urgently; and his sweat was like clots of blood falling to the ground" (Luke 22:44). Was there only sweat? Could there not have been tears also? But how is one to paint the weeping Jesus in Gethsemane?

In the Bible there is an attempt to lift suffering to apocalyptic dimensions. The "little apocalypse" in Mark 13 is a typical example. "The desolating sacrilege" (13:14) could be an "apocalyptic code" for the desecration of the temple of Jerusalem in the war of A.D. 66–70.[3] The suffering the war brought to the Jews in that city must have been great. It is said that "in those days there will be such tribulation as has not been from the beginning of the creation, which God has created until now, and never will be" (Mark 13:19, RSV; par. Matt. 24:21).

War, any war, must be spoken about in apocalyptic terms. It is a destruction of lives and civilization. It is an assault on God's creation. That is why the war that destroyed Jerusalem, desecrated the temple, and slaughtered so many persons was a horror of apocalyptic dimension. According to the eyewitness account of Josephus, the Jewish historian, writing immediately after the war ended:

> Pouring into the alleys, sword in hand, they [the Romans] massacred indiscriminately all whom they met, and burnt the houses with all who had taken refuge within. Often in the course of their raids, on entering the houses for loot, they would find whole families dead and the rooms filled with the victims of the famine . . . running everyone through who fell in their way, they choked the alleys with corpses and deluged the whole city with blood, insomuch that many of the fires were extinguished by the gory stream. Towards evening they ceased slaughtering, but when night fell the fire gained the mastery, and the dawn of the eighth day of the month Gorpiaeus broke upon Jerusalem in flames.[4]

Was this not the end of the world? Was this not the creation raging in fury? If Mark wrote his account after the war—almost certainly the case—how could he describe it except in apocalyptic language?

A MUSTARD-SEED PARABLE

Life is suffering. It is consumed by suffering. The world is also in suffering. It is a sea of bitterness. A great sensitivity to suffering has touched the core of Asian humanity. It also touches the core of the world. In Christianity suffering leads to the cross, the symbol and reality of God's saving love for the human being. In Buddhism suffering gives rise to the Bodhisattva consumed with compassion for suffering humanity.

There is a Buddhist parable of the mustard seed that describes human suffering and the Buddha's compassion in a most exquisite, touching, and moving way.[5] In the parable Kisagotami, "a woman dove-eyed, young, with tearful face," comes to the master with her dead son in her arms, beseeching him to bring her son back to life. The master says to her:

> Yea, little sister, there is that might heal
> Thee first and him, if thou couldst fetch the thing;

> For they who seek physicians bring to them
> What is ordained. Therefore I pray thee, find
> Black mustard-seed, a tola; only mark
> Thou take it not from any hand or house
> Where a father, mother, child, or slave hath died;
> It shall be well if thou canst find such seed.

The grief-stricken mother, with hope rekindled in her heart, sets out on visits to relatives, friends, and others, to find the mustard seed as the master had told her. There was such a seed, but . . . she has to listen to the same story over and over wherever she went:

> Here is the seed, but we have lost our slave!
> Here is the seed, but our good man is dead!
> Here is the seed, but he that sowed it died
> Between the rain-time and the harvesting!

Utterly dejected, she comes back to the master and tells him that she has not been able to find the kind of mustard seed he must have to cure her son. With gentle eyes and tender voice the master then says to her:

> My sister! thou hast found,
> Searching for what none finds—that bitter balm
> I had to give thee. He that thou lovedst slept
> Dead on thy bosom yesterday: today
> Thou know'st the whole wide world weeps with thy woe:
> The grief which all hearts share grows less for one.
> Lo! I would pour my blood if it would stay
> Thy tears and win the secret of that curse
> Which makes sweet love our anguish and which drives
> O'er flowers and pastures to the sacrifice—
> As these dumb beasts are driven—
> I seek that secret; bury thou thy child!

At the death of Lazarus Jesus wept. The master in this parable, in saying these words to the mother of the dead child, must have wept too.

But it is the compassion of the master that strikes us. "I would pour my blood," said the master, "if I could stay thy tears and win the secret of that curse which makes sweet love our anguish." One can hear the master's anguish in these words. One can see his face covered with grief. One can feel compassion going out from his heart to the mother in tears and sorrow. Here is the beauty of humanity created by God in this world of suffering. Here we are in the presence of a deeply compassionate soul in communion with the God of love. And here in the voice of the grieving master one hears the voice of God in anguish.

Reading stories and parables such as this in Oriental religious literature written with vivid imagination and finesse, without haste or compulsion, I often wish that the writers of the Gospels in the New Testament had given us more glimpses into Jesus' heart stirred and moved by the suffering of others. There are some such glimpses in the story of Lazarus's death and in the accounts of Jesus in Gethsemane. But these are rare. Jesus must have shown much emotion. He must have sighed often. He must have wept more than once. He must have said many, many gentle words to the sick, apart from the brief formulas of healing. He must have spoken many, many assuring words to those in anguish of spirit, apart from the words of forgiveness. And his presence with men and women stricken with grief and sorrow at the death of their dear ones must have made his empathy, anguish, and hope palpable. All this we have to image for ourselves from the Gospel stories. For these stories are very eager, almost too eager, to show how God's mighty work is done through Jesus. They are impatient with details. They want to move quickly to the manifestation of God's power and glory.

But God seems especially patient in Asia. Space is vast. History is long. Culture is rich. Persons are numerous. The heart nourished by such culture embraces deep emotions. The soul formed in such history is very patient. And the mind grown out of such vast space has plenty of room.

We Asians are by nature religious. We revere heaven and respect earth. We find affinity with nature and seek harmony with God. And for us human relationships are shaped and conditioned by our religious beliefs. It is this kind of Asia that was able to produce religious teachers such as Shākyamuni in India and Mo Ti in China. We Christians in Asia must learn to read our Bible with that vast heart, grasp its message with that rich soul, and comprehend its meaning with a patient mind. Then the God of compassion in Jesus may become related to us more personally, speaking to us more deeply and confiding to us secrets unknown to us before.

SALVATION IS COMMUNAL

We must now return to the story of the spider thread told by Akitagawa Liunosuke. As in the parable of the mustard seed just discussed, the burden of the story is also the compassion of the Buddha. Even in Paradise the Buddha does not forget the world in turmoil and the human community in suffering. His gaze is not directed upward but downward. That is why he is acclaimed as "Regarder of the Cries of the World":

> [he has] regard of pity, compassionate regard,
> Ever longed for, ever looked for!
> Pure and serene in radiance,
> Wisdom's sun destroying darkness,
> Subduer of woes of storm and fire,
> Who illumines all the world!

Law of pity, thunder quivering,
Compassion wondrous as a great cloud,
Pouring spiritual rain like nectar,
Quenching the flames of distress![6]

It is this Buddha, the Regarder of the Cries of the World, who saw Kandata suffering in Hell from the lotus pond in Paradise. Thus began the tragic drama of Kandata who betrayed the Buddha's compassion and fell back down to Hell.

So much depends on that fragile spider thread! Men, women, and children suffering in the sea of bitterness depend on it. Multitudes of living beings (*chung sheng* in Chinese) depend on it. The whole world depends on it. But it is such a thin thread. It is so frail. It can hardly stand any stress or strain. At the slightest use of force it will break in two. But it is a really astonishing sight! This thin, frail, and fragile thread bears the weight of hundreds and thousands of persons desperately hanging on to it! How did it become so strong, so durable? It looks as if it will break at any moment. But it does not. Carrying an enormous weight, it holds fast and even gives out light in the world of pitch darkness, illuminating the way out of suffering into joy. This is a ghastly picture of human beings struggling for salvation. But it is also a sublime picture of the slender, silvery spider thread bearing the burden of the world. It is a thread of hope. It is a thread of light. And it is a thread of life.

But where does the spider thread get its strength? How does it have the power to sustain so much weight? It does not have the power and strength of its own to do it. It is the Buddha who gives power to it. It is he who makes it strong. But there is more: that spider thread is strong, durable, and capable of bearing such a weight because of the Buddha's compassion. The Buddha pours all his compassion into it. His compassion transforms it into an unbreakable thread. That thin, frail spider thread turns into a thick, strong, and durable thread. It has become the Buddha's compassion itself! And perhaps even more, that spider thread is the Buddha himself, who was represented as saying:

> The burden of all creatures must be borne by me. . . . It is better indeed that I alone be in pain than that all creatures fall into the place of misfortune. There I must give myself in bondage, and all the world must be redeemed from the wilderness of hell, beast-birth, and Yama's world, and I for the good of the creatures would experience all the mass of pain and unhappiness in this my own body.[7]

How can that spider thread not be strong and durable because of the Buddha? It can bear not only Kandata's weight, but also the weight of so many others holding it with all their might and climbing out of the pond of blood in Hell, looking neither to the right nor to the left.

From the edge of the lotus pond in Paradise above the Buddha must have been watching all this in compassion and with much anxiety. His heart must have gone out to those clinging to the spider thread and climbing with so much effort. The distance was so enormous. He only wished that all of them would make it to the top as soon as possible. He must also have been praying that his strength would last until each and every one of them got out of Hell.

The Buddha then saw Kandata, who was heading the climb, stop. He must be tired; but he should not stop. The Buddha was perhaps about to urge him to make the last mile when he heard him shout to those following from below him: "Hey, you sinners! This spider thread is mine. Get down! Get down!" The Buddha could not believe his ears. It was not Kandata's thread. It was *his!* And the next thing he heard was the snap of the spider thread, a piercing sound. And Kandata, together with all the others, fell headlong back into the pool of blood far down below. The thread of the Buddha's compassion could bear "the burden of all creatures" in suffering, but it could not bear the burden of even one person's trying to save himself at the cost of all the others. The Buddha was very sad and resumed his lonely walk along the edge of the lotus pond.

Compassion is a communal thing. It is com-passion: together-passion or passion-together. Passion is both suffering and loving. Hence compassion is together-loving and together-suffering. It is suffering together and loving together. It is this togetherness that makes a community a community. Community is born out of compassion. It is correct that human beings traditionally regard the family as the basic community. The community called family is the result of compassion, passion-together of husband and wife. But compassion does not stop at the family level. It goes on to become the basis of society, nation, and even the world. When compassion weakens and disappears, families break up, society becomes the pit where persons consume one another—the rich consume the poor, the strong consume the weak, government becomes oppressive, and the world turns into the arena of power politics.

Compassion is the heart of religion, of course. But compassion can disappear from it. When a religion loses its heart of compassion, it becomes demonic. Religion then becomes law and a burden imposed on its adherents. A religion can start a religious war to destroy its enemies. It can set up an inquisition to condemn those who disagree with religious authorities in matters of morals and doctrines. It may still retain many of the characteristics of religion—rituals, liturgies, teachings, but it is no longer a religion of compassion. And religion without compassion, religion that ceases to love and suffer together with its believers within and nonbelievers without, is no longer religion. It is an institution that administers religious affairs. Even many governments in the world today, especially those with authoritarian systems, have a department of religious affairs. That department is not set up to care for believers with compassion. It is not meant to love them and suffer with them. Its sole function is to control them, intimidate them, and force them to comply with its oppressive rules. A religion, if it is to be faithful to its calling, must not become a department of religious affairs. It must be compassionate; it must have a compassionate heart and spirit.

Jesus had to contend with a religion lacking in compassion, a religion that wanted to stone a woman caught in adultery, a religion that refused to save life on the Sabbath day. He was grieved by a religion that created outcasts. He had to tell the religious authorities and his followers stories and parables about compassion, about how God loves and suffers together with people and about how people must love each other and suffer with each other.

In the parable of the good Samaritan (Luke 10:29–37) a priest and a Levite went past the man who had fallen victim to highway robbery on his way from Jerusalem to Jericho. Their religion made them incapable of compassion. Religious law did not allow them to touch a dying person while on their religious duties; it deprived them of the ability to love and suffer together with injured persons. That kind of religion destroyed community—the very thing it was ordained to build. In contrast, the Samaritan, considered a heretic, with whom the Levite and the priest would have nothing to do, went out of his way to help the wounded man. He was capable of compassion, and could be referred to as an example for others.

Jesus told other parables and stories to illustrate God's compassion:

> If one of you has a hundred sheep and loses one of them, does he not leave the ninety-nine in the open pasture and go after the missing one until he has found it? How delighted he is then! He lifts it on to his shoulders, and home he goes to call his friends and neighbours together. "Rejoice with me!" he cries. "I have found my lost sheep" [Luke 15:3–6; par. Matt. 18:12–13].

It is the compassion of the shepherd for the lost sheep that is the single most important point made by the parable. One could also stress that the community of ninety-nine, though safe and sound, is impaired and incomplete with one member lost. That impaired community must be restored. Only the recovery of the stray can bring wholeness to the community.

Matthew's concluding remark is right to the point: "In the same way, it is not your heavenly Father's will that one of these little ones should be lost" (Matt. 12:14). As a matter of fact, these concluding words fit in better with the Lukan version of the parable. The Lukan conclusion, "In the same way, I tell you, there will be greater joy in heaven over one sinner who repents than over ninety-nine righteous people who do not need to repent" (Luke 15:7), seems to express more what Matthew had in mind in his version of the parable when he said that if the shepherd found the lost sheep "he is more delighted over that sheep than over the ninety-nine that never strayed" (Matt. 18:13). Obviously this was directed to the self-righteous Pharisees and doctors of the law in whose eyes tax-collectors and other "pariahs" had no place in God's salvation.

At any rate, Jesus did not only talk about compassion. He practiced it. "When he saw the crowds," we are told, "he had compassion for them, because they were harassed and helpless, like sheep without a shepherd" (Matt. 9:36, RSV; par. Mark 6:34). Jesus loved and suffered together with others. He formed with them a community of loving and suffering. Wherever he went, a community of compassion came into being. It was a loving, saving, and suffering community. And Jesus brought that community all the way to the cross, where he loved the whole world and suffered with it. Salvation takes place within a community of compassion.

This was also the Buddha's compassion. Kandata wanted only himself to be saved. But there was no salvation for him outside a community of compassion. The power of compassion that made the spider thread strong was obstructed. The thread broke. It could bear the weight of the community of compassion but not the weight of even one uncompassionate person.

13

Broken Humanity

PASSION WITHOUT COMPASSION

Passion must be transformed into compassion. Passion developed into compassion becomes the basis of human community—communion of loving and suffering in pursuit of salvation. Community is where persons are able to share life in common and be united in search of its meaning. A community, large or small, is in trouble if its members have little in common and are not willing to be united in loving and suffering together. The disintegration of community in modern civilization should be a matter of grave concern. Often it takes a crisis—personal, national, or global—to bring persons back into community. The great number of persons in the world today who are united in search of peace because of the threat of nuclear warfare is an example.

Without togetherness, without commonness, passion can be a dangerous thing. Passion without compassion loses its twofold meaning of loving and suffering. It becomes an inordinate will-power to consume other persons, to control them, even to destroy them. Blind passionate love can be a terrifying thing. In politics, the passion for power becomes a deadly passion. In an authoritarian regime a ruler's passion for power may not tolerate an opposition political party, the right of dissent, or the freedom to express different views on the state of the nation. Passion then becomes a demonic power, filling prisons with political dissidents, permeating society with fear, and destroying freedom of conscience. It is a dehumanized power.

In religion, too, passion without compassion can be a dreadful thing. That kind of passion, when applied to God, turns into wrath. A passionate God can be a wrathful God who must be placated with prayers, incantations, and sacrifices—even human sacrifices. In the hymns of the Rig Veda, current in India fifteen centuries before Christ, Varuna, a Vedic deity and the guardian of Rita, the physical and moral order of the universe, is supplicated:

Whatever law of thine, O god, O Varuna, as we are human beings,
Day after day we violate,
Give us not as prey to death, to be destroyed by thee in wrath.
To thy fierce anger when displeased.
To gain thy mercy, Varuna, with hymns we bind thy heart,
as binds
The charioteer his tethered horse. . . .[1]

Why does anger play such a predominant role in religion? Is it part of "primitive" psychology? Is it because of the awe and fear caused by the awareness of some inscrutable power? Is it a reflection of a patriarchal society in which masculine power overcomes feminine love? (In Japan four things are to be feared: earthquake, thunder, fire, and one's father!) Or is it an extension of the absolute power that chieftains, kings, and emperors exercised?

In the Bible also there is cataclysmic wrath and anger, especially in the Old Testament. The God of Sinai was an angry God. At the foot of Mount Sinai the people had a taste of what their God was like. "Mount Sinai was all smoking because the Lord had come down upon it in fire," says an account in the book of Exodus, "the smoke went up like the smoke of a kiln; all the people were terrified. . . . Whenever Moses spoke, God answered in a peal of thunder" (Exod. 19:18–19). Who would not be afraid before such a fiery and thundering God?

God's wrath is sometimes incomprehensible. Men and women have to bear the brunt of it, not knowing why. In the hymns of lament in the book of Psalms we encounter persons struggling with an angry God. Psalm 88 is an example:

O Lord, my God, by day I call for help,
by night I cry aloud in thy presence.
Let my prayer come before thee,
hear my loud lament [vv. 1–2].

What is the cause of lament? What is troubling the psalmist? It is the threat of death:

I am numbered with those who go down to the abyss
and have become like a man beyond help
like a man who lies dead
or the slain who sleep in the grave [vv. 4–5].

But why does one have to be cut off from the world of the living in the prime of life? What did one do to deserve it? Here is the psalmist's answer:

Thou hast plunged me into the lowest abyss,
in dark places, in the depths.
Thy wrath rises against me,
thou hast turned on me the full force of thy anger [vv. 6–7].

So it is the God of wrath! Before that angry God there is nothing but death! Was the author of the letter to the Hebrews reflecting this when he said: "It is a fearful thing to fall into the hands of the living God" (Heb. 10:31)?

In fact, however, it is *not* a fearful thing to fall into the hands of the living God. It is blessing! It is hope! It is life! The angry God is a God with passion but without compassion. But is there a God with passion but without compassion? Such a God is the fabrication of the revengeful human mind, a product of an autocratic feudal society, the creation of an authoritarian religious hierarchy. God can only be a compassionate God, loving us and suffering with us. That is the God who enables the psalmist to say:

> God is our shelter and refuge,
> a timely help in trouble;
> so we are not afraid when the earth heaves
> and the mountains are hurled into the sea,
> when its waters seethe in tumult
> and the mountains quake before God's majesty [Ps. 46:1–3].

Shelter is a place without fear. Refuge is a place of security. This is our God—the God who not only does not make us fear but removes fear from us. This is the God of Jesus Christ. It is the God who speaks to us through Jesus: "Come to me, all who labor and are heavy laden, and I will give you rest" (Matt. 11:28, RSV). It is also the God who spoke to Jerusalem through Jesus: "O Jerusalem, Jerusalem, the city that murders the prophets and stones the messengers sent to her! How often have I longed to gather your children, as a hen gathers her brood under her wings" (Matt. 23:37). Jesus' God is the God of compassion.

A CHILD-SOLDIER

In our world there is more passion than compassion. The cross is inevitable in such a world as ours. In world history and in the history of our own nations we see how the passion for power destroys human community and creates broken humanity. This is still true today the world over. And to our infinite sorrow, it is most true in Asia. There are so many pieces of broken humanity scattered all over Asia. There are so many fragments of broken humanity to be gathered up and put back in place.

But how can this be done when Asian humanity is forever being broken? Asian humanity is broken faster than it can be put back together. But these pieces of broken humanity must be gathered up. And it is the task of theology in Asia to pick up some of these fragments of broken humanity and put them back together. It is no accident that Shākyamuni Buddha taught and practiced compassion in Asia. Nor was it by chance that the gospel of the cross borne by Jesus was brought to the Asian world.

We must listen to the stories of broken Asian humanity. There are many such stories to tell out of all the rubble of the wars fought on Asian soil.

Here is such a story—the story of Gora (a fictitious name), a Cambodian youth in a refugee camp in Thailand who fought as a child-soldier under the Lon Nol regime in Cambodia before the communist takeover:

> For a few years under Lon Nol's rule, when Phnom Penh was a city isolated from the country, there were entire regiments composed of little boys, aged 10-14, making war, killing, severing heads, firing heavy artillery—all under the weight of helmets and machine guns that were too heavy and too large for their frail bodies. They weren't only attacking. They were also targets. Like flies, they died of badly treated wounds, unchecked infection, and total exhaustion. What has become of this army of little boys? What do they think of their childhood spent in blood, amid the sound of heavy artillery fire, far from affection, toys, studies, and joys of adolescence?
>
> Gora is one of them. He wears the traditional Asian smile on a face tainted by a scar born of a badly treated wound; he sports the charm of a child's innocent look. Gora is 16 years old, a soldier at the age of 12.
>
> "I left grandfather a long time ago to earn a few pennies in the city. I followed street boys . . . we did silly things and finally the police got us. They gave us the choice of prison or the army."
>
> "Why choose the army?"
>
> "I don't know, but it was less frightening. To start with, there are walls in prison. In the army, there are uniforms, arms, and things to earn."
>
> "What for example?"
>
> "What you can get from the enemy."
>
> "Weren't the enemy also Cambodians?"
>
> "Yes . . . but they were from the other side."
>
> "You killed some of them?"
>
> He smiles. Is it awkwardness, nostalgia, or anguish?
>
> "Yes, of course I killed . . . you had to. . . ."
>
> "You had a gun?"
>
> "Yes, and a hatchet."
>
> "To cut wood?"
>
> "To kill in silence . . . to chop off heads . . . the more heads of the other side we could bring, the more food we got."
>
> "You never hesitated at the time?"
>
> "No, the others killed too. We watched each other, each wanted to be the champion."
>
> "You come from a Buddhist family?"
>
> "Of course, everybody was Buddhist then."
>
> "What have you done with the peace, the silence, the forgiveness, the tolerance, and the love taught by the Buddha?"
>
> He looked at me without a smile this time. He avoids my eyes and scratches the scar on his face.

"He wasn't there. He was never there during the war."

After a moment he adds, "We had driven away the Buddha in asking him to help us kill better."

"Do you think about that sometimes?"

Gora's face regains a little of the light from the Thai sky when he looks up. "There are so many headless Buddha statues in the countryside," he says.

"The traders decapitate them and steal them to sell to foreigners. We only severed the heads of our enemies who also wanted to chop off ours; are we more or less guilty than those thieves who robbed holy statues?"

"It's not the same thing," I say.

"I don't know," he replies with surprising conviction. "We were fighting dangerous people. Thieves don't fight. They take no risks. They are Buddha's real assassins. They are the criminals."[2]

This is a grim and sad story, especially grim and sad because it comes from a Buddhist country. But it is also a sophisticated story—a story of a boy who had grown prematurely old in the world of broken humanity.

BUDDHA'S ASSASSINS

War is a time for generals and admirals. It is a time for soldiers, marines, and aviators. But it is also a time for thieves who rob a country of religious emblems and sell them as art objects. How many such "art objects" are to be found in museums, large and small, particularly in the West? And how many of them are in private homes, decorating living rooms and lining bookshelves? A large number of such "art objects" are from Buddhist countries in Asia. Buddhism has developed magnificent art. Like Christian and Hindu art, Buddhist art expresses profound reverence for the Buddha and deep respect for his teachings. It tells the story of Buddhist spirituality seeking liberation from human greed and lust, achieving the compassion of Bodhisattva, attaining fulfillment in nirvana. It reminds Buddhists that there must be good over against evil, life beyond death.

Since the first century A.D. the Buddha has been the favored motif of Buddhist religious art. "In the course of time the positions of the Buddha's hands and body were standardized" in pictures and statues.[3] There is a famous sculpture from the Gupta period (fifth century) depicting the Buddha "in the gesture of setting the wheel of the doctrine in motion; his legs are crossed in the lotus posture. The ear-lobes are elongated from the bearing of heavy jewelry, which Gotama discarded when setting out for a homeless life. They so symbolize renunciation."[4] A Japanese scroll of the twelfth century shows "the Buddha expounding the Dharma," his right arm raised, forming the wheel of the teaching with the thumb and the ring finger of his right hand.[5] A rather striking statue is a Thai bronze of perhaps the fifteenth century showing "the Buddha granting consolation and appeasement of passions."[6] His right hand, bent at the elbow, is half raised with the palm open toward the front. The left hand, which points downward, seems to form with the right hand a gesture of acceptance.

And the faces of the Buddha, seen by themselves apart from the hands and the body, all look the same. The eyes are closed, giving the impression of deep contemplation. It is a picture of serenity itself, oblivious to the noise of the world, unaffected by disturbances from outside. But seen with the hands and the body, the faces begin to look different. In the posture of teaching and expounding dharma, the wisdom gained from deep contact with the woes of life seems to radiate from the Buddha's placid face. And in the posture of giving consolation the Buddha's face becomes compassion itself, extending to all suffering humanity his grace and mercy. It is to this Buddha—hands, head, body, soul, and all—that his devotees bring their petition and prayer:

> O Pure One of the Bodhi tree,
> To your feet I bring my plea.
> I praise you, compassionate one,
> Who loved all beings as your own.
> You implanted in their hearts
> The hearts of those who prayed to you
> The ways of truth and light
> To dispel ignorance and gloom. . . .
>
> Why did you abandon your crown,
> The throne at whose feet kings knelt in homage?
> You left behind a kingdom and pomp,
> Why, O Lord, for whose benefit?
> Was it not to serve the poor,
> To wipe the tears of the destitute?
> The lamp of wisdom and knowledge you lit,
> To drive out fear and ignorance.[7]

The Buddha is not God. Statues of the Buddha are not idols. They testify to the wisdom and compassion of the Buddha. They also are signposts of the wisdom and compassion Buddhists seek in this vale of tears. They are not art objects. For that matter they are not religious art objects. They are the Buddhist faith in visible forms. They manifest the Buddhist spirituality longing for truth and eternity.

But merchants—Gora calls them thieves—turned the spirit and soul of Buddhist faith into art objects. And what a hideous thing they did! They severed heads from Buddha statues and sold them to foreigners. What a sacrilege they committed! A Buddha head without the hands and body has nothing to tell. It is an eternal silence. Severed from its teaching hands, cut off from its consoling hands, a Buddha head is just a mass of particles and molecules. It has no spirit. It has no compassion. It becomes just an object to be smuggled out of the country, destined not for a shrine or temple, but for a museum or a living room.

And what about those hands and bodies of the statues left behind without heads? The face through which the hands and the body convey wisdom and consolation is there no more. The Buddha's disciples no longer hear his wisdom. They do not receive his compassion any more. Deprived of the wisdom and compassion of the Buddha, they become capable of anything. They can be driven by the passion for power to turn their country into a battlefield. Without the Buddha's wisdom to guide them, they give vent to greed and exploitation. Without the Buddha's compassion to hold them in check, they resort to violence and murder. They become capable of genocide. Is this not what happened in Cambodia, now called Kampuchea?

Vietnam, another Buddhist country in Indochina, went through the baptism of fire and brimstone of the Vietnam war. Hundred and thousands of heads must have been severed from Buddha statues by thieves, gunners, and bombers. The country with decapitated Buddha statues suffered beyond description. Nhat Chi Nai, a Buddhist nun who burned herself as an offering for peace in May 1967, left this poem behind her:

> O Vietnam, Vietnam,
> Why this hatred among people?
> why this killing of one another?
> who will be the defeated?
> who will be the winner?
>
> Oh please remove all labels!
> we all are Vietnamese
> we all are Vietnamese
> let us take each other's hand
> to protect our country.
>
> O Vietnam, Vietnam.[8]

Why?, the nun cried out from the depth of her agony. Her cry must have risen with the flame that devoured her, echoing in the streets of Saigon and the battlefields all over Vietnam. The Buddha has been assassinated by thieves, politicians, militarists, the superpowers. Compassion has fled the country. That is why. When compassion deserted the Vietnamese, they became mere objects to one another—objects to be maltreated, cast aside, annihilated. The Buddha with his head severed was not able to save Vietnam. Nor was he able to rescue Kampuchea from Pol Pot's genocidal insanity.

A CRITIQUE OF RELIGIONS

The Buddha with his head severed is no longer the Buddha. A headless Buddha statue symbolizes the tragedy of a people and a nation. Even children as young as ten to twelve years old were engulfed in that tragedy. They were made into soldiers, donning oversize uniforms and carrying heavy machine guns to shoot and kill their "enemies." They even asked the Buddha to help them kill better. Of course it was not the Buddha they asked. How could they dare ask the Buddha to help them—the Buddha who, they must have known from their parents and Buddhist monks, is all compassion, who forbids killing as a most heinous sin? The Buddha they asked was not the real Buddha. It was the headless Buddha statue that they turned to with their horrible request. The headless Buddha statue was not the Buddha.

Those boys, ten, eleven, and twelve years old, went about severing the heads of their enemies with their hatchets. But with each head they severed, they severed a Buddha. Each person, whether friend or foe, is a Buddha; this is one of the basic teachings of the Buddhist faith. Those boys, born and brought up in a Buddhist country, ought to have known it. The "Sutra of Wei Lang" (Hui Neng) says:

> Within our mind there is a Buddha, and that Buddha within is the real Buddha. If Buddha is not to be sought within our mind, where shall we find the real Buddha?[9]

If Buddha is within the mind of a person, to kill that person is to kill the Buddha.

Those boys were wrong, however. The Buddha was still there, even though the statues with severed heads did not represent him anymore. The Buddha was within each and every person. The Buddha was each and every enemy whose head they removed with a hatchet. They thought they were doing this behind the Buddha's back. Little did they know they were doing the killing right in his presence. They were doing it to him.

What a profound tragedy this is! The Buddha was betrayed by politicians and generals who had only the passion for power and no compassion for fellow human beings. The Buddha was also betrayed by those children who resorted to killing, thinking that the Buddha was not there. This is the broken humanity that replaces the religion of compassion with the practice of violence and turns a culture of compassion into a culture of dispassion.

Does not this betrayal of the Buddha disclose to us a very dark side of human nature? Does it not tell us that human beings have an enormous capacity to achieve broken humanity despite the power of compassion at work in the world? Does it not warn us that religions do not always enable their followers to discern what is good, beautiful, and true, and to become committed to it? Does it not tell us that religious faith does not automatically lead believers to liberation from bondage to sin?

Jesus had some very strong words to say about his own religion. It was a religion that tithed mint and dill and cummin but neglected the weightier matters of the law—justice, mercy, and faith (Matt. 23:23). It was a religion that "cleanses the outside of the cup and of the plate, but inside is full of extortion and rapacity" (23:25). It was like a whitewashed tomb, outwardly beautiful but inside full of all kinds of filth (23:27).

This is a severe critique of religion. Jesus' critique is not based on a comparison of doctrines and teachings. For him the critique of religion is not a theoretical exercise, as is often the case with theologians. Some theologians have this incurable urge to speculate and compare. They speculate that God has a limited presence in a place such as Asia, which remains largely outside the sphere of Christian influence. They mistakenly assume that God's presence is Christianity. They compare Christian faith with other faiths under the overt or covert assumption that what Christians believe is superior—not only superior but unique and absolute. That is why the study of other religions in most of our theological schools remains a comparative study.

But a *theological* study of these religions has hardly begun. Theologically we do not know what to make of them, although we have come to know them a little better. Our chief difficulty is that we do not know what to do with them theologically. To add to our problem, traditional theology has taught us that these religions are prone to revolting against God. All this points to the urgent need for us to become engaged in a theology of religions, not speculating about and comparing religions as a theoretical exercise, but feeling them, experiencing them as the spiritual forces that have shaped or failed to shape the lives of peoples, the mores and ethos of societies.

Jesus critiqued the religion of his day: it betrayed God! That is what Jesus was saying. But that religion had many splendors to its credit. It had been quickened by a deep awareness of the exodus from Egypt as God's liberating and saving act. It was inspired by a strong sense of humanity in the care of a merciful God who was remembered to have said: "If you take your neighbor's cloak in pawn, you shall return it to him by sunset, because it is his only covering. It is the cloak in which he wraps his body; in what else can he sleep? If he appeals to me, I will listen, for I am full of compassion" (Exod. 22:26–27).

It is this God full of compassion that Jesus tried to reintroduce into his own religion. He wanted his coreligionists to regain their faith in such a God. He did not do it by constructing a doctrine of God but by telling the story of the good Samaritan. And he did not conclude his story saying, "Write it all down in your notebook," as we do in our theology classrooms. What he said was: "Go and do as that good Samaritan did" (Luke 10:37).

The story of the good Samaritan was a monograph in Jesus' theology of religions. The Samaritans did not see eye to eye with the Jews in matters of faith and religion. It would have been disastrous if Jesus had begun comparing the religious beliefs of the Samaritans with those of his own religion. There would have been a clash at the very beginning. A heated debate would no doubt have arisen. The swords of the two religions would have joined in conflict. But Jesus began with life—a parable related to a real-life situation. After all, religion is a part of life; or better, it has to do with the whole of life. It is in the real-life situations of this uncertain world that a religious faith has to be tested.

And what a surprise! From the life of faith that that Samaritan exemplified on the dangerous road to Jericho, Jesus was able to help his hearers find their own God full of compassion in their own religious traditions. He did something more. It was not only their own religious traditions that pointed to a compassionate God who stipulated that the neighbor's cloak be returned for the night. The religion of the Samaritans also pointed to such a God. In this way, Jesus clearly indicated that God full of compassion is not the God of Jews only. That God is also the God of Samaritans. That God is also the God of the Gentiles, the God of women and children, the God of tax-collectors and adulteresses. There is so much we must learn from Jesus' theology of religions.

14

Struggle for Wholeness

HUMAN COMMUNITY AND COMMUNION WITH GOD

Broken humanity is humanity at war. It is human beings at each others' throats. It could even ask the Buddha for help to kill better. It could even crucify Jesus, the savior filled with the God of compassion. Broken humanity destroys human community—the community that is possible only when persons are able to love and suffer with each other. In destroying human community, it also destroys communion with God.

Human community and divine communion are interdependent. It is not a question of either-or, but of both-and. Nor is it a matter of which comes first—communion with God or community with other human beings. They both come first: they take place simultaneously. Communion with God without human community may be possible in the world of metaphysics but not in the real world of human persons. Human community without communion with God inevitably yields broken humanity. It is no longer community. It is hell.

Writing to a group of Christian believers, John, the author of the Gospel that bears his name, says in his first letter:

> We love because [God] loved us first. But if a man says, "I love God," while hating his brother, he is a liar. If he does not love the brother whom he has seen, it cannot be that he loves God whom he has not seen. And indeed this command comes to us from Christ himself: that he who loves God must also love his brother [1 John 4:19–21].

Love is mentioned here not by accident. Love is creative. It creates humanity. It creates community. Nor is love created by us: before we know it, we already have it. We love because we are made to love. To be able to love is a sign of humanity. The depth of one's capacity to love is a sign of the depth of one's humanity.

It is through love working in us, making us a community of persons, that we come to know God as love. God is creative love. This is not a theological hypothesis. It is the truth about God disclosed to us through living in community. First we come to know that if there is no love, there is no community. But we do not stop there. We go on to learn that love comes from the God who is love. God is the source and ground of love.

That is why John in his letter says that our love for God is not genuine unless it is manifested in love for our brothers and sisters. There is no other way of showing our love for God except in human community. God's love cannot be grasped and expressed apart from the community in which we live. To separate love of God from love of neighbor is to cripple love. Such a separation, according to John, makes one a liar. Such a liar ends up loving neither God nor neighbor. Broken humanity is made up of such liars. Community is destroyed by them. And communion with God becomes false even if they go through all the prescribed exteriorizations of official church membership.

Jesus was also at pains to show how closely love brings together community of persons and communion with God. On one occasion he said to his listeners: "If, when you are bringing your gift to the altar, you suddenly remember that your brother has a grievance against you, leave your gift where it is before the altar. First go and make peace with your brother, and only then come back and offer your gift" (Matt. 5:23–24). Bringing a gift to the altar is bringing one's own self to God. A gift is not something separate from you. It is a part of you. It is the love of which you are capable. You offer that gift of love to God who is love ultimately and primarily.

But if there is a grievance between you and your brother or sister, that love of yours, that love which is you, is breached. Your gift, then, is also breached. You cannot offer that broken gift to God. There will be no communion with God as long as that broken love of yours harms the community of which you are a part. The community has lost its wholeness. It is no longer healthy. It has no peace. Health and peace are essential to wholeness. A community without health and peace is also a community without justice. Human relationships are disrupted and communion with God is impaired. The struggle for wholeness, for health, peace, and justice, is a religious struggle. It is a struggle for the wholeness of communion with God, for the peace, health, and justice of that communion.

For us Christians there is no social action that is not at the same time religious action, and no political concerns that are not the concern of our faith. You may think that giving food to the hungry has nothing to do with religion, but was not Jesus remembered as saying to those who gave food to the hungry: "When *I* was hungry, you gave *me* food"? You may think that a donation of money or clothing to refugees or famine victims is a matter not related to the Christian faith." But did not Jesus say: "When *I* was a stranger, you took *me* into your home"? You may think that involvement in activities for the cause of freedom and democracy is purely political in nature and should not be confused with the mission of the church. But did not Jesus also say: "When *I* was in prison, you visited *me*" (Matt. 25:31–46)?

Struggle for the wholeness of community is a religious vocation. It is service rendered to one's neighbor and also to God. It is effort for the healing of broken humanity and for restoring peace and justice to human community. Loving God and loving one's brothers and sisters are two sides of the same coin. Communion with God and the wholeness of human community are closely interrelated. Reading the words of the prophets of the Old Testament, one cannot but wonder whether such struggle is not their main preoccupation. There is, for example, that resounding denunciation from the lips of Isaiah:

> Shame on you! you who add house to house and join
> field to field,
> until not an acre remains,
> and you are left to dwell alone in the land. . . .
>
> Shame on you! you who call evil good and good evil,
> who turn darkness into light and light into darkness,
> who make bitter sweet and sweet bitter. . . .
>
> Shame on you! you mighty topers, valiant mixers of drink,
> who for a bribe acquit the guilty
> and deny justice to those in the right [5:8, 20, 22].

Is what is said here not social and political through and through? These words did not come from a social or political activist, but from the prophet who was in the temple at the critical time of the nation when Uzziah, king of Judah, died (Isa. 6). He was the prophet who confronted king Ahaz with a sign from God at a time of national crisis (Isa. 7). The more he spent his time in the temple, the more he realized the depth of the social and political responsibility of his faith. His social and political tasks, derived from his faith, was to expose the injustice committed by rulers and to bring about health and wholeness in the community.

PLEA FOR JUSTICE

If struggle for wholeness is a Christian vocation, it is also a Buddhist vocation, a Hindu vocation, a Confucian vocation, a Muslim vocation. Compassion, for example, is the heart of Buddhism, as we have seen. Compassion, with its twofold meaning of love and of suffering with others, demands justice. How can you love and suffer with others unless you believe in justice and take up its cause? Justice without compassion becomes a coldhearted law that hears no cry from the anguish of the soul. It can become a pretext for those in power to oppress the powerless. Compassion that does not oppose injustice is not true compassion; it becomes an accomplice of unjust power.

It is to the compassion of the Buddha that the Tamil-speaking plantation workers, mostly Hindus, in Sri Lanka appeal. They were originally brought to Sri Lanka to work coffee and tea plantations. But, in that predominantly

Buddhist country they became the targets of religious discrimination and racial hatred. There is no compassion and justice for them and there is no end to their tragedies. In a poem entitled "To the Buddha—a Plea," part of which I cited earlier, a Tamil estate worker presents his appeal for compassion to the Buddhist community in Sri Lanka:

> But, my Lord, in this land of righteousness,
> Where truth should prevail and justice rule,
> Your dreams have come to nothing,
> Your visions are a vain hope.
> Your name these people invoke day in day out
> And proclaim your goodness with their lips;
> But the hearts of many are filled with hate
> And to cause suffering they wait their turn. . . .
>
> Your words are like a grain of sugar
> Cast into a bitter sea.
> O king of righteousness, you came
> A shining star to save the world.
> Through your coming were redeemed
> Those in distress and without hope.
> Yet today like a rootless tree
> Your goodness and justice wither. . . .
>
> O Compassionate One, Merciful Lord,
> All life was precious in your eyes;
> All humanity you love.
> As your own you treated them.
> But these people invoke your name
> When all their goodness is a sham;
> Your teachings they have thrown away,
> And gross self-seeking rules their lives.[1]

If these words would not move the Sinhalese Buddhists who make up the culturally, religiously, and politically dominant community in Sri Lanka, they would move the Buddha. They must also inspire Christians, both Tamil and Sinhalese, to redouble their efforts to be a community of love and justice for the entire Sri Lankan community.

There is in this plea a strong echo of the prophets of the Old Testament. Justice is mentioned in the same breath as compassion. The Buddha, the compassionate one, is the just one. It is on compassion with justice and justice in compassion that the Buddha founded the Sangha, the monastic community. What should life be like in the Sangha? These words said to be from the Buddha toward the end of his life indicate what it should be like:

> So long as the monks shall persevere in kindly acts, words, and thoughts towards their fellows both in public and in private—so long as they shall share impartially with their modest companions all that they receive in accordance with the recognized discipline of the Sangha, even down to the contents of the food bowl—so long as they shall live among the worthy in the practice, both in public and in private, of those qualities that bring freedom and are praised by the wise.[2]

Sharing things in common "down to the contents of the food bowl"! This is an ideal difficult even for monks in the Sangha to attain, to say nothing about lay Buddhists who live in the rough and tumble of this world. Still the ideal should make Buddhists sensitive to the needs and plights of others. A society that betrays the faith on which it is founded deserves protest and anger from a prophetic figure such as that Tamil estate worker turned poet.

It must be with a heart in anguish that this estate worker has to remind his Sinhalese Buddhist neighbors what the Buddha stood for. In his plea to the Buddha he says: "All life is precious in your eyes; all humanity you love, as your own you treated them." But the Buddhists who profess to follow the Buddha care little about the life of the Tamil workers. They do not love those workers who have contributed so much to the life of the nation for many years. And they have not treated them as their own. That is why so many of them—nearly five hundred thousand—are still deprived of citizenship. And "this community of nearly one million people remains politically powerless, economically exploitable, and socially and culturally ostracized."[3]

This plea to the Buddha is a heart-cry of the Tamils in Sri Lanka. As long as their suffering continues, the community of that nation is without peace, justice, and health. The struggle of the Tamil people is, then, a struggle for community wholeness in Sri Lanka. The active participation of the Christian community in that struggle is its mission both as Christian and as Sri Lankan.

VANGUARDS FOR JUSTICE

Broken humanity has created broken community. It has marred our communion with God and made it difficult for us to hear and meet God in our broken community. But God seems to have chosen other ways to commune with us. God has chosen to be heard, seen, and met in the struggle for the wholeness of human communality, in efforts toward peace, in demands for justice. It must be God's hope that out of such struggle a new community will emerge. It is a sign of hope that today the struggle for wholeness takes place in many societies in Asia and elsewhere. Our era may be remembered as an era of struggle for wholeness in community of persons in communion with God.

The *Korea Communiqué* once printed the following news item under the heading, "Dead Worker Hard-Core Labor Union Leader":

> Miss Kim Kyong-suk, 21, who died in a clash between riot police and her colleagues at the headquarters building of the opposition New Democratic Party (NDP), was an executive member of the labor union at the controversial Y. H. Industrial Co.
>
> Miss Kim had read a workers' resolution and appeals representing the protesting workers only hours before the police raid.
>
> Born in Kwangju, Chollanamdo, Miss Kim lived with her mother Mrs. Choe Yong-ja, 43, and her younger brother, now 18, after her father's death until she came to Seoul in 1972. . . .
>
> Miss Kim, known to have a strong will and sense of responsibility, had already become a skilled worker when she moved to the Y. H. Industrial [in August 1976]. . . .
>
> She was widely known to be faithful to her family among colleagues as she had sent 50,000 won to 60,000 [US $ 68–81] every three months to her brother for education expenditure since 1975.
>
> Miss Kim bought a TV set and electrical goods last March in preparation for her marriage.
>
> Her mother heard the news of Miss Kim's death while peddling popcorn and collecting scrap materials as usual. Her brother hurried to Seoul after borrowing 30,000 won [$40] from the landlord of their rented room.[4]

This is a plain news report. It presents factual statements. There is no commentary, no handing down of value judgments. It is a good and truthful report of what happened on a certain day in April 1979.

But what a wrenching cry one hears from this report! Its burden of anguish, of that unrequited spirit groaning in the heart of a people, makes this information very heavy reading indeed. This is a tragic human drama involving a young woman who died with her dreams unfulfilled. She wanted her brother to have an education. She hoped to make the life of her mother easier. She was getting married. And above all, she was striving to have workers' rights respected and fulfilled.

There was her mother in the news report. And what a tragic figure she makes! One could almost see her, shabbily dressed, collecting scrap materials and selling popcorn in the streets when someone brought her the news of her daughter's death. She must have stared at the bearer of cruel tidings, not able to comprehend what was said to her. And when she realized what had happened, she must have collapsed and burst out in a cry of deep distress.

Then there was her brother who depended on her for his education and for a better future. One can picture before one's eyes this brother in grief and panic, borrowing from his landlord some money to take him to a final meeting with his murdered sister.

But there is something more in this news report. It has to do with the society and the nation that could bring about this young woman's death and heap untold misery on her family. This plain factual news report is a vehement protest against a society that could allow this kind of human tragedy to happen. It is a strong indictment of a nation that uses police power to brutally suppress the powerless—in this case, women workers—mercilessly trampling workers' rights underfoot and even cold-bloodedly taking their lives. This is a society without justice. This is a nation without health and peace. What one sees in such a society and such a nation is a community disrupted by the broken humanity of its rulers who have the passion for power but no compassion for the ones they rule. It is a jungle where the strong consume the weak. It is a wilderness where respect and love for humanity, especially the humanity of the powerless, is conspicuous by its absence.

What is this Y. H. Trading Company? Why did the workers there, including Miss Kim, have to go on strike for days, only to be crushed by the police sent in by the government? The Y. H. Company, according to a report made by the members of the Y. H. Trading Company Branch of National Textile Workers Union,[5] "was the biggest wig manufacturing company in Korea with 4,000 employees in 1970. The net profit of the company in 1970 was 1,273.9 million won (US $17.2 million)." This was a giant enterprise bringing enormous profit to management and contributing to the "economic prosperity" boasted of by the government. It is not surprising that it enjoyed the strong support of bank and government officials.

One would hope that the workers whose sweat and labor turned out so much gain for the company and for the government would fare well. But such was not the case. The average daily wage of a woman worker was no more than 220 won (US $3). Job security was nonexistent. "The management flaunted its one-sided rights through illegal firing of workers without pre-notice, unjust transferral, and salary reductions." This was a factory, a company, run by dictatorship. What was important to it was not the welfare of the workers and their families, but profit to management and the "economic progress" of the nation.

The workers were treated as units of labor, not as persons. What the company needed was a labor force, not human beings. It would extract as much as possible from the workers and do as little as possible for their well-being as human persons. This was evident also from the conditions in which the workers at the Y. H. Trading Company and those at similar companies and factories had to do their work:

> In most working places the conditions are bad and workers suffer from dust, noise, and bad smell of raw chemicals. Besides, temperature and humidity are often disagreeable and even unbearable. It has been reported that among the 3.6 million workers who are insured against industrial accidents, 1,537 were killed and 17,245 became disabled by accidents in 1979. . . . If the cases of noninsured workers were taken into account, the accident rate would be far higher than is reported officially. Many factories have the barest facilities such as dining room

and clinic (without doctor or nurse). Cultural facilities such as entertainment facilities, library, or bathrooms are not provided for the workers.[6]

What kind of economic progress is it that reduces human beings to mere units of labor? What kind of national prosperity is it that does not treat workers as human beings? This must remind us of what Amos the prophet said about the ruling class of Israel in his day:

> . . . they sell the innocent for silver
> and the destitute for a pair of shoes.
> They grind the heads of the poor into the earth
> and thrust the humble out of their way [2:6].

Human beings cannot endure such inhuman treatment indefinitely. There was bound to be an outburst sooner or later.

For the Y. H. Trading Company the outburst came in 1979. It was the passion for power and the greed for gain that determined the policy and operation of the company, and it was the same passion for power and greed that was going to destroy it. The company became infested with corruption and mismanagement and had to lay off over two thousand workers. The workers were not going to accept all this meekly anymore. They had to struggle for their survival. But it was not merely a matter of survival. They had to struggle for their humanity. The community broken by greed and the passion for power must be restored to its wholeness again. Thus they began a peaceful sit-in strike. But the police intervened with brutal force. Women strikers were beaten and humiliated. And Miss Kim suffered death.

That particular struggle for the recovery of human wholeness ended in tragedy. Those who had the power to rule did their utmost to prevent the recovery of humanity and the emergence of wholeness in community. They would do all they could to prevent a situation in which the powerless would have a little more power and the powerful a little less power. They would suppress as much as possible a call for compassion and justice, for sharing power and powerlessness, richness and poverty. Those in power would not readily accept such a new community—a community in which wholeness is restored to humanity. The struggle continues.

But there is hope and a future. For those involved in struggle come to know what it means to be human. Their desire for a healthier community is strengthened. They begin to see a future arising out of the pain and agony of their struggle. That is why they can sing a hymn such as this one called "Vanguards":

> Our sisters have always known sorrow,
> but with hearts fixed on tomorrow
> they fought as a vanguard for right
> and quickened our spirits to fight.

Our sisters have always known pain,
but our lives can be ours once again;
when you've cried overnight in a jail,
nothing against you can prevail.

Despised and oppressed for so long,
at last we can join in the throng
struggling for justice and peace in our land,
along a straight road, hand in hand.[7]

Struggle for the right to be human—peaceful struggle—brings pain and sorrow, but it also generates strength and hope. It awakens in us the power of love and compassion for ourselves and for our society. It is part of a painful and hopeful process of restoring community to its wholeness. Is this not the way of the cross?

AN AUSTRALIAN CREED

Many persons today, Christians among them, are struggling for community with compassion and justice. This is a movement of the people that is stirring in our world today. The human spirit, long incarcerated in the bondage of humiliation, oppression, and injustice, has been released from apathy, resignation, and self-pity. It has emerged from the abyss of suppressed oblivion, calling to humanity, challenging oppressive powers, and striving for wholeness in human community. In this stirring, calling, and struggling of the human spirit, Christians should be able to recognize the Spirit of God working to bring love, justice, and peace to humankind. What we are witnessing today is a great movement of the human spirit awakened to the calling to be human. In this movement we are also witnessing the movement of God.

It is small wonder that more and more Christians and churches find themselves caught up in this great movement of the human spirit and are becoming active participants in it. They are no longer spectators, watching someone else's struggle. They are also active in the movement, contributing to it and accepting the challenge to reflect deeply on their faith and mission in order to practice the faith in a new and responsible way. "An Australian Creed" gives us an example of Christians who cannot remain unmoved as the Spirit of God mobilizes others toward community in wholeness and toward a fuller communion with God:

I believe in God
 and I believe in humanity
 as the image of God.

I believe in Australians
 in their black aboriginal beauty
 in their migrant struggles
 as they come into their own
 having given up their own.

I believe in an Australian place
in its ambiguous possibilities
of Asian growth and European decline
in dream time, southern time, our time . . . .

I believe in our hopes for a great human family as Christ wishes it:
in hopes fostered by memories,
and banishing from the land of the Holy Spirit
the stupor of despair.[8]

One hopes that all Australians heard this creed, that all Christians in that land felt inspired by it and took it to heart.

It is time that Christians of Western origin in Australia took a second look at the creeds and confessions their forebears brought from the old world and had them recited in the new world. These creeds made them always nostalgic about their home in the West that they had left for good. These confessions continued to make them aliens, and superior aliens at that, in the vast world of Asia teeming with peoples speaking different tongues, practicing different customs and religions, and cherishing their own rights in their own lands. These confessions of faith and creeds of life always reminded white Australians that they were Europeans, not Asians. They made Australia into a Europe—much, much bigger than their own countries of origin in Europe taken together—in the midst of Asia. They were never able to become Asians.

That is the heart of the problem for white Australians. They came as invaders to an Asian land, inhabited by its own people for more than thirty thousand years, took it by force from them and drove them into "reservations." Their victory was the woe of the Australian aborigines. For two centuries they were denied the beauty of their own mountains, the awesome expanse of their own space, the fruits of their own soil and forests. The aborigines were also robbed of their humanity and their right to live and prosper in their own land. They faced extinction and became the objects of anthropological field study.

But even the Australian aborigines have been caught up in the worldwide movement toward a restoration of broken humanity and broken human community—a movement inspired by the Spirit of the Creator God. They are no longer willing to accept their miserable status. They cannot remain silent anymore. Their spirit stirs in the depth of agony and sorrow. They have begun to get organized, making their voice heard both inside and outside Australia, carrying out their struggle to claim back the rights that are theirs by creation and by birth. A new future is still far away, but they have begun their trek toward it.

In a joint statement made by an Australian aboriginal action group and the Black Protest Committee, opposition was voiced to the Commonwealth Games held in Brisbane in 1982. It was a cry out of the suffering of the Australian aborigines' and one must listen to it:

> Black Australians have been in a state of crisis since the whites first invaded our land. We have been the victims of exploitation, genocide, and racism for two centuries. There is no indication of conditions improving for us. Black Australia has to take the initiative for her own survival. The Brisbane Games provide us with an opportunity to expose the racism of Australia to the rest of the world. . . . Black Australia asserts herself as an active part of history. We are part of the family of humankind.[9]

This is a cry from the heart of the Australian aborigines. It penetrates one's soul and moves it deeply.

Christians and churches in Australia began to hear that cry. How could they remain unaffected by it? How could they go on reciting their ancestral confessions and creeds as if all were well in this Asian land of Australia? They must rewrite their creed, confessing their faith in the beauty of the black aboriginal Australians. They must also make this the creed not only of the church, but also of the entire community of Australia. Armed with such a creed, they must learn to stand on the side of the aborigines, struggling with them for the rights that are theirs. Then, and only then, can they also understand their own struggle as migrants in a new world. Then, and only then, will they understand what it means to be part of Asian humanity. Then, and only then, their ancestral time, their European time, will become a dream time and southern time, Asian time, and their own time. Then they can confess and say: "I believe in God and in humanity as the image of God."

This is quite a confession to recite and practice. But it must be recited and practiced if the broken community of Australia is to be healed and if a new community of wholeness is to emerge—community with the Australian aborigines and with other Asian brothers and sisters. And theology in Australia, if it has anything to contribute to the struggle, has to shed its nostalgia for shallow metaphysics and cold logic inherited from the West, and embrace wholeheartedly the passion that inspired Asian spirituality and created Asian cultures. It has to be, above all, a theology of compassion.

15

God of Compassion

LOVE WITH NO STRINGS ATTACHED

Compassion is not an abstract notion in a theological textbook, but a living force working in us. Compassion is the power to love others and suffer with them. And compassion is ours because it is first God's. We are told by the author of the fourth Gospel that "God loved the world so much that he gave his only son" (John 3:16) to it.

To love someone "so much" is to give oneself to that person. "So much" means without limits and conditions. Such love has no strings attached to it. "So much," when used with the act of love, means that that is the most deeply one can love. "So much" is not "much more." It is not even "most." When you love someone "so much," you love that person more deeply than most deeply.

Are we human beings capable of such love? Obviously we are not. There is always a ceiling to our love. There is always a bottom to it. Our love has strings attached to it. We bind a person we love with those strings. With strings attached to it, our love changes its nature. It becomes a command. I command the person I love to do what I desire. It becomes an order. I order that person to behave according to what I think is right and proper. It can also turn into hate when the person I love does not reciprocate. That love can even transform into a violent power to destroy the person I love when my love is not accepted. It is this love with strings attached that often creates misery in our lives and tragedy in this world. Is this not the reason why there are so many broken families today? Has not this love with strings attached created so much racism in our world? And is it not on account of such love that prisons for political prisoners in totalitarian countries are never empty? Love with strings attached to it is an indiscreet love. It is dictated by our desires and whims. And it can become a power of destruction.

In traditional theology love often has strings attached to it too. Theology, it is said, can decide, at least in certain cases, who can attain salvation and who not. But, by what authority is it entitled to do so? Jesus has abundantly shown that authority gained from the traditions and teachings of religion can be a false authority, that it has no business deciding such a grave matter as the salvation of any individual. The woman caught in adultery had to be stoned, according to the religious authorities. The Pharisees and scribes who brought her to Jesus had the authority of tradition behind them. But that authority crumbled when Jesus bade the one among them without sin to cast the first stone (John 7:53–8:11).

Theology, it is also stressed, must not compromise salvation. It is through Christ understood, interpreted, and preached by the Christian church that God's salvation is made known. That is true salvation. But this amounts to saying that only the Christian church has the key to God's saving love. The assumption is that the church alone is capable of understanding who Christ is, interpreting him correctly, and preaching him authentically. But again Jesus himself seems to have disputed this. When that Roman centurion beseeched Jesus to heal his servant but did not dare trouble Jesus to come all the way to his house, Jesus, deeply astonished, said to those following him: "I tell you this: nowhere, even in Israel, have I found such faith!" (Matt. 8:10). This was a very disturbing statement to make in the presence of Jews. A number of them, especially religious leaders and theologians, were terribly offended by it.

Luke, who showed a particular interest in tax-gatherers, sinners, and Gentiles, tells the story of the ten lepers healed by Jesus (Luke 17:11–19). Nine of them were Jews. They happily went away to show themselves to the priests, the cultic officials in Jerusalem who alone had the authority to certify their health and restore them to the religious community. They never bothered to return to Jesus to thank him for curing them. But one leper healed by Jesus did come back. He "turned back praising God aloud and threw himself down at Jesus' feet and thanked him" (17:15–16). Luke at once added: "And he was a Samaritan." Jesus must have had terribly mixed emotions at that point. He expressed it when he said: "Were not all ten men cleansed? The other nine, where are they? Could none be found to come back and give praise to God except this foreigner?" (17:17–18). Where are the nine men from the "chosen" people of God? Did they think they were entitled to the gift of healing? They obviously regarded showing themselves to the priests more important than returning to Jesus to give praise to God. But that foreigner was not from the "chosen" people. He had no ritual requirements to fulfill. And he knew he had to come back to Jesus to thank him and to praise God. "Your faith has cured you," Jesus said to him. *Your* faith! It was not the faith cultivated by the religion of the Jews, but his faith as a Samaritan, that cured him. Is it, then, not evident that the man who helped the wounded person on the road to Jericho in Jesus' parable (Luke 10) had to be a Samaritan also?

Love with no strings attached is compassion. That was Jesus' love. That was Jesus' theology, theology of compassion. His theology was the theology of "God loving the world so much that God gave the only son" to it. Jesus was that love of God. And the love that was Jesus was nailed to the cross. The cross is the love of God with no strings attached. It is the compassion of God loving and suffering with all humanity. That is why the cross has had such compelling power throughout the centuries and throughout the world. Divine providence ordained that the love incarnate in Jesus should be found in Asia also. Palestine alone could not contain it. Europe could not keep it to itself. And the West cannot monopolize it. That love of God has no strings attached to it. It recognizes no boundaries. It is not conditioned by the color of the human skin.

That compassion of God for all humanity did not come to Asia as if to a foreign land. Jesus praised the good Samaritan. He commended the faith of the Samaritan cured of leprosy. And he was deeply moved by the Roman soldier who had faith such as he had not found even in Israel.

God's compassion in Jesus must have always been attuned to the rhythms of love vibrating in the heart of this vast area of God's creation. It must have heard its own *hibiki* (echo) in the souls of those selfless followers of the Buddha who dedicated themselves to struggling and suffering humanity. These rhythms Christian missions did not hear. These *hibiki*s Christian theology did not feel. Even when these rhythms and *hibiki*s have grown much, much louder in recent years, we are still very uncomfortable with them. They still sound strange to our ears. We have not developed the spiritual capacity and theological sensitivity to listen to them intently, understand them deeply, and let them tell us the stories of God's mercy and compassion working in the heart of Asia and its peoples since the beginning of God's creation.

Theology of compassion is the theology of love with no strings attached to it. It does not predetermine how and where God should do God's saving work. It does not assume that God left Asia in the hands of pagan powers and did not come to it until missionaries from the West reached it. That would have left Asia without the God of Jesus for millions of years. Jesus' God could not have been such an irresponsible God. If that was Jesus' God, Jesus would not have commended the faith of the Gentiles who crossed his path.

We must put behind us that kind of theology; it is not inspired by God's compassionate love working without interruption in Asia. Asians themselves have often misunderstood and distorted that love. They have shown a propensity for turning that love into pantheons of gods and idols. Many of our Asian brothers and sisters—in the past, at present, and probably in the future also—deserve St. Paul's anger when he wrote in his letter to the Christians in Rome:

> Although they knew God they did not honor God or give thanks to God, but they became futile in their thinking and their senseless minds were darkened. Claiming to be wise, they became fools, and exchanged the glory of the immortal God for images resembling mortal human beings or birds or animals or reptiles [Rom. 1:21–23, RSV].

We must confess that there has been no lack of such fools in Asia. But can Christianity—in all its myriad traditions and denominations—boast of a lack of such fools?

We must take to heart St. Paul's words. There is always a danger in religion, any religion, to idolize—idolizing everything from power, pomp, doctrine, and creed to some minute detail of how a believer is to be initiated into the mystery of faith. It is such idolizations that fragment the Christian church, split Islam into warring sects, and start religious wars. We are all guilty of St. Paul's accusation.

Theology of compassion, however, ought to be able to see something besides the sin of idolization. It must be able to perceive some divine sparks in the midst of human darkness. It should be able to catch sight of God's compassion in a temple dimmed with the smoke of incense offered by religious devotees. And it must be able to hear some divine words of comfort and assurance out of many wrong and misleading things said and done in the name of gods and lords. There is a lot for the theology of compassion to hear, see, and feel in Asia. It must be attentive to the voice of the compassionate God arising out of the heart of Asian humanity. It may find that voice strangely familiar, resembling the voice of Jesus who said: "The Son of Man did not come to be served, but to serve, and to give up his life as a ransom for many" (Matt. 20:28).

THE BLOOD OF KANNON

The study of religious faiths other than the Christian cannot be left to the history of religions or the science of comparative religion alone. It has to be an inseparable part of theological disciplines. Even after we have understood all the doctrines of God in the history of Christian thought and passed our examinations on them, we cannot be said to know all about God. We must also know how God is perceived in Hinduism, Mahayana Buddhism, in Islam, in religious beliefs and practices centered on ancestor worship. To approach religious faiths as doctrines, systems of beliefs, cults, and rituals, even organizations, is valid and important. But these alone do not give us the inside stories of these faiths. They give us the framework for understanding them, but they do not introduce us to the persons who hold these faiths. And in fact the persons who are born, live, and die in cultures shaped by these faiths are of the utmost interest to Christian theology.

In the study of religions, theology of compassion makes human beings the subject of theological inquiry, the persons who toil and labor, who hold anguish and hope in their hearts, who long for an emancipated life in a world of conflict and strife. It is they who will tell us true stories of their faith. That is why we must listen to their stories—stories of the life they have lived, stories they tell in parables and in legends. Theologians should read such stories and draw theological meaning out of them.

Folktales are a fascinating wonderland where theologians can spend endless hours reading, reflecting, pondering, and feeling inspired. They are stories in the language of imagination told by persons who continue to believe in God despite their sad fate, continue to long for glimmers of light in the midst of darkness, and search for signs of goodness in humanity in this ugly world of hate, malice, and violence.

Let me tell you a folktale from Japan entitled "The Kannon who Substituted." Kannon (Kuan-yin in Chinese) is a Bodhisattva known as the Goddess of Mercy, venerated and held dear by hundreds of millions of persons in East Asia, especially by those whose arduous lives have special need of divine mercy. The folktale begins:

> Looking up from a small village nestled at the foot of a certain mountain, one can see a little shrine of Kannon on the very top. A young couple used to live in that village. The wife, for all her youth, believed in Kannon with utmost sincerity. Every night, after she had finished her daily housework, she visited the shrine to worship the image. Her husband did not know the reason for her going and became suspicious of the wife who went out and returned to the house every night at the same time. One day he finally lost his patience with his wife and determined to kill her. So he hid in the dark woods by the roadside and waited for his wife to come back. At the usual time she returned. The husband watching her coming near and, carefully aiming at her shoulder, swung down his sword askance. At this moment the wife felt her blood run cold throughout her body.
>
> The husband wiped the blood from his sword and put the sword back in its sheath. When he returned to his home, he was astonished to see his wife, whom he thought he had slashed to death. He marvelled, and went back to see the place he had struck his wife. Sure enough, there were the dots of blood on the ground. He retraced his steps homeward, and asked his wife: "Didn't you feel something strange at such and such a time in such and such a place?" Then the wife answered: "Just at that time something made my blood run cold." The husband could not but confess all that had happened.
>
> The next morning he awakened early and was surprised to see blood dotted all the way from the entrance of his house to the shrine on top of the mountain. When he looked at the statue of Kannon, he was again surprised to see a scar on the statue's shoulder, on the place where he had struck his wife the night before.[1]

Is this just a story of a jealous husband? Is it merely a tale from those days in Japan when samurai—swordsmen—could kill persons, even their wives, for the slightest offense or unintended provocation?

The folktale tells us something more. There must be something more if such a story could survive those days of violence practiced in the name of honor and chivalry. Or perhaps it was the uncertainty of life in such a society that strengthened faith in a merciful God, a God who not only would not kill, but who would protect defenseless men, women, and children, even taking their place in time of danger.

Most Chinese-speaking readers are familiar with the classical novel *Hsi yu chi* ["Journey to the West"] by Wu Ch'eng-en (ca. 1506–82) of the Ming dynasty.[2] It is a superb comic fantasy about the adventures of a devoted monk,

San-tsang or Tripitaka, through treacherous lands, inhabited by gods and demons, in search of Buddhist sutras. He was accompanied by Monkey and Pigsy, two bizarre animals turned pilgrims appointed by Kuan-yin (Kannon in Japanese) to protect the sage-monk on his dangerous journey to the West. The novel revolves around these two characters, especially Monkey, as much as around the monk himself, showing both the very religious and the human side of life in search of truth and salvation. But the novel is not the product of pure imagination. It "has its historical basis in the epic pilgrimage of Hsuan-tsang [San-tsang] to India. . . . He traveled abroad for seventeen years (629–45) and brought back from India 657 Buddhist texts. Upon his return, he devoted the remainder of his life to translating these scriptures and establishing the abstruse Mere Ideation school of Chinese Buddhism."[3]

His travel was full of dangers and hardships common in those days. In one of the accounts about the journey, Hsuan-tsang, having crossed the Chinese border, upset his water container and spilled the supply that was to sustain him until he was safely across the desert:

> All around me was a vast expanse: no travellers or birds. At night there were glimmerings of monstrous fires, shining like stars; in the daytime the frightening winds hugged the sand and scattered it like rain. Even though I had met with this disaster, my heart was not afraid. My only worry was the lack of water because in my thirst I could not push on. For four nights and five days I had not a single drop to moisten my throat. My mouth and intestines became so parched that I was on the point of dying. I could not go on, and lay in the sand. But no matter how debilitated I was, I kept repeating the name of Kuan-yin in silence. I also prayed to the Bodhisattva, "This trip of Hsuan-tsang's is not undertaken for profit or fame: it is solely to seek the right law of the incomparable truth. I have always known that your mercy extends to all living things and that your task is to save them from distress. I am now in distress—have you not noticed it?" Thus praying, I kept my heart in a state of unceasing hope.[4]

Help came in time. Suddenly there was a cool breeze. Feeling refreshed and strengthened, he went on. And there was "a pond of water sweet and clear like a mirror."

Here was a monk in great distress praying to the Goddess of Mercy, "whose mercy extends to all living beings" and whose task is "to save them from distress." It is this belief in the all-merciful Kuan-yin or Kannon, and trust in her readiness to save them, that has sustained East Asians in their journey of life full of difficulties, hardships, upsets, and tragedies. Kuan-yin symbolizes the spirituality of compassion deeply embedded in cultures of East Asia. One cannot truly understand those cultures apart from this spirituality. To those who have no grasp of that spirituality, cultures of East Asia appear only in the form of exquisite art, elaborate social manners, inscrutable silence in a Zen temple, and the deafening noise of the crowds in the streets and marketplaces.

These are merely the surface of Asian culture. Deep down is that spirituality of compassion tempering restless hearts, giving assurance to souls in anguish, and kindling hope in spirits verging on despair.

The theology of compassion must be able to touch that soul, feel that heart, and be in tune with that spirit. Then Christians and theologians in Asia will begin to see the deeply troubled human beings in search of mercy and compassion.

In the poems of eternally pessimistic Li Ho (791–817), a Chinese poet of the late T'ang dynasty, who sang about the transience of life and the anguish of heart, one hears longing for that compassion in Asian spirituality. Here is an excerpt from one of his poems, "Don't Go Out the Door":

> Heaven is inscrutable,
> Earth keeps its secrets.
> The nine-headed monster eats our souls,
> Frosts and snows snap our bones.
> Dogs are set on us, snarl and sniff around us,
> And lick their paws, partial to the orchid-girdled,
> Till the end of all afflictions, when God sends us
> the chariot,
> And the sword starred with jewels and the yoke of
> yellow
> gold.[5]

After all the afflictions one has to go through in life, how could heaven still remain inscrutable?

The poem is about a great poet-statesman Ch'u Yuan at the turn of the third century B.C. in China. Unjustly banished from his service at court and exiled to a remote place far from the human community, he "roamed among the mountains and marshes, crossed over the hills and plains, crying aloud to the Most High and sighing as he looked at heaven."[6] It is compassion one seeks behind that inscrutable heaven. That compassion was sought by the Chinese in all ages—kings and paupers, great government officials and ordinary men and women, the literate and the illiterate. That compassion they found, after the introduction of Buddhism into China, in Kuan-yin, the Goddess of Mercy, who hears the sounds (prayers) of the world.[7] Could that voice of compassion they hear from Kuan-yin have nothing to do with the voice of the merciful God whom Jesus has shown to us Christians?

Coming back to that Japanese folktale of the blood of Kannon, one does not fail to see its central message. The folktale is not about a jealous husband. It is not even about a pious wife. It does not mean to divert its readers to wonder why there was not more communication between the husband and the wife. There was seldom such heart-to-heart talk anyway within a matrimonial relationship in a culture that made a virtue of suppressing one's personal feeling as much as possible, especially in those days of samurai ethics. The folktale is about Kannon, the Goddess of Mercy, and its message is her compassion. The husband aimed his deadly blow at his wife. With his swordsmanship he could not have missed her. He did not miss his aim, but it was not his wife but Kannon that he struck. The blood he saw on the road was not his wife's blood. It was Kannon's blood. That blood led him all the way to the shrine on top of the mountain and showed him a scar on the shoulder of the Kannon statue.

One perceives a deeply sensitive spirit in this folktale. One cannot dismiss the blood of Kannon as of no significance. One cannot treat the message of compassion in the folktale as unimportant. There is human warmth in that compassion, in a bleak world of swords and spears. There is tenderness of heart in a harsh society of impassiveness. And there are tears of compassion in a culture in which tears are a sign of weakness and cowardliness. This folktale shows us the side of Asian culture hidden from casual observers and doctrinaire theologians. The folktale is not exceptional. In fact it is just one of many tales of a merciful and compassionate God. There is even a folktale telling "how the painting of Fudo, the God of Fire, shed bloody tears and took to itself the sickness of his young worshipper Shoku, in the thirteenth century."[8] The painting with its bloodstained tears is said to exist. It is to be found in Miidera, Otsu, Shiga prefecture, Japan.

Weeping Buddha? Perhaps none of us has seen a painting or a statue of a weeping Buddha. The Buddha does not weep. He does not shed tears. He should be beyond weeping and tears. That is why he is called the Enlightened One and the Awakened One. He has already left all human sorrows and worries behind him. Nothing in the world, neither life nor death, would move and stir him from his bliss in nirvana. This is what enlightenment means, does it not? That is what most of us are taught about Buddhism.

Yes, there is this cold, aloof, and unworldly side to certain schools of Buddhism. But there is the other side too, the side showing that the Buddha could weep, could shed tears, at the sight of human misery. The Buddha is not calmness itself. He is not the personification of aloofness and indifference. Until we are able to stare at the serene face of a Buddha statue and see tears welling from his eyes half-closed in contemplation, we have not touched the hearts of our brothers and sisters in Asia. Until we perceive that tranquil face of the Buddha distorted with pain, we have not seen their souls in pain. Perhaps these are not only their tears and their pain; they may be our own tears and our own pain. After all, we Asian Christians are also Asians. And after all, we are also human beings, like the rest of the human race. And that Kannon who shed her blood to save the Japanese wife from her samurai husband, that Fudo who shed tears for a sick young worshiper, will they not strengthen our faith in the compassionate God disclosed to us by Jesus Christ?

MY BODY BROKEN FOR YOU

In the three years of his public ministry, Jesus encountered many persons. There were Pharisees and doctors of the law, to whom he had many harsh words to say. At times he had some strong words to send to the Roman rulers too. But it was mostly ordinary folk—men, women, and children, uncertain about their future, ostracized from their religious community—with whom Jesus associated. With them he had many words of comfort and encouragement to share. He touched many aching hearts. He embraced many weeping souls. He restored many sick persons to health. And he gave power and strength to men and women in despair. His must have been a ministry full of excitement and thrill. But his must also have been a life full of struggling to bear all the pain and suffering that those around him had to endure. Jesus absorbed all this into his own self.

It must have been no easy thing to absorb so much sorrow and pain into his own person. But it was not just the sorrow and pain of other persons. In them Jesus must have recognized his own sorrow and pain as a fully human person living in a community torn apart by broken humanity. And his recognition of himself in them must have enabled them to recognize themselves in Jesus too. The relationship was reciprocal. And it was the compassion of God that bound Jesus with them in pursuit of a community that would be healthy and whole, in search of communion with God in its richness and joy.

After he had entered Jerusalem to the tumultuous welcome of the people, Jesus must have sensed that all this was coming to an end. He was going to bear that broken community to the cross where a new community would be born out of the abyss of death. It must have been the longest journey for Jesus, a journey starting with his entry into Jerusalem and ending with his death on the cross. It must have also been the most painful journey. But that journey of death turned out to be a journey of life. That journey of defeat became a journey of victory.

One of the things his disciples remembered most vividly must have been the last meal they had with Jesus the night he was arrested. According to the account in Mark's Gospel, the supper was surrounded with a mysterious aura from the beginning (Mark 14:12–17; par. Luke 22:7–14). There was something unusual in Jesus' instructions for the preparation of the supper. Everything seemed to have been prearranged. They were to meet a man who would show them "a large room upstairs set out in readiness" (Mark 14:15; par. Luke 22:12). Who was that man? How did Jesus get to know him? Was he entrusted with some secret? Jesus' instructions sounded like coded language. Was this going to be a decisive night? Was Jesus going to lead them in an uprising against Roman rule? They must have wondered, especially those disciples covertly embracing the Zealotist cause.

But an uprising did not take place. Jesus was arrested, tried, and executed on the cross. His disciples deserted Jesus during the final hours of his struggle with life and death. That last supper they remembered distinctly. But they remembered it very differently from the time they were having it with Jesus. Yes, that last supper did have an extraordinary meaning illuminating the reason why Jesus lived the way he did, said what he said, and had to do all the things he did. It was not a meal in preparation for a political uprising, but a meal in anticipation of Jesus' imminent death—a death closely related to God's saving love for the world. In the account of that last supper, this was what they remembered Jesus doing and saying:

> During the supper he took bread, and having said the blessing he broke it and gave it to them, with the words: "Take this; this is my body." Then he took a cup, and having offered thanks to God he gave it to them; and they all drank from it. And he said, "This is my blood, the blood of the covenant, shed for many" [Mark 14:22–23; par. Matt. 26:26–28; Luke 22:19–20].

Body broken for you and blood shed for you! That was the meaning of that last supper! That was the meaning of the cross! Out of this last supper and out of the cross a new kingdom of Israel did not come; but something far more important, something that was going to have a lasting significance: a new community of persons and a new communion with God.

In that body of Jesus is the compassionate God. That body broken on the cross should have been our body. The blood shed from the cross should have been our blood. But the God of compassion in Jesus accepted Jesus' body in place of our body, and accepted Jesus' blood in place of our blood. And from that broken body of Jesus a new life was born, a new community of compassion became a possibility. That last supper was not a political event. It was a meal of redemption prepared by the compassionate God.

It had to be Jesus' body and it had to be his blood. Our body, once broken, remains broken. Our blood, once shed, vanishes. How could a new life come into that broken body of ours? And with our blood that vanishes, our life vanishes too. Out of death, life will not come. Out of broken humanity, no healthy humanity will emerge. In the community torn by our passion for power, greed, and violence, communion with God is strained, disrupted, and distorted.

But the broken body of Jesus is different from ours. It is the body of the compassionate God. It is broken to release the redemptive power of God. Its blood is shed to give rise to a community of wholeness. It is the reign of God that breaks out of that broken body of Jesus. And there are signs of that reign in Asia as individuals and groups seek love and compassion in the life they live and in the faith they possess. How should Christian theology testify to such signs? It is a question we cannot evade.

PART FOUR

VISION

16

Reign of God

DOMINION OF LIGHT

Night does not have absolute dominion over the surface of the earth. There is always a morning to come. It breaks out from within the night.

Have you ever watched a sunrise from the vantage point of a seaside beach? It can be watched only with wonder. There is darkness on the horizon. Night still reigns over the skies. You are shrouded in darkness. Then you realize that the color of the night is changing. From pitch darkness it becomes pale darkness. Then from pale darkness it turns slowly—very slowly—to misty white. The change does not come from outside. It comes from inside the darkness. It is born out of it.

You look at the horizon far away. You are watching the miracle of morning; it is dissipating the darkness of night. Light grows out of the womb of creation steadily and surely. At first it resembles a smoking flicker of fire about to be extinguished. But that moment of weakness does not last long. Before your very eyes light expands in all directions—vertically to illumine the sky, horizontally to make the sea glitter with milliards of tiny sparks. As the light grows, the darkness fades. Then suddenly a fireball leaps from the horizon to command the day. It is the sun, light itself. It has emerged from the womb of the night to brighten the morning of God's creation.

It makes one think of the description of creation in the first chapter of Genesis: "In the beginning of creation, when God made heaven and earth," the priestly text reads, "the earth was without form and void, with darkness over the face of the abyss. . . ." It was night. The miracle of creation began at night. God did not make the darkness; it was just there. The writers in the priestly tradition did not know where it came from. And they simply admitted their ignorance: darkness was there when God made heaven and earth.

But those zealous priests of Israel at the time of the Babylonian exile were not the only ones who did not know the origin of night. Our Asian ancestors did not seem to know it either. This, for example, is how the Maoris of New Zealand understood the beginning of creation:

> The universe was in darkness, with water everywhere. There was no glimmer of dawn, no clearness, no light.[1]

Did our African forbearers know more? An account from the Boshongo, a central Bantu tribe of the Lunda Cluster, says:

> In the beginning, in the dark, there was nothing but water. And Bumba [the creator] was alone.[2]

Darkness was there and nobody knows why and how. But it was not allowed to prevail. Darkness does not differentiate anything. It is an abyss that swallows up everything—good as well as bad, true as well as false, beautiful as well as ugly. It has no feeling, no compassion. It is sheer chaos, *tohu wābohu* "formless and void" (Gen. 1:1). God did something about it. God made the light and separated it from the darkness. God "called the light day, and the darkness night" (1:4). This was a giant first step, a revolutionary step. It changed the whole character of the universe. With light as well as darkness, day will be different from night; what is good can be distinguished from what is evil; what is true can be distinguished from what is false; and what is beautiful can be distinguished from what is ugly. Night still returns, but there will be morning. Evil continues to make havoc of the world, but one can count on the good too. There will still be false words, false deeds, false promises, but true words, true deeds, and true promises will stand up to challenge them. Ugliness will keep raising its head, but the comely soul will no longer be muted. The era of light has arrived. There will be a sunrise every morning—the miracle of day breaking out of night, light dispelling darkness.

The Maori creation myth cited above and in Chapter 1 has some deep insight to share at this point. After mentioning darkness, it continues:

> And lo [the Supreme Being] began by saying these words—
> That he might cease remaining inactive:
> "Darkness become a light-possessing darkness."
> And at once light appeared.
> He then repeated those self-same words in this manner,
> That he might cease remaining inactive:
> "Light, become a darkness-possessing light. . .
>
> Let there be one darkness above,
> Let there be one darkness below. . .
>
> Let there be one light above,
> Let there be one light below. . .
>
> A dominion of light,
> A bright light.[3]

"Light-possessing darkness" and "darkness-possessing light"! Who says the Asian mind is incapable of dialectic? Who has decided that the Asian mind can only go round and round for eternity, producing nothing new? Who has determined that it can only say: "What has been is what will be, and what has been done is what will be done; and there is nothing new under the sun" (Eccles. 1:9, RSV)? The Asian mind can say much more than that. It is capable of perceiving, smelling, and imaging something new. It goes round in circles. This is the wisdom that nature imparts to all human beings, not just to those of us in the Orient. Who can deny that "everything has its season and every activity under heaven its time"? Even the rational modern mind cannot deny it. As is observed in Ecclesiastes, there is indeed

> a time to be born and a time to die;
> a time to plant and a time to uproot;
> a time to kill and a time to heal;
> a time to pull down and a time to build up;
> a time to weep and a time to laugh;
> a time for mourning and a time for dancing. . . .
> a time to embrace and a time to refrain from embracing;
> a time to seek and a time to lose. . . .
> a time to tear and a time to mend;
> a time for silence and a time for speech;
> a time to love and a time to hate;
> a time for war and a time for peace [Eccles. 3:1–8].

Sometimes it seems that things happen only in circles—there seems nothing new in life. But this is not what this wisdom, this marvelous dialectic, is telling us. The life that is born is new. The plants sprout from the earth, grow, and bear fruit. Laughing and dancing after weeping and mourning give power to live anew. Loving and embracing create life and vitality in the world of hate and death. Timely speech after deep silence can explode into revolution. And signs of peace in the midst of war generate hope for a new world in which human beings will no longer inflict inhumanity on one another.

This is the dialectic of "light-possessing darkness" and "darkness-possessing light" in the Maori hymn of creation. That dialectic is not the product of abstract reasoning. It comes from sense organs that feel, smell, touch, hear, and see. That dialectic sees the light already in the darkness. It hears the morning already in the night. It touches the heart of love when the world rages in fury. It embraces life in the midst of death. This dialectic comes from the Asian mind richly endowed with the ability to image things, to picture them, to paint them, to become absorbed in them with compassion—loving and suffering together with them.

This is God's dialectic of creating heaven and earth out of the undifferentiated chaos and making light shine in the midst of darkness. It is the Maori dialectic of light-possessing darkness and darkness-possessing light. It is a dialectic of hope: out of the struggle for dominance between light and darkness, a bright light appears. The morning arrives. And life continues its journey toward the future. A dominion of light, says the Maori hymn of creation. The light is good, says the priestly creation account in the Old Testament. "The light shines in the darkness, and the darkness has not overcome it!" (John 1:5, RSV), says John, the theologian-author of the fourth Gospel in the New Testament.

DO NOT GO SILENT INTO THE NIGHT

Faith in a dominion of light is a religious faith. Without that faith a religion has nothing to offer its members. It becomes a religion of darkness, speaking no words of comfort, forgiveness, or hope. That faith is also a political faith. Without it the struggle for freedom and democracy becomes a struggle for the power to dominate and enslave. When that light of faith becomes dim and vanishes, oppression rules.

That faith is the faith that sustains life. Without it, hope is easily defeated by despair, joy drowned in sorrow, and life surrendered to death. That faith is the strength to live and the courage to hope, even when life is overwhelmed by suffering.

The following story of a Philippine Christian is a testimony to the pervasive impact of darkness:

> He was coming back from a meeting in Europe and stopped over in Bombay. There some friends took him to visit the slums. Though he had worked in Manila's slums for years . . . he became physically sick when he saw the immense sea of misery. As they were leaving toward nightfall, they passed one hut the size and shape of a raised coffin, covered with burlap. A man stood by the low doorway, and in the doorway or entry hole, a woman sat. Maybe it was the fading light, but when he looked closely at the woman, he saw his wife's face. He was stunned. It only lasted a second or two. They walked on. As they did, he began to think what suffering it must be for the husband standing there by the coffin-house. How would you feel to see your own wife in such a sad condition; to be able to do nothing better for her and the children, not because you weren't trying, but because the rich and the powerful cheated you; to have no hope, for life has always been one unbroken suffering; and to have a religious explanation that only tells you it is your own fault you are in this sad condition and that you must bear it patiently till the wheel turns again and perhaps will give you a better life?[4]

This is a very dark story. The husband's face was dark. The wife's face was dark. And that little coffin-sized hut was dark. The image of a coffin intensifies the darkness that surrounded the husband and wife, their fate, and the entire slum quarter.

Suffering makes everything dark even in broad daylight. It covers everything with the shadow of darkness even in bright sunshine. But that darkness has to be a light-possessing darkness. That Philippine Christian saw in the face of that Indian woman in the slum hut the face of his own wife. That was light in darkness. It was a fleeting light. It lasted only a second or two. It was quickly eaten up by darkness, leaving no trace.

It was not only that Philippine Christian who saw his wife's face in the face of that Indian woman. Many Christians and many others have also seen the faces of their wives, children, or parents in the faces of suffering men, women, and children in many other places. Each time it is just a small light, indistinct and fragile. Many lights seen in this way must have disappeared as quickly as they appeared. But some such lights must have endured. And when these small lights come together, they add up to bigger and stronger lights. It is these bigger and stronger lights made up of many small lights that can turn into the movements of harijans, God's people, in India, of aborigines in Australia, women workers in Korea, movements for freedom and human rights in many countries of Asia.

These movements are composed of the many seconds of time when men and women see in the faces of suffering persons the faces of their own loved ones. A second is just a twinkling of an eye. It passes away as quickly as it comes. It disappears into eternity noiselessly. But when your seconds and my seconds are brought together, when the seconds of many persons are pulled together in one place, they are not just a volatile flash; they become minutes, hours, days, months, and years. They create a mighty flow of time not to be carried away by the wheel of fate. That time will be registered in anxious hearts, mobilize those who suffer injustice, and create possibilities for change. That flash of a second seen by one person—is it not a flash of God's reign in the world ruled by darkness?

We recall Gora, that Cambodian child-soldier, who calmly talked about severing the heads of his enemies, about asking the Buddha to help him kill better. That was darkness—pitch darkness. In a nation in which twelve-year-olds thought nothing of severing the heads of others, darkness must have reigned supreme. There could have been no light at all. Nobody saw anything in the faces of others. How could they see anything when the whole nation was covered with thick darkness? How could they feel anything when their hearts were paralyzed by the power of darkness?

Still, light was not totally absent in that darkness. There was a second or two in which some light was seen in that dreadful darkness. Listen to this story of Nop Narith, another Cambodian boy in another refugee camp in Thailand:

> Nop Narith . . . has shaggy black hair and great buck teeth that gleam in a smile. He holds his left arm below the table. Narith had polio when he was younger, and the arm is withered. Both his parents are dead. "When

the soldiers came to my house, they took our whole family away. Me they took to a mobile team. I never saw my parents again. But I have a photograph of my father. My father was worried that I could not take care of myself. Yet I feel guarded by his spirit. I dreamt that I saw him, and he promised that his spirit would protect me. In the dream he told me to gain knowledge and to take revenge on his killers."

"Do you seek revenge against the soldiers, then?"

"Yes."

"What do you mean by revenge?"

"Revenge is to make a bad man better than before."[5]

One's heart cannot help but go out to that boy who firmly believed that the spirit of his dead father guarded him. This is a heart-breaking story. How many such stories Cambodian children in Thai refugee camps have to tell!

The spirit of his dead father tells Nop Narith to gain knowledge and take revenge on the Pol Pot soldiers who killed him and the boy's mother. Nop Narith will gain knowledge, once he gets the chance to leave the camp and study somewhere. And take revenge? Nop Narith will do that too, but how? "To make a bad man better than before"! This is quite an answer for a child to make—a child who has gone through so much. Could those who killed his parents be made better? The boy probably did not think too much about the question. It is a difficult question for an adult, not to say for a boy such as Nop Narith. But does one not see in that reply a flash of light in the heart of that boy—a heart not destroyed by hate for his parents' murderers? Does one not perceive in that heart a fleeting shadow of God's reign?

Nop Narith's reply to the question on revenge shows us a little seed of God's reign in his heart. His may not be the only heart among those refugees who fled to Thailand from their homes in Cambodia. At least one hopes not. There must be many hearts like that of Nop Narith among them, not consumed by hatred for the murderers of their loved ones, but cherishing somehow a vague hope that even cruel soldiers could become better persons. The world will be a more hopeful place with such hearts. There will be a chance for the recovery of human community if such hearts grow into movements for love and peace.

At the conclusion of the story of the Philippine Christian who visited the slums in Bombay a poem is quoted:

> Do not go silent into that dark night
> Rage, rage against the dying of the light.[6]

Is this not the message of creation? Is this not the challenge of the reign of God? God broke silence when darkness and chaos threatened to gain the upper hand. God charged into the darkness and brought light out of it. That is why the darkness has become a light-possessing darkness. God established a hold in the world of chaos. That reign of God came in Jesus born in a humble place from humble parents. It was a small beginning. Many a time that light of God's reign was almost put out. It was thought to be totally extinguished on the cross. But that light survived. It not only survived, it has since grown into a mighty flame shining in this bleak world of ours and kindling the light of hope in the hearts of men, women, and children. This is the way of the reign of God, and Jesus has a lot to tell us about that reign of God.

THE SMALLEST OF ALL THE SEEDS

The reign of God (*basileia tou theou*) is a theme that the writers of the gospels often return to, especially in the parables taught by Jesus. "How happy are you . . . yours is the kingdom [reign] of God" (Luke 6:20–23, JB; par. Matt. 5:3–10). This is what his hearers must have been waiting for. The reign of God must be coming. God is great and glorious, and God's reign must be great and glorious too. And in that reign of God they will reign with God. They will not be poor any more. They will not have to go hungry any longer. And of course the injustice and humiliation heaped upon them will be a thing of the past.

Jesus began his mission with a solemn proclamation: "The time has come; the kingdom [reign] of God is upon you" (Mark 1:15). His hearers must have wondered what that reign would be like. What price would have to be paid for it? Did it mean war or peace? They wanted to know. They waited for Jesus to tell them more about it and, if possible, point it out to them so that they could understand it better.

"How shall we picture the reign of God?" Jesus asked the expectant crowd waiting to be initiated into the glory of God's reign. This was their own question. They had their own secret answers. Their poverty and humiliation colored their vision of God's reign. But what is Jesus' answer? Is it the same as theirs? What is his vision of God's reign? "It is like the mustard-seed, which is smaller than any seed in the ground at its sowing," Jesus said matter-of-factly. And he told them the parable of the mustard seed (Mark 4:30– 32; par. Matt. 13:31–32; Luke 13:18–19).

The hearts of those listening eagerly to Jesus must have sunk. This was not what they had expected to hear. They were thinking of something spectacular. God's reign would have to be something big. God's reign would have to be bigger than the Roman empire. The Roman empire is very big. From Rome, its capital far away, it had extended its territory to the whole region of the Mediterranean world. It had added Palestine to its map. It is a big empire. But God's reign would have to be bigger than the Roman empire.

Bigness means powerfulness. The Roman empire is a powerful empire. It has a powerful Caesar. It has brave generals and soldiers. Roman troops are victorious everywhere. To overcome Roman colonial rule God's reign must be more powerful than the powerful Roman empire.

It was not only in Jesus' day that bigness and powerfulness were so attractive. Bigness fascinates contemporary nations, on an alarming scale. Bigness has become a symbol of "advanced civilization." A nation must be big—big in economy, big in science and technology, big in skyscrapers, and big in armaments. Bigness brings power—power over other nations and other peoples. The two superpowers—the United States and the Soviet Union—have entered into an escalating arms race. Each wants to be bigger and stronger than the other. This is a vicious circle of power and more power, bringing the world to the brink of nuclear destruction.

But not only the superpowers are addicted to bigness. The developing countries, in which most of the poor of the world live, are also affected by it. They have contracted the urge to become big and strong in a military way. They spend as much as one-third of their gross national product on arms. All nations, big and small, are caught up in this frenzy to outdo one another in bigness and powerfulness.

What is most frightening is the fact that the bigness the world is after is the bigness of destruction. Modern civilization has sustained two world wars. The magnitude of the destruction wrought on human lives and on faith in humanity was horrendous. But the power of bigness has continued its work of destruction in the Third World since the end of World War II. It has been calculated that in the Third World since 1945 "there have been more than 130 wars involving more than 70 countries and the armed forces of more than 80 states. More than 20 million people have been killed in these wars."[7] The obsession with bigness and the pursuit of it has turned the world into a jungle of cannibals!

But the reign of God, says Jesus, is like a mustard seed, smaller than any other seed. Jesus' stress on smallness was so conspicuous. Jesus' listeners must have stared at him in disbelief. How ridiculous! A tiny mustard seed? It is too small to be taken seriously. It does not impress anybody. It does not catch anybody's attention. But Jesus insists that "it is the case with the reign of God as with a grain of mustard-seed."[8]

The crowds around Jesus must have looked at him with uneasiness. The mustard seed Jesus referred to seems to contradict everything they believed that the reign of God should be. It does not meet their need of a powerful advocate for their cause. They must have murmured to themselves that they were too small already, small in the sight of those important dignitaries holding religious, economic, and political power over them. A reign of God the size of a mustard seed would make them even smaller.

But Jesus goes on as if he is not aware of their apprehension. That tiny insignificant seed grows! It takes some time—no, a long time—for it to grow. It requires a lot of patience and hard work. And there is a lot of sacrifice involved in its growth too—the sacrifice of not being able to talk big and act big, the sacrifice of not being powerful and not being admired. If this is the case also with the reign of God, then it is not all happiness and joy, power and glory. It requires patience. It demands sacrifice. It refuses to be part of a megalomaniacal civilization. The reign of God is going to be a different kind of civilization altogether.

The mustard seed grows. And Jesus begins at last to talk about bigness. The mustard seed "grows up and becomes the greatest of all shrubs and puts forth large branches, so that the birds of the air can make nests in its shade" (4:32, RSV). The stress now is on bigness. Yes, the reign of God does grow big; it becomes bigger than any other kingdom and empire in the world! If it is big, it must also be powerful. Yes, God's reign is a powerful reign. It will be more powerful than the most powerful regime in the world!

But what kind of bigness is it? What kind of powerfulness is it? And here Jesus brings the parable to its dramatic conclusion: the reign of God grows so big that the whole world can settle in its shade; it grows so powerful that all persons can be sustained by it. This is the secret of God's bigness—the bigness of grace. This is also the secret of God's powerfulness—the powerfulness of love. This is the grace of being able to see in the face of those who suffer the face of your own dear ones. It is the grace of seeing Jesus in persons in anguish. The reign of God grows out of the seed of compassion that God has sown in the hearts of men, women, and children everywhere.

Have Jesus' hearers understood him? He sees they are not fully convinced. He tells them another parable of the reign of God. "The reign of God," he says, changing the metaphor, "is like leaven, which a woman took and mixed with half a hundred weight of flour until it was all leavened" (Matt. 13:33; par. Luke 13:20f.). A ridiculously small amount of leaven and a ridiculously large quantity of flour![9] This is an unfair contest from the start. The leaven will completely disappear in the flour. It will lose its identity. And worst of all, it will be lost to sight.

For those just recovering from the parable of the mustard seed, this leaven parable represents a challenge to their logic, to their hope and aspirations. One thing they know for certain: invisibility is the last thing the power of this world wants. Power must be visible in all sorts of forms. Persons must see it to be impressed by it. They must be confronted by it. They must taste it to have fear and respect for it. That power must be concentrated in a ruler. It must be institutionalized in a strong government. It must take form in police power and military power. This is the power exhibited by authoritarian governments in the present day. That is the power around which the powerful nations in the world today ceaselessly turn in geopolitical struggles at the cost of small and weak nations.

Power is essentially exhibitionistic. It must show itself in public. It must demonstrate itself before the eyes of the world. It must prove itself to its rivals. The world is in the clutch of such power. That is why all nations, rich and poor, want to arm themselves with the newest weaponry. That is why the military parade becomes a patriotic duty. And that is why heads of state are surrounded with an aura of invincibility and heralded with martial music.

This is the kind of power Jesus' hearers understood. They must have expected nothing different from the power of God's reign. They must have expected Jesus to organize that power into a revolutionary army. They must have wanted Jesus to proclaim it in the form of a provisional government. They must have hoped that Jesus would consolidate that power in the form of a political party.

But contrary to their expectations and contrary to the logic of our world, Jesus quietly affirms that God's reign will be out of sight. It will function in the manner of leaven. The power of God's reign is not exhibitionistic. It is self-effacing, self-concealing. That power, like the leaven buried inside the mass of dough, is a fermentative power in the depth of humanity, in the womb of God's creation. It is the power of compassion. It is the power of the cross.

17

A Messianic Banquet

WASTING OF PERSONS

The Christian Conference of Asia, holding its sixth assembly in Penang, Malaysia, in June 1977, summarized the Asian situation as follows:

> The dominant reality of Asian suffering is that people
> are wasted:
> Wasted by hunger,
> torture,
> deprivation of rights.
> Wasted by economic exploitation,
> racial and ethnic discrimination,
> sexual suppression,
> non-relation
> non-community.[1]

Wasting of persons created in God's own image—persons given life by having God's own breath breathed into them! Does not this amount to wasting God also?

We have been wasting the limited resources of nature. Mother Earth is limited, not unlimited, in its resources. It has "a limit to the amount of renewable resources such as food and timber that can be produced, a limit to the amount of non-renewable resources that can be produced and consumed, and a limit to the pollution-absorbing capacity of the planet."[2] But we have been treating it as if there were no limits to its resources.

There are limits, severe limits. One report after another has been telling us just that. The United Nations, in its 1976 report, "The Future of the World Economy," said: "The World is expected to consume during the last 30 years of the 20th century three to four times as many minerals as have been consumed through the whole previous history of civilization."[3] The report goes on to predict that at this rate of consumption lead and zinc would run out by the end of the century.

This is a very critical situation. The biggest offender in this mindless consumption of world resources is the United States. It has been pointed out that "the American people consumed in the decade 1959–69 more of the world's resources than had been consumed by all the people of the world throughout history." The implications are frightening, for "if everyone in the world were to consume resources at the American rate, the total known reserves of petroleum would be used up in six years and the annual consumption of timber, copper, sulphur, iron, and water would exceed available known reserves of these resources."[4] This is a truly apocalyptic picture of the limited resources of the world at the mercy of a rapacious appetite.

Wasting of the natural resources of the world has reached an alarming degree. It has at last brought home to those "big wasters" in the developed countries the absolute imperative of conserving the resources and energies of the earth. But there is a far more serious waste that modern technology and industrialization have created: the wasting of human resources. The modern culture of industrialization has given rise to a picture of "the average person in the developed world today . . . surrounded by tons of steel, copper, aluminum, lead, tin, zinc, and plastics, and . . . every day gobbling up 25 kilos of raw steel and many kilos of other minerals."[5] How is one to visualize such a "developed" human being walking in the streets of an industrialized nation? Perhaps as that human monster in the Frankenstein movies, moving heavily and laboriously, leaving destruction behind it wherever it goes.

That is what has been happening in the world today, especially in the Third World: wasting of human resources and destruction of human beings:

> "We eat only once a day, a ball of millet with a few chillies," says the prematurely aging man squatting on the wet pavement in the city. . . . "After going round me and my nine children, precious little is left for my wife," he adds, looking at his emaciated wife, struggling to suckle a baby on her lap, a wrinkled, malnourished little human body. The children are either naked or near naked and sprawl on newspaper for beds. On this sparse diet they . . . work from morning until late in the night. At the street corner waits the burly money-lender, who gave them loans at the exorbitant interest when the father was sick, when his daughter had to be married off, and when he had to make some repairs to this ramshakle tin and cardboard structure he calls home. The money-lender takes away the major portion of the family's income merely for interest and that means their taking another loan from him. All their lives they toil, without hope.[6]

Such tragic drama of life is the rule rather than the exception in Asia. Does it not shame the conscience of this "civilized" world?

On the one hand there are persons grown fat gobbling up twenty-five kilos of raw steel a day, and on the other hand there are persons grown thin because they can afford to eat only once a day, "a ball of millet with a few chillies." There are men, women, and children who have become grossly overweight with many kilos of various other minerals each day, and there are those who are dangerously underweight. A world wasting so many persons is an immoral world. A part of the human community that wastes a great number of human beings through consumption and exploitation is an unethical part. The shape it gives to the world is contrary to God's intention. It does not reflect a community of persons created in God's image. And if we take into account the persons being wasted in prison because of their struggle for freedom and human rights, and those oppressed for reasons of sex, race, or religious faith, is not our world a very godless world?

A RICH FOOL

Jesus lived in a community much smaller than ours. He labored in a world not divided into the rich north and the poor south. But it was an immoral community like ours, dominated by the rich and powerful, an unethical world in which the poor and the powerless were wasted. His compassion went out to the poor and powerless and his warning of God's judgment was beamed to the rich and powerful.

One is reminded of Jesus' parable of the rich fool (Luke 12:16–20). Jesus was talking about the coming judgment, cautioning his followers not to be taken by surprise. What is it going to be like? How are the unprepared going to fare? In his usual manner Jesus must have tried hard to communicate his message simply but pointedly. The case of a wealthy farmer came to his mind, not just a wealthy farmer but one who was also a fool. The harvest from his rich land was plentiful. But he was a fool: there was no room for God in his heart. The psalmist warned: "The fool says in his heart, 'There is no God' " (Ps. 14:1). That is why he did not thank God for the good harvest. But he was also a fool in that he neglected his tenant-farmers who toiled and labored all the year round to make that good harvest possible. Those poor tenant-farmers had families to feed. They had debts to pay. They put their hope in a good harvest so that they might also receive their fair share to provide for their families and pay their debts.

But that rich fool was heartless. Although he had more crops than his storehouses could take, he was not going to share anything with his tenant-farmers and others in need. He pulled down the old storehouses and put up larger ones to store "all his corn and other goods." One can picture Jesus' hearers—many of them must have been poor tenant-farmers and their wives—shaking their heads and sighing. But Jesus was not finished. The rich fool, after storing all his crops away safely in his new storehouses, was content with himself and ready to enjoy life. "Man," he said to himself with great satisfaction, "you have plenty of good things laid by, enough for many years: take it easy, eat, drink, and enjoy yourself" (12:19). But he was not going to be able to eat, drink, and enjoy himself. For God said to him that very day: "You fool, this very night you must surrender your life; you have made your money—who will get it now?" (12:20).

Jesus was not wreaking psychological revenge on the rich and powerful for the benefit of the poor and powerless. Jesus was no Robin Hood. Catastrophes strike the poor as well as the rich, the powerless as well as the powerful. But Jesus must have been both incensed and saddened by the rich and powerful of his day—what insensitive, selfish fools they were!

There is another rich fool in Jesus' parable of the rich man and Lazarus (Luke 16:19–31). Jesus drew a sharp contrast at the outset of this parable: the rich man dressed in costly garments, feasting all day, and Lazarus, a beggar, suffering from a skin disease, barely surviving by begging in the street. Jesus sketched the pathetic sight of Lazarus fighting with street dogs for "pieces of bread which the guests [at the rich man's table] dipped in the dish, wiped their hands with, and then threw under the table."[7]

If Jesus' parable had ended here, his hearers would have drawn their own conclusions from the religious beliefs implanted in them by their religious traditions. They would have thought that the rich man deserved his honor, luxury, leisure, and well-being because he was in God's favor, whereas Lazarus was a sinner receiving due punishment from God. This was karma. The rich man was reaping happiness from his good karma and Lazarus unhappiness from his bad karma. And as surely as the sun would rise the next morning, the same karma would bring them the same fate in the next life.

But to the surprise of his listeners, Jesus went on to draw another contrast—a complete reversal of the first one. The scene now shifted from this world to the next. That rich man was suffering miserably in Hades, in the land of the dead, whereas the beggar Lazarus was with Abraham, clean and happy. The torment of that rich man must have been great, for he was beseeching Abraham to ask Lazarus "to dip the tip of his finger in water, to cool my tongue" (16:24). He called Abraham "father," hoping perhaps that as a member of the chosen family of Israel Abraham would pity and save him. But nothing availed. Abraham's reply was final: "There is a great chasm fixed between us; no one from our side who wants to reach you can cross it, and none may pass from your side to us" (16:26).

Again Jesus broke karma with one stroke. He broke it definitively in favor of the poor. Good karma or bad karma, what moves God is the miserable life of those who go hungry, naked, and homeless through no fault of their own. And the rich are fools if they have no feeling for the wretched of the earth, their brothers and sisters. They are fools because they say there is no God—if not with words, then with what they do not do for persons like Lazarus. This is sin. Sin for Jesus is insensitivity to human suffering, indifference to the plight of others, enjoying the good things of life when the world around you cries out in pain. Sin is the inhumanity that allows you to throw pieces of bread to the floor for beggars and dogs to fight for. Sin is the self-satisfaction gained from your storehouses filled with crops, your factories working to full capacity, at the cost of the health and well-being of your tenant-farmers, wage earners, and their parents, spouses, and children. Sin is bureaucratic rigidity and arrogance of those in government, in business, or in the church, depriving others of their freedom, dignity, and livelihood, exposing them and their families to danger, uncertainty, and desperation.

Jesus has radically altered the meaning of sin. Sin is not the breaking of the Sabbath if you heal, comfort, or do something good for those in pain and agony on that day. Sin is not the ritual uncleanness brought about by your contact with a wounded or dying person on your way to a religious service. Sin is not the discarding of a legalistic tradition when that tradition is enslaving, not liberating. Sin is the self-righteousness that condemns the faults and failures of others but is indulgent about one's own. Sin is the audacity to say to them: "Let me take the speck out of your eye, when all the time there is that plank in [one's] own" (Matt. 7:4; par. Luke 6:42). Sin has not come from a devil outside you. Rituals cannot make a person a sinner. Canon law cannot turn its offender into an outcast of God's grace. Sin comes from the heart, from the loveless heart, from the heart hardened against loving others and suffering with them. Sin is inside our humanity—self-righteous, self-centered, self-important, and self-seeking humanity.

Sinners are fools. They are not fools because they are stupid. Often they are cunning and sagacious. That is why the rich man under whose table Lazarus fought for discarded bread with street dogs has grown so rich. Sinners are fools not because they are lazy, wasting their time away. They can be very industrious. For them every second and every minute is important. They do not waste their time in small talk. They have no time to stop and think how others are faring. They spend their time making splendid plans for their future.

But sinners are fools. They are sinners because they proclaim by their deeds that there is no God, even though they may go to church every Sunday and observe every possible requirement as faithful church members. And since there is no God in their hearts, they have no people at heart either. Their mind is insensitive to the needs of other people, although it becomes very sharp when gaining power and wealth for themselves is concerned. Their eyes do not see the sorrow behind a resigned face. Their ears do not hear a heart beating in pain in an undernourished body. And their hearts never go out of themselves to those in suffering and agony.

This is what Jesus meant by sin. And he did have some very hard words to say to the rich who were at the same time such fools:

> Alas for you who are rich; you have had your time of happiness.
> Alas for you who are well-fed now; you shall go hungry.
> Alas for you who laugh now; you shall mourn and weep
> [Luke 6:24–25].

This is a very scathing thing to say. Jesus must have sounded like one of those uncouth prophets of old.

Jesus was not rejecting riches outright. He might have made a good and authentic socialist, though not an orthodox communist, certainly not a communist corrupted by capitalism. Do you remember an episode in the house of Simon the leper on the eve of his final struggle in Jerusalem, told in Matthew's Gospel (26:6–13)? That is one of the most beautiful and memorable gospel stories. It is a story of a woman who anointed Jesus with costly oil. She must have been one of his secret admirers and devout followers. In her sensitive mind she must have realized Jesus was facing mortal danger. She came to Jesus "with a small bottle of fragrant oil, very costly, and as she sat at the table she began to pour it over his head" (26:6–7). We are not told who that woman was. She might have been from a rich family, able to afford such "very costly" oil. In their complaints the disciples said that the oil "could have been sold for a good sum and the money given to the poor" (26:9). The disciples, after all this time with Jesus, saw only the costly oil and the money represented by it. They could not see the pain in the woman's heart anointing Jesus in preparation for his death. They were not able to perceive the agony in Jesus' soul facing the cross. At this stage they were still "fools," enslaved to the market value of the oil, and unable to see the vital cause it was serving.

Jesus had to say to his disciples:

> "Why must you make trouble for the woman? It is a fine thing she has done for me. You have the poor among you always; but you will not always have me. When she poured this oil on my body it was her way of preparing me for burial. I tell you this: wherever in all the world this gospel is proclaimed, what she has done will be told as her memorial" [26:10–13].

Jesus was not a long-faced ascetic. He often ate and drank with "sinners and tax-gatherers"—that is, persons outside the respectable religious community. He was aware that he was accused of being "a glutton and a drinker, a friend of tax-gatherers and sinners" (Matt. 11:19; par. Luke 15:2). Jesus could not eat and drink comfortably with rich fools. But with the poor and oppressed he ate and drank to his heart's content, although the food and drink would be of a lower quality. But of rich fools Jesus was prompted to say with bitter sarcasm, adapting a local saying: "It is easier for a camel to pass through the eye of a needle than for a rich man to enter the kingdom of God" (Matt. 19:24).

A BIG DINNER PARTY

Both Matthew (22:1–4) and Luke (14:15–24) relate the parable of the great supper, but with marked differences. In Matthew's version it was a king who held a marriage feast for his son, whereas in Luke "a man was giving a big dinner party," not saying what the party was for. In both versions the first invitation was followed by a second one just before the feast. This has been the way of social etiquette in Asia too. The host shows courtesy and sincerity to some of those invited by sending his servants or others to their homes and urging them to come. They in turn make sure they show some hesitation at the first invitation, as required by unwritten social custom, and wait to be persuaded to come by the messenger from the host. In Matthew this second invitation came with the information about how splendid the feast was going to be, with oxen and fattened calves killed and prepared for it. Luke omits this information.

In both accounts those invited declined to come. Luke goes into some detail describing the reasons why they have declined the invitation as a way of leading to his main point: getting all sorts of the lowly to come to the dinner in place of the disrespectful rich who had been invited, making the feast a messianic banquet for the poor and the oppressed. Matthew at this point differs from Luke completely. The servants sent to the guests were seized, brutally attacked, and killed, incurring the great wrath of the king who sent his troops to destroy "those murderers and set their houses on fire," obviously referring to God's judgment of the world at the end of time. Matthew also has the king invite "unworthy" persons to the wedding feast after the bloody encounter is over, but his story is almost another version of the parable of the vineyard in which the tenants killed the servants whom the landowner had sent to collect the rent due to him (Matt. 21:33–41).

Both Matthew and Luke must have drawn from the same source for their versions of the parable. But Matthew allegorized it heavily and related it to God's judgment on the day of reckoning. Luke adhered to the basic thrust of his Gospel, highlighting the difference between the rich and the poor, stressing God's acceptance of the latter. Luke must have stayed closely with the parable as he found it. And it is Luke's version that I shall use in our reflections here.

We must once again let our imaginations go back to the scene where Jesus was telling his hearers what God's reign was going to be like. By now they must have become accustomed to unexpected twists and turns in the stories and parables Jesus told them. They were familiar with such stories and parables. They grew up with them. Parables are folk wisdom—wisdom of the people, handed down from one generation to the next, undergoing changes here and there on the way. These stories are folktales—stories telling how their forebears fought and struggled in an oppressive society and how they managed to retain hope and love despite their agony and pain. These folktales and parables are a precious source of wisdom, courage, and hope. They give them the power to live and enable them to go on believing in God. There is a lot of people theology in them. Is this not also the case with our folktales in Asia? Do they not contain a lot of people theology ?

It is no surprise that Jesus often turned to folktales and parables. He was essentially a folk theologian, a people theologian. In his theology one hears the people speak, murmur, sing, groan, sigh. There is so much of the people in it. It is filled with sounds from the depths of souls. It echoes the heartbeats of the people and vibrates with the longings of their spirit. Jesus knew much about the people and experienced deeply their humanity. It is because Jesus was such a people theologian that he was also a God theologian. He told us so much about

God, and shared with us so much of his experience of God's love. Jesus did not merely *have* the image of God. He *was* the image of God.

"A man was giving a big dinner party," Jesus began, "and had sent out invitations" (Luke 14:16). A big dinner party? Jesus' hearers must have wondered, How big? How many tables are set up? How many guests are invited? But they must have quickly felt a disappointment: they who are poor, hungry, and oppressed have no part in that big dinner party. For them the parable is going to be a fairytale.

But Jesus went ahead with his parable as if he was not aware of what was going through his hearers' minds. Who gets invited to the big dinner party? Persons of means and prestige, of course! A man who could afford to buy a piece of land was the first to be invited. He must be a wealthy man and an important person. Another person invited was a landowner. He had just bought five yoke of oxen. Inasmuch as "in general, a farmer owns as much land as one or two yoke of oxen can plough, that means about 10–20 hectares," he must have "owned at least 45 hectares, probably much more."[8] Five yoke of oxen! It is beyond the dreams of the poor. And there is a third person who declined the invitation to that big dinner party on the ground of his recent marriage. To be invited to such a party is a great honor. Social custom dictates that only men be invited to a banquet and the man married just recently is not willing to leave his wife alone at home. He himself must be a man of great prestige to be able to treat the invitation so lightly.

Jesus was slowly leading his listeners to the point he wanted to make. But they did not seem to be aware of it. True, they must have thought to themselves, those rich and prestigious persons have all spurned the invitation. But there will be other important persons who will be invited to that big dinner party.

But Jesus had a surprise for them. The invitation was not going to be extended to other important persons. Jesus' parable took a critical and dramatic turn that must have jostled his hearers out of their disappointment. Jesus had the host of that big dinner party issue orders at a rapid pace: "Go out quickly into the streets and alleys of the town, and bring me in the poor, the crippled, the blind, and the lame!" (14:21). These are beggars like that poor Lazarus. How incredible! Even if the rich host of the big dinner party was angry at those insolent guests, he had no need of the company of beggars. If he did get beggars to come to the party, he could not be doing it out of compassion for them. He must have done it to slight those who had rejected his invitation.

Then, suddenly, Jesus' hearers got the point. Why, this is not the rich host speaking. It is Jesus speaking! It is our compassionate God speaking through Jesus! Jesus who eats with us, drinks with us, and embraces us, showing us for the first time that God is love and compassion—it is Jesus who gives that big dinner party for us. At last it dawned on them: it is they—the poor and the outcasts—who are going to sit at the banquet given by God! It is they who are going to reign with God in God's kingdom! The world is going to be different. Just imagine: 800 million undernourished persons in absolute poverty in the world today will be the honored guests in God's great banquet and responsible decision-makers in God's glorious reign!

But Jesus had another surprise ready. He had the rich host issue a second order: "Go out on to the highways and along the hedgerows and make them come in; I want my house to be full" (14:23). Those were persons outside the city, beyond the borders set up by the Jewish religious traditions, who had to live and die without God's salvation. Again the people realized that this was Jesus' order. It was God's order through Jesus. The gentiles were also to sit at God's banquet and reign with God! This is a religious revolution! It is at this point that Matthew also came round to this main theme in Luke's version of the parable, for at the end of his account of the parable he also has the king issue the order: "Go out to the main thoroughfares, and invite everyone you can find to the wedding!" The servants dutifully "went out into the streets and collected all they could find, good and bad alike" (Matt. 22:9).

Jesus in this parable is not talking about an ordinary dinner party. A dinner party to be attended by outcasts and Gentiles cannot be an ordinary dinner party. It has to be an extraordinary dinner party. What should one call it? How is one to characterize it? It is a messianic dinner party! It is a banquet of God's salvation! In that party God's saving love is spread out on the tables. The food served in that banquet is prepared with God's compassion. Sitting happily at the party are sinners, beggars, and outcasts—not rich fools. Looking contented at the banquet are the gentiles and not those orthodox theologians and church leaders who gave them up for lost. A truly remarkable messianic banquet. This is Jesus' vision of God's reign.

18

Space of Salvation

SPACE IN THE MARGIN

Yoji Inoue, a Japanese Catholic priest, has written a book with the title *Watakushi no naka no Kirisuto* ["Christ within me"]. It is a thought-provoking work. In it the author tries to grasp Jesus as would a Christian caught in the dilemma of being a Japanese embracing a Christianity deeply rooted in Western culture. This is an important and timely undertaking. Here and there he has made attempts to bring his Japaneseness to bear on his account of Jesus. Here is one of his penetrating insights:

> These were the days shortly after the end of the war. The sight of a few American soldiers with chewing gum in their mouths was still part of the scene when one entered the subway.
>
> One night during the visit of one of my father's friends, he told us the following story. A certain American army officer became so interested in a picture scroll hanging on the wall of an alcove in his house that my father gave it to him. The officer then cut off the margins on the scroll and framed the picture. I remember how my father and his friend exchanged glances and sighs, disgusted at what that American officer had done to the picture scroll. I also laughed at the story, but at that time I did not know why the picture was completely spoiled without the space on its margins. . . .
>
> Some fifteen years later . . . I visited Liuan shrine in Kyoto one summer afternoon. . . . It was about two o'clock and all was quiet; only the shrill chirrup of cicadas could be heard, giving one an oppressive feeling. . . . Looking at the nineteen stones placed on the white sand in the yard, vaguely wondering whether they represented a group of islands, imagining a tigress with its cubs crossing the river by means of those stones . . . I suddenly became aware of something. . . .
>
> It occurred to me that the tense beauty that those garden stones possessed was precisely the beauty of space forming a margin. When I

became aware of this, I felt I grasped the secret of those garden stones—why they attracted one's attention so powerfully. I also remembered the story about that American officer.[1]

Yoji Inoue then goes on to relate his insight into the meaning of marginal space to the Buddhist concept of emptiness, stressing that emptiness is fullness, giving power and beauty to objects surrounded by a given space. He also relates it to Jesus' teaching on the kingdom of God—the world of emptiness giving grace, love, and beauty to the world surrounded by it. This is a very important insight, and I should like to develop it further, but in a different way, in relation to our doing of theology in Asia surrounded by the space of God's salvation.

We live in a very crowded world. The world population of more than four billion competes for space on this tiny planet Earth. It is no wonder that nations will allow no violation of their precious space. They guard their air space with vigilance. Intrusion into their territorial waters will be met with loud protest and swift retaliation. Disputes over national borders often lead to military confrontation. To protect the borders of a nation is a sacred duty. Wars are fought and blood shed in the name of national sovereignty.

But space is not the concern of nations only. It also concerns persons personally. It has to do with living space in a crowded city in an overpopulated country. Take South Korea, for example. The population of 37 million shares 98,859 square kilometers of land area; that is about 375 persons per square kilometer. But two-thirds of the land area are covered by forests, reducing the habitable area to a mere one-third of the total. The number of persons per square kilometer escalates dramatically—from 375 to 1,123 persons.

Hong Kong, as is well known, lives under nightmarish conditions. A population of some 5 million lives in the land area of 1,052 square kilometers. That amounts to 4,753 persons per square kilometer![2] This is what the Taiwanese call "people living on top of people" (*lang thiap lang,* in Taiwanese). Hong Kong has been a marvelous place in many ways, marvelous in every sense of good and bad. But behind that brave facade are fierce struggles of human beings like caged animals, trying to survive, to outdo one another, to live on top of one another. Something similar obtains in every crowded Asian city—Taipei, Tokyo, Seoul, Jakarta, and so on. But in Hong Kong one sees the human struggle in a most brutal and naked way.

The fight for living space and breathing space is a particularly intense fight for us in the contemporary world. Modern industrial civilization has brought prosperity and progress to many. But it has also brought poverty, enslavement, and inhumanity to many others, especially in the Third World. It has more and more deprived human beings of space. And this is perhaps one of the worst tragedies that we have brought upon ourselves.

We human beings are spatial beings. We are also temporal beings. We live in time. We move with time. We leave time behind us, and anticipate time before us. But on balance one must say that space is more important to our well-being. We can choose to forget time, not to be bothered by the ticking of the clock. But we cannot choose to forget space, for space is where we stand. Space is the room in which we eat, work, and sleep. It is that visible and invisible part of the creation that supports us, sustains us. Life is born into a particular space. There must be a space to receive it, to make it grow and develop.

Because space is as essential as the air that persons breathe and the food they eat, to deprive them of space amounts to depriving them of their very being. A space-less person has only a ghostly existence. That is what that American soldier did to the picture scroll. Removing from the picture the space in the margin around it, he spoiled it. It had no more life in it. Imprisoned in a frame without space around it, the picture was dead.

The invention of prisons shows that we human beings know this by instinct. And it is totalitarian rulers who implement this knowledge to their utmost. They put behind bars political dissidents and those who struggle for freedom and human rights, depriving them of space to move about freely, reducing them to a subhuman level. By controlling the space of their prisoners, they not only control their lives, but also crush their humanity. A totalitarian government is an antihuman government. It is a government that invades the space to which persons are entitled as human beings. It is a government that reduces them to nonspatial beings.

What antihuman authoritarian rulers can do to humanity is testified to in a poem written by an unknown Vietnamese prison poet in 1970. It has the title "My Verses":

> My verses in fact are no verses
> They are simply life's sobbings
> Dark prison cells opening and shutting
> The dry cough of two caving-in lungs
> The sound of earth coming down to bury dreams
> The exhumation sound of hoes bringing up memories
> The chattering of death in cold and misery
> The aimless contractions of an empty stomach
> The hopeless beat of a dying heart
> Impotence's voice in the midst of collapsing earth
> All the sounds of a life not deserving half its name
> Or even the name of death:
> No verses are they![3]

Prison is no space of life. It is the space of death. There one's dreams are buried. All that one can hear is the sound of death coming from "caving-in lungs, empty stomach, and dying heart." That unknown prison poet must have dedicated this poem to death too, for he concludes "My Verses" by saying: "No verses are they."

Poets must dedicate their poems to the beauty and truth of humanity even in the midst of pain and anguish. But when they dedicate their poems to death, hope is gone, life is extinguished, and a future is precluded. That is when poets cease to sing. And when poets stop singing, life becomes lingering death, light reflects the terror of darkness, truth tells of the horror of nothingness. The struggle for space is the struggle for life, for meaning, for hope, for humanity, for salvation.

COMFORT MY PEOPLE!

Salvation has a very strong physical sense. It has to do with your body and the space your body occupies. Salvation means to have space restored to you so that you can move freely in it. Salvation means you are fully human again because you are fully spatial again. When you reach out, it is not the cold walls of a prison cell that you feel, but the warm delicious air in the wide and open space surrounding you. In that space of yours, you hear the surging cry of joy from your lungs, the rhythms of gratitude from your contented stomach, and the echoes of your heart beating in hope. This is what salvation means. A fully spatial human being with a living heart, a singing stomach, and shouting lungs! This is salvation we can see, hear, and feel.

It is this kind of salvation that the great prophet Second Isaiah proclaimed in Babylon, the land of captivity. The Babylonian era is drawing to its close and the Persian age is about to begin. With a most profound foresight the prophet envisions a tremendous space to be created by tumultuous change in world history. It is not going to be a matter of one nation taking the place of another nation, or simply a new and vigorous political power forcing an old and ailing political power off the stage of history. A big space is going to open up for the people in exile at this momentous juncture in the life of the nations.

The prophet can scarcely conceal his excitement. He cannot suppress his sense of wonder. In front of him he sees the space of God's salvation appear in glory and triumph. His deep and robust prophetic mind is also a great and sensitive poetic mind. He pours out in superb and noble verse what he sees with his mind's eye. It is as if his whole being burst out in a hymn of joy, a song of praise, a poem of heavenly music:

> Comfort, comfort my people;
> it is the voice of your God;
> speak tenderly to Jerusalem
> and tell her this,
> that she has fulfilled her term of bondage,
> that her penalty is paid;
> She has received at the Lord's hand
> double measure for all her sins
> [Isa. 40: 1–2].

What a way to begin a proclamation: "Comfort, comfort my people!" How much has that people been longing to hear such words! The memory of its recent past gives it little comfort. That a people who believed it was the special concern of God could fall so low! Jerusalem was in ruins and the people of Israel was held in captivity in Babylonia. And now it is hearing words of comfort proclaimed to it? Can this be true?

It must be true. The prophet says, "it is the voice of your God." Israel thought that voice had been buried in the ruins of Jerusalem. It had shut it out from its captive heart. But that voice comes back, not from the temple of Jerusalem, but from the heart of God to the heart of the people. This is what "speak tenderly" means. It means "to speak to the heart." It is heart-to-heart talk. It is a heart-to-heart proclamation.

Heart language is serious language. Each syllable echoes the heartbeats of the speaker. Each word is heavy because it is filled with the whole person of the speaker. Salvation language must be heart language. It cannot be a language just from the lips and the brain. Salvation language must be person language. It cannot be language that speaks of objects, principles, or theories. Salvation language must be compassionate language.

This language of the heart turns into the language of space. The prophet shows the people what God's salvation is like in images of space:

> There is a voice that cries:
> Prepare a road for the Lord through the wilderness,
> clear a highway across the desert for our God.
> Every valley shall be lifted up,
> every mountain and hill brought down;
> rugged places shall be made smooth
> and mountain-ranges become a plain
> [Isa. 40:3–4].

Is God not the God of space? Do we not hear in this the voice of God in the beginning when God made heaven and earth?

Wilderness and desert—are they not the darkness and chaos that confronted God when God began the work of creation? Light and darkness had to be distinguished; heaven and earth had to be separated; a course had to be set for the stars. God made space out of nonspace. And God made animals and created human beings to inhabit this space. The whole creation process is a space-making process. It is a redeeming process.

In the prophet's proclamation there are wilderness and desert. Is not the wilderness chaos? Is not the desert darkness? This is what the wilderness and the desert lying between Jerusalem and Babylon are like. The Jews in exile know it by experience, for that was the way they came. Wilderness is no space for the living. Nor is the desert. Space has to be created out of the wilderness and the desert. This is what the prophet is saying God is going to do. There will be a road through the wilderness and a highway will be built across the desert. Is this not creation? Is this not salvation? And when the exiles walk on that road and traverse that highway to return to Jerusalem, they will know what salvation means. It means a road to walk on with joy and a highway to travel in hope. To create space where there is no space—salvation has this strongly physical dimension to it.

Among the religions in Asia it is Zen Buddhism that seems to have the best grasp of this spatial meaning of salvation. The feeling of spaciousness that a temple yard gives is a feeling of emancipation. To create space out of nonspace, to make a large space out of a small space, to project space beyond the horizon of the human mind—this seems to be the emancipation and freedom that Zen understands and experiences. If we ponder the following description of a tearoom in a Zen temple, we may better understand why:

> Where a series of flag-stones irregularly arranged comes to a stop, there stands a most insignificant-looking straw-thatched hut, low and unpretentious to the last degree. The entrance is not by a door but a sort of aperture; to enter through it a visitor has to be shorn of all his encumbrances, that is to say, to take off both his swords, long and short, which in the feudal days a samurai used to carry all the time. The inside is a small semi-lighted room about ten feet square; the ceiling is low and of uneven height and structure. The posts are not smoothly planed, they are mostly of natural wood . . . . The flower-vase contains no more than a single stem of flowers, neither gorgeous nor ostentatious; but like a little white lily blooming under a rock surrounded by in no way sober pines. . . . Now we listen to the sound of boiling water in the kettle as it rests on a tripod frame over a fire in the square hole cut in the floor. The sound is not that of actually boiling water but comes from the heavy iron kettle . . . [and] greatly adds to the serenity of the room. . . . One here feels as if one were sitting alone in a mountain-hut where a white cloud and the pine music are one's only consoling companions.[4]

That little hut seems to grow into the whole of the universe. A vast space is created in that small tearoom. Everything in that hut and in that tearoom is unobtrusive. Even the flower vase has one stem of flowers only. And the sound the kettle makes only adds to the vastness of the serenity of the place. No wonder one feels as if one were sitting in a mountain hut surrounded by mountains and clouds, by heaven and earth. It is almost a miracle for a ten-square-foot room in a crowded city to be able to project such a huge space. The sense of emancipation and freedom from taking a cup of tea in this vast small space is aptly expressed by Suzuki, the Japanese Zen master:

> To take a cup . . . in this environment . . . wonderfully lifts the mind above the perplexities of life. The warrior is saved from his daily occupation of fighting, and the businessman from his ever-present idea of money-making. Is it not something, indeed, to find in this world of struggles and vanities a corner, however humble, where one can ride above the limits of relativity and even have a glimpse of eternity?[5]

Eternity of space in the limits and preoccupations of this world! Is this not the emancipation that brings human beings closer to the source of life?

To enter that infinite space of the tiny tearoom, one has to leave all the baggage of life outside—"shorn of all encumbrances." Even a samurai has to take off his swords, both long and short. To a samurai swords are life. Not only during the waking hours, in sleep too he must not part with them. They make a samurai a samurai. But just because of this, he is not allowed to take his swords with him into the tearoom. In that infinite space there is no room for his swords. It has room only for his naked self, his humble humanity, his simple person, not burdened with pride, glory, or the vanity of this world. It has no room for the cares, anxieties, and naggings of this life. Only when you enter that tiny tearoom just as you are, will you be lifted above "the limits of life" and given "a glimpse of eternity."

I often wonder if there was a touch of Zen in the deeply religious mind of Jesus. "Look at the birds of the air," he said to his hearers almost worn out by the cares of life. "They do not sow and reap and store in barns, yet your heavenly Father feeds them: (Matt. 6:26). This is true. His listeners would have agreed with him readily. But what about us? We sow very diligently, but we do not always have enough after reaping and often nothing at all to store in barns. We are no better off than the birds of the air! But Jesus went on to say: "You are worth more than the birds!" Jesus turns from the vertical space of the sky to the horizontal space of fields: "Consider how the lilies grow in the fields; they do not work, they do not spin: and yet, I tell you, even Solomon in all his splendor was not attired like one of these" (Matt. 2:28–29). Again the people could not agree with Jesus more. But look at us, Jesus. We work and spin from morning till night, and yet we are poorly clothed, if not in rags.

Jesus' reply was: How little faith you have! There is no space in their faith. All the room in their faith is taken up by worries of this world. There is of course no room there for the birds of the air and the lilies of the field. How, then, can there be room for God? But if there is no room for God who gives the power to live and the strength to believe, how can there be that power of the spirit to fight the injustice done to them, to resist the oppression of the rich and powerful, and to struggle for freedom from poverty and inhumanity imposed on them by the powers of this world?

Jesus was no dreamer. He was no smooth-tongued preacher. All he wanted to do was to create space in his hearers' minds and hearts, so that they would have God within them to rise above the limits of life and to gain power to strive for space within those limits. This is emancipation. This is salvation. Jesus has transformed the space of salvation outside in the wilderness into the space of salvation in the inner world within ourselves and within our community. "Do not be anxious about tomorrow!" (Matt. 6:34). This is the faith created in that inner space of salvation. And only with that faith can one face the hardships of the world without despairing, struggle for riddance of injustice in hope, and envision God's reign here and now.

Is this not what Jesus meant when he said: "The reign of God is within you"?

You are not to look for God's reign only in the external. Nor do you have to wait for it until tomorrow, or next year, or the year 2000. You are not kept waiting for it endlessly. This is what traditional faith has been telling the people. But Jesus is no ordinary rabbi. He is not a traditional theologian. He is refreshingly unconventional in his outlook. He is liberatingly unorthodox in his teachings. And he is boldly untraditional when it comes to the reign of God. God's reign, he proclaims, is within you. God's reign is that inner space in your heart where God is present. It is that space in your soul that can contain the suffering and pain of other persons. It is the space in your spirit that can house the groanings of the oppressed. That space within you is the reign of God. It is made up of those little spaces within you, fledgling reigns of God in those little spaces. But what a mighty reign of God it is going to be!

MY REDEEMER LIVES!

The "outer" space of salvation is transformed into the "inner" space of salvation. But that inner space of salvation does not remain inert. It is transformed back again to the "outer" space of salvation. This is what God's reign is. Salvation in the inner spiritual sense does not exist apart from salvation in the outer physical sense. And salvation in the outer physical meaning does not exist in separation from the inner spiritual meaning. The "inner" has to become the "outer," and the "outer" has to become the "inner." This is what the reign of God is as the space of salvation. This is the quality of salvation that persons of deep faith manifest in the world of suffering, pain, and conflict.

We must recall Job once again. We have already seen how that paragon of piety was stricken with horrible disasters, cursing the day of his birth in his untold woes. His friends came to console him but became instead his accusers, trying to make him admit that he must have committed some grave sin against God. Job's "outer" space of salvation was reduced almost to nothing. He pours out a heartbreaking lament:

> My kinsfolk and my close friends have failed me;
> the guests in my house have forgotten me;
> my maidservants count me as a stranger;
> I have become an alien in their eyes.
> I call to my servant, but he gives me no answer;
> I must beseech him with my mouth.
> I am repulsive to my wife,
> loathsome to the sons of my own mother.
> Even young children despise me;
> when I rise they talk against me.
> All my intimate friends abhor me,
> and those whom I loved have turned against me
> [Job 19:14–19, RSV].

Is there a more tragic sense of life than this? This is a description of hell. Hell is created when no space is left on the margin of life. In hell there is no room for expansion. Everywhere one turns, one encounters hostility, malice, and rejection.

Job could not help crying out, begging for pity even from his friends who came not to console him but to accuse him:

> Have pity on me, have pity on me,
>   O you my friends,
>   for the hand of God has touched me!
> Why do you, like God, pursue me?
>   Why are you not satisfied with my flesh?
>   [19:21–22, RSV].

This could have been the end of Job. He would have gone to the world of the dead with his soul not vindicated, tormented with his deep anguish.

But just as when those who filled his space of salvation—his loved ones, relatives, friends, servants—had deserted him, a little light was lit in his inner space of salvation, and one hears his confession:

> For I know my Redeemer lives,
>   and at last he will stand upon the earth;
> and after my skin has been thus destroyed,
>   then from my flesh I shall see God
>   [19:25–26, RSV].

My Redeemer lives in the midst of the tragedy that struck me. My Redeemer lives when I am afflicted with a dreadful malady. My Redeemer lives when those dear and close to me have rejected me. My Redeemer lives even when street urchins taunt me. My Redeemer lives. . . .

This is the faith hidden in that inner space of salvation in Job's heart. This is the confession that comes out of that space in spite of Job himself. That inner space has not been destroyed by the destruction of the space outside filled with his wealth, loved ones, friends, and relatives. It is that inner space that now speaks. It confesses that the Redeemer lives despite all Job has to go through. It confesses that even after his skin has been destroyed, even after the "outer" space of salvation is gone, he will still see God from the flesh remaining to him, from that inner space of faith that is still his. It is this inner space that expands under the barrage of his friends' sharp arguments and counterarguments. And it is this inner space that is to grow into the vision of God that enables Job to say later: "I had heard of thee by the hearing of the ear; but now my eyes see thee; therefore I despise myself; and repent in dust and ashes" (42:5–6, RSV). To despise oneself before God is redemption. To repent in God's presence is salvation. A new space of salvation has been created within him and around him. There he has experience of his true God, the Redeemer.

"My Redeemer lives!" When these words are uttered, no matter where, space of salvation is created. When this confession is made, no matter by whom, the nonspace of despair is turned into the space of hope; the nonspace of death becomes the space of life. And when these words are whispered by prisoners from one cell to the next, the human spirit breaks out of prison bars and soars into the vast space of freedom that brings salvation. That is why prisoners of conscience can be the freest of all human beings. This is what the poem "From Prison Window," which originated in a prison camp in the Philippines, attests:

Of triumph the lakebirds sing as they fly
Shafts from the sun on their fervid wind.
My poems of freedom take to the sky.

This lake is a spring where deep hopes lie,
Borne too by songs of the flock coming in.
Of triumph the lakebirds sing as they fly. . . .

When mountains are palled and coldly sigh,
Winds ever rise: and behold! the clearing. . . .
Of triumph the lakebirds sing as they fly.

Then I see heaven: like a god on high
My spirits soar. And my dreams begin.
My poems of freedom take to the sky.

Off with the deathbound on earth, all cry:
Who yearns for that heaven, unbound him!
Of triumph the lakebirds sing as they fly,
My poems of freedom take to the sky.[6]

Does this poem not show us that salvation is a matter of space created in the human spirit? It is an enormous space: it reaches to the sky.

Is this not ultimately the space created by the cross of Jesus? The cross at first appeared to be the defeat of what God intended for salvation in Jesus. The space of salvation seemed to shrink until it became that narrow space of the cross—the space framed by two wooden beams. That was no space at all. The cross was nonspace—the nonspace of shame, torture, and death. It was reported that "at midday a darkness fell over the whole land, which lasted till three in the afternoon" (Mark 15:33; par. Matt. 27:45; Luke 23:44). Midday ought to be bright; all the space surrounding you ought to be clearly visible. But darkness swallowed it all up.

There was no more space. Darkness does not have space. It is only a fearful abyss. When the space of God's salvation is reduced to the nonspace of the cross, darkness covers everything. The death of Jesus would have been the death of humanity and the end of God's creation.

But on the cross there was not a criminal, but Jesus; not a diminished human being, but a full human being; not a demigod, but the full presence of God. After three days, out of darkness light broke out; out of the nonspace of death the space of life emerged. Jesus rose from the dead!

Resurrection is the confession that our Redeemer lives. It is the testimony that although our skin can be destroyed, with our flesh that remains we shall see God. Resurrection is the poem of freedom from prison bars. It is the song of victory after defeat in the struggle to be human. It is the hymn of life surrounded by death. Resurrection is the new space created by God for us in the world of toil, labor, pain, and anguish. It is both the inner and outer space of salvation that is ours from God through Jesus. Theology is possible because of such space, both inner and outer. And it can be immensely enriched and deepened by the experience of such space in Asia.

19

Vision of Tomorrow

TOMORROW OUT OF THE WOMB OF TODAY

Vision begins with down-to-earth reality. Reality is what we see, hear, smell, touch, and feel. Reality is ourselves and the world in which we live. If we do not see with our eyes and our mind's eye, then vision is not real. It is illusion. If we do not hear with our ears and our mind's ear, then what we think we hear is hallucination. If we do not smell with our nose and our mind's nose, then what we fancy we smell is imaginary. Our vision is a dream that disappears as soon as we wake up from sleep. We want to touch it again, but it is not there anymore. We should like to feel it again, but it eludes us completely.

Vision is not vision if it does not begin with down-to-earth reality. It not only begins *with* reality, it begins *in* reality. Vision has to be born out of our seeing, hearing, and smelling reality. It has to grow from our touching and feeling reality.

The reality in which vision begins and grows is life as we live it yesterday and today, the life that we live, touch, and feel, the life that gives us joy and hope, but also much, perhaps more, sorrow and despair. Life brings us enough blessings to make us know there is meaning in it; but it has also much, perhaps more, disappointment to make us wonder if it is worth all the toil and pain. Reality consists of the life that began yesterday in the great joy of parents and blessings of well-wishers and ends tomorrow in the great sorrow of loved ones and the tears of dear ones.

Real vision has to be related to such reality—the reality that greets us as we walk into the streets, as we enter the marketplace, and as we begin our daily work at home or in an office or factory. It is the reality that faces us as we open the newspaper to read, switch on the radio to listen, and turn on the television to watch. That reality is not hiding in a philosopher's mind, but is there right in front of us. We cannot miss it. That reality is not concocted in a theologian's brain. It takes place in physical reality and is brought to our notice through powerful communications systems. We cannot escape it.

True vision is inseparable from true life—the life of flesh and blood. It is the life we live as a family sharing joys and agonies, torn between union and separation, sustained by the love that has its ecstasy and pain. The life from which our vision has to be born is also the life we live in community, large or small. That life can be beautiful with genuine sympathy and care, but it can also become ugly with pettiness and selfishness. That life can be uplifting with encouragement and good will, but it can also be destructive when hatred and jealousy reign. That life enables you at times to increase your faith in humanity, but it can also destroy that faith.

The reality with which and in which vision begins is not an ideal life. Ideal life may exist in God's future but not in our here and now. It seems that some theologians have assumed such an ideal life as the basis for their reflection, teachings, and system-building. They begin with a future that is fulfilled and glorious. And when they touch on life here and now—life unfulfilled and less than glorious—their theology takes on a flight back to the future. It invites Christians to that future, ignoring the present, with its doubts, sighs, and tears, besides its moments of joy and happiness. Theirs is a theology that disowns the past and present, giving Christians the impression that the pain of yesterday would have no meaning for the joy of tomorrow and the struggle of today only obscures the vision of fulfillment in some indefinite future. It gives them a faith that will be active in the future but not today. It discourages them from taking seriously all the things that make life real today—history, culture, and human relationships, within which Christians also live as part of their society, nation, and world.

Christians and theologians in Asia are learning that our vision of the future must begin within the reality of life today. This is how biblical faith came into being. The vision of the exodus began with the reality of life of enslavement in Egypt. The call to God's love and justice was issued by prophets from within a society that had become corrupted with human avarice and violence. And the vision of that great prophet Second Isaiah was born in the midst of a life of exile in a foreign land. That biblical faith never let the future run away by itself. The future was always in the firm grip of the present that had just struggled out of the past. It is that kind of future that made sense to the prophets. And only a vision built on the life of reality as actually lived made an impact on it.

It was the same with faith in the first decades of the New Testament—perhaps even more so. Jesus' ministry was filled with the present. It was the present that dared to challenge the past and project the future. As we have seen, his vision of God's reign was born out of the life of the people lived in poverty and oppression. That is why his message touched their hearts. It made sense to them. It brought God very close to them.

Jesus also spoke about the future. In response to a threat on his life by King Herod, Jesus said: "Today and tomorrow, I shall be casting out devils and working cures; and on the third day I reach my goal" (Luke 13:32). Yes, Jesus had his goal. He had his third day. But that future had to be brought to the present as Jesus went about casting out devils. That goal had to be projected into the here and now as Jesus continued working cures. His third day would come only after today and tomorrow. His resurrection had to take place through the cross. The life of tomorrow must overcome the death of today. The vision of tomorrow must be built on the reality of life today. It must be born out of the womb of today.

MORAL CODES TO BE DISCARDED

The vision of tomorrow must be built on the reality of today. This is not to say that the reality of today has to be accepted without question. The opposite in fact is often the case. The reality of today has to be resisted and even rejected in order that the vision of a new tomorrow may be a real vision. That vision requires the courage to say in the hearing of all the world, "Not Today":

I always do the right thing
But not today.
I always do what people ask
But not today.
No!
In Nilchander valley
Where nothing grows old,
Nothing changes,
Flawless,
Starless,
Stormless,
The blood in my hot veins is rebellious.
Passionate as my blood,
Giant hills
Demonic stones,
I want to see the clouds
Breaking their heads
And I want to see the clouds
Fall into those gulfs,
Their limbs shattered.
I don't like pure blue sky.
I always do the right thing
But not today.
I know society has a loud voice
But my purse is full
I can buy the voice.
I know religion will be outraged
But I shall bow my head for a while
And it will be appeased.
I know something will cry in my soul
But psychology will find me an explanation
And keep my soul quiet.
I always do the right thing
But not today.[1]

No! Not today! This is a loud and emphatic no! It is a cry from the lungs of women in India. It is a shout of determination from the hearts of Asian women. And it can also be a chorus of pent-up bitterness from the souls of all the oppressed persons in the world—women, men, and children.

Women in India, for whom the poem speaks, and women in Asia are expected to do the things determined by tradition, prescribed by society, and required of them because they are women. They "in traditional view are seen as weak creatures, ornaments in the house, happy domestics who should not express anger, always look nice, etc. In addition, the feudal system makes women surrender to the man, who is the father, husband, or eldest son who is the king or heir."[2]

In those parts of Asia where Chinese culture dominates, there are the "three obediences and four virtues" (*san ch'ung su te*), the age-old moral codes imposed on women. The three obediences require that a woman before marriage should obey the father, in marriage the husband, and after the husband's death, the son; the four virtues expect them to be proper in behavior, language, appearance, and observance of duty. For women in traditional society these three obediences became fetters, making them prisoners within the family and society controlled and dominated by men. For them these four virtues severely restricted their activities, suppressed their true feelings, and confined them to a small world hidden away from the world of men. How much tragedy was created by the tyranny of these obediences and how many tears were shed under the bondage of these virtues will never be known.

But women in Asia are now saying that they are not going to do the "right thing" today as prescribed by these traditional virtues, which had held them captive in a world dominated by the male. These obediences deprived them of their humanity and their creative activity in society and made them inferior to men. The father can be wrong. The husband does not always have the truth. The eldest son can go astray. They have to be restrained, reprimanded, and corrected. Women are not going to keep quiet and comply, not anymore. At home and also in society when something is not right, it is no longer appropriate for women to swallow their anger and put on a smiling face. It is correct for women in Asia today to be outspoken in the family matters, social affairs, and political issues. It is also correct for them to be economically active and to become financially independent. Today they will do what their needs demand, not what the virtues of yesterday demanded. Today they will do what their conscience dictates, not what the moral codes of a male-dominated society dictated.

The stereotyped Asian social landscape must change. It must have new stars to shine over it. And a storm must rage through it to sweep away the three obediences and the four virtues of feudal society. There will be pain not only on the part of women but on the part of men. There will be the debris of the wrecked past after the storm. There will be a lot of crying for the lost past on the part of men and perhaps a lot of nostalgia too. But women have decided not to do the "right thing" today. Things that were right yesterday are not necessarily right today. It is their duty not to do what would be wrong. The vision of tomorrow can arise only out of their courage and determination to do what the exigencies of today prescribe.

LIFE BEGINS ON THE CROSS

In Asia, not only women are building their vision of tomorrow on the rejection of the wrongs of yesterday; outcasts too—the untouchables in India, the Burakumin in Japan, the aborigines in Australia—have begun to do the same. Here is a story of an "untouchable"—a story that tells us the kind of treatment they are subjected to:

> "Keep to the side of the road, oh low-caste vermin!" he suddenly heard someone shouting at him. "Why don't you call, you swine, and announce your approach! Do you know you have touched me and defiled me, cock-eyed son of a bow-legged scorpion! . . . "
>
> Bakha stood amazed and embarrassed. He was deaf and dumb. His senses were paralyzed. Only fear gripped his soul, fear and humility and servility. . . .
>
> Bakha hurried aside and, putting his basket and broom down, wrapped the folds of his turban anyhow. Then, wiping the tears off his face with his hands, he picked up his tools and started walking.
>
> "I am a sweeper, sweeper—untouchable! Untouchable! Untouchable! That's the word! Untouchable! I am an Untouchable!"
>
> Like a ray of light shooting through the darkness, the recognition of his position, the significance of his lot, dawned upon him. It illuminated the inner chambers of his mind. . . . A shock has passed through his perceptions, previously numb and torpid, and had sent a quiver into his being, stirred his nerves of sight, hearing, smell, touch, and taste, all into a quickening. "I am an Untouchable!" he said to himself, "an Untouchable!" He repeated the words in his mind for it was still a bit hazy and he felt afraid it might be immersed in the darkness again.[3]

Does this not remind us of the Old Testament injunction about those who have "a malignant skin disease" (leprosy)? They had to "wear their clothes torn, leave their hair dishevelled, conceal their upper lip, and cry: 'Unclean, unclean'" (Lev. 13:45). They were outcasts, ostracized by society. They had to live outside the city.

What devastating harm society has done to these persons! They have to bear the stigma of *hinin*—nonpersons, as the Burakumin in Japan were called of old. A society that brands certain individuals nonpersons—is it still a community of persons itself? A religion that consigns persons to the category of untouchables—can it be said to be a religion of compassion? Human beings who treat some other human beings as less than human—are they themselves truly human?

This is the reality of many societies in Asia today. But today *hinin* must refuse to be treated as nonpersons. They must shout out loud until others realize that there are no *hinin* in the human community. They must struggle until their brothers and sisters can touch them, embrace them, and take them into their homes and hearts. They must strive until those around them who have deprived them of their rights give those rights back to them. A vision of a world with no untouchables, no *hinin,* no persons without rights, must be the result of struggle against the inhuman reality of yesterday and today.

That struggle has begun in Asia. Harijans in India—"people of God," the name Gandhi gave to the untouchables—have started to organize themselves to fight their "untouchable" lot. They go to the police and say to their face: "You people have all your laws and regulations regarding Harijans and you publish in the newspapers that there are welfare facilities for Harijans, but you are doing nothing. We are standing on our own legs" to fight for justice for ourselves.[4] This must be a new voice for the police to hear. Not until a community is resonant with such a voice, and changed by it, will it be a fully *human* community. Is this not the reason why Jesus stayed close to outcasts—to have dignity and humanity restored to them? And was not a fully human community part of his vision of God's reign?

The vision of tomorrow extends as well to economic and political reality in Asia. It is the reality of economic progress at the cost of workers forced to sell their labor for a pittance. It is the reality of political oppression by those who hold power—the power that breaks families and destroys lives. The lament of a Korean wife whose beloved husband was beaten, tortured, and finally hanged by the Korean Central Intelligence Agency in 1974 reminds us of the tragic reality of many countries in Asia today:

> Where should I go,
> where should I go
> from now on, to meet you again?
>
> > Turning your head again and again
> > you'd leave our home in the morning,
> > and always come back in the evening,
> > always you came back to me. . . .
>
> Last spring, all of a sudden
> you were taken away
> without any reason.
>
> > After the spring, summer came
> > and autumn passed without
> > any sign of your return.

All through the long winter
I waited for spring to come
for, if spring came, I could see you
and I kept dreaming of that joyous day.
Even that dream I'm deprived of now,
I am refused even to feel the pain
that I had gone through
by waiting for you.

You were all that I lived for,
the spring where my strength to live came from,
Beloved one!
I would rather,
I would rather lie next to you
holding your pale tortured hands,
holding them tightly, tightly
and with a smile.
I would rather lie next to you
peacefully,
peacefully, and quietly.[5]

The lament moves one to tears. It is heartrending. It fills one with anger at the brutal political power that thinks nothing of destroying such a beautiful union between husband and wife.

This is a dirge. It is the dirge of a bereaved wife for her departed husband. But it is also a dirge for a government that cruelly took the life of her husband and the lives of many others. It is a dirge for a political power that multiplies widows and orphans.

But it is also a love song. The song is a dedication to that tender love of the husband who would, on his way out to work in the morning, "turn his head again and again" toward his wife standing at the door to see him off. The song is a confession of the love of the wife who "would rather lie next to her dead husband, holding his pale tortured hands tightly." Such love is indestructible. Police brutality cannot break it. Political cruelty cannot destroy it. It still binds the wife to her husband. It puts to shame those whose love is weak and calculating. It will kindle hope in those who have a vision of tomorrow built on the ruins of today.

With such love, tomorrow will become possible—not only possible but real. That love is the power of tomorrow, the energy of the future, and the glory of God's reign in the world. One recalls Jesus on his way to the cross. "Great numbers of people followed," Luke tells us, "many women among them, who mourned and lamented over him" (Luke 23:27). How much these women loved Jesus! They were like mothers and sisters to him, and he was to them like a son and a brother. But he is being taken to be executed on a cross. How could they not mourn? Who could stop them from lamenting? Their mourning and their lament must have filled the air. It must have gone into the hearts of spectators. It must have reached the hearts of those religious leaders who conspired to have all this happen; it must have shaken their souls. And it must have also reached Pontius Pilate, the Roman governor who became, against his better judgment, an accomplice in the hideous abuse of law and sent an innocent Jesus to die a shameful and painful death on the cross. It must have given unrest to his heart the rest of his life.

The crying of these women must have deeply touched Jesus. What he saw were tears of love. He "turned to them and said, 'Daughters of Jerusalem, do not weep for me; no, weep for yourselves and your children' " (23:28). Yes, for the city of God that is going to be deprived of Jesus, the Son of God, they should weep. Over the nation favored by God, the nation that murdered prophets and now is going to murder God's only Son, they should lament. And for themselves who looked for a messiah in him and now have to accompany him on his way to death, they should cry.

But Jesus had something else to say to those weeping women: "For the days are surely coming when they will say, 'Happy are the barren, the wombs that never bore a child, the breasts that never fed one' " (23:29). These are words of strong warning about God's judgment. This is an apocalyptic warning. This is a striking parallel to that apocalyptic passage in Mark's Gospel where it is said: "Alas for women with child in those days, and for those who have children at their breast!" (Mark 13:17). A city that is going to crucify the Son of God—is there a warning of future catastrophe strong enough for it? These words could have been put on Jesus' lips by the earliest Christian community. But if they had indeed come from him, Jesus must have said them with deep compassion.

But Jesus had to face up to the cross. He had to walk that road of death to the end. But that road to Golgotha was not the final end. It was the beginning of the road to life. The tomorrow of the resurrection dawned out of the yesterday and today of the cross. Some of those women who wept at the foot of Jesus' cross were the first ones to meet the risen Christ and announce his resurrection. It was Mary of Magdala who went to the disciples and broke the incredible news: "I have seen the Lord!" (John 20:18).

FAITH THAT MOVES MOUNTAINS

From the reality of today to the vision of tomorrow! A short statement; it can be said in a single breath. But what a long, long way it always is! From hours it becomes days. From days it turns into months, from months to years. And from years it can often extend to generations. But as long as there are the wrongs of yesterday, there must be the struggles of today. And as long as the struggle of today continues, the vision of tomorrow will not be expunged. After all, is not the seed of that vision of tomorrow contained in struggle within the reality of today?

For Hsu T'ien-Hsien, pastor of Lim-a-lai Presbyterian Church in Tainan, Taiwan, that journey from the reality of yesterday to the struggle of today took three years. Arrested for his participation in the Human Rights Day Rally in December 1979, he was sentenced to three years imprisonment. He was released on December 23, 1983, and returned to the joyous embrace of his family and to the hearty welcome of his own church members and other Christians. Such a welcome was ample testimony in itself that Hsu T'ien-Hsien did not commit the crime of sedition—a crime fabricated by government prosecutors to put behind bars those who strive for freedom, justice, and democracy in Taiwan.

A thanksgiving service was held in his small country church. It was filled to overflowing with members of his own flock, friends, and colleagues from all over Taiwan. It was a magnificent worship service filled with the tears of participants from beginning to end. Hymns were sung in tears. Scriptures were read in tears. The message was delivered in tears. Words of welcome home were said in tears also. God must have been in the midst of them shedding tears too. Hsu, standing on the pulpit from which he was taken away by the police three years earlier while he was conducting Christmas worship, concluded his words of thanks with these verses he entitled "On Leaving Prison":

Three long years.
I remember them in my heart.
It was a dark, dark night
Without a single star in the sky.
Intimidation, threat, and isolation
Torture, insult, and sarcasm
Were my constant companions.
Trials were open but ridden with bias.
Rampant in prison was political discrimination,
Dear ones were torn apart north and south.
Blessed that the Lord was my Refuge. . . .

Remembering brothers and sisters still in prison,
Sorrow and pain are beyond words.
May the Spirit of the Lord be with them
And rescue them from the pit of suffering,
Enabling them to sing with us hymns of praise
With one heart giving glory to the Savior Lord.
Wake up, O people of this land!
For our future and our destiny
Let us rouse ourselves and struggle together.
Water our own soil and fields
Bearing fruits of freedom, democracy, and human rights.[6]

It had been a long journey. And how long a prison journey can be! It is not just three years. It must have been ten years, fifty years, a hundred years. The psychological year in a prison cell must be many, many times longer than the calendar year. It is a bottomless time.

The past is still very much present in these verses—torture, threat, and rigged trial. The present is also there—the brothers and sisters serving their unjust sentences in prison. But the future is also very much present—fruits of freedom and democracy someday. The journey will still take a long time, but it is a journey lightened and guided by the vision of tomorrow.

It is a journey of faith. Without faith one cannot rise above the wrongs of yesterday. Yesterday will take hold of you, enslave you, imprison you. You become something that belongs to yesterday. Prison is the tomb that buries you with yesterday. For those who have conspired to put you there, you are no longer an active member of society. You are deleted from the lists of those who enjoy the rights to which citizens are entitled. You have no right to vote. You have no legal protection. But it is faith that keeps you alive in the tomb of prison. It is faith that maintains your rights as a human being. And it is faith that rescues you from yesterday and gives you today. It is this faith that gives you power to live today in the midst of yesterday and even to see the vision of tomorrow.

Faith is the power to see the vision of tomorrow in the darkness of today. The fact that you are released from the prison that failed to bury you in the tomb of yesterday does not mean you are free to create your own tomorrow. You are released from the prison of yesterday to face the struggle of today. You have to report to a police station regularly. Your whereabouts are closely followed. What you do and what you say are checked and rechecked to determine whether they are of a nature to initiate rebellion against the government. To live in such a today without faith is not possible. Without faith how can one cling to a vision of tomorrow in such a today?

Faith is not merely a pledge of loyalty to the traditions of the church. It is the living power that enables you to maintain your sanity in this maddening prison of threats, torture, and solitary confinement. Faith is the energy that makes it possible for you to maintain balance of spirit in this world of change and insecurity. Faith is the grace given to you by God, enabling you to reach out for life when confronted with death. Faith is the power of God's love that makes you strong when you are weak, gives you courage when you fear, and supports you when you falter. This must be the kind of faith Jesus meant when he said to his disciples: "If you have faith no bigger than a mustard-seed, you will say to this mountain, 'Move from here to there,' and it will move" (Matt. 17:20). Faith as small as a mustard seed, the smallest of all seeds, could move mountains! That must be a powerful faith. It was the faith of Jesus. And because of that faith, the light of life shines on the resurrection day out of the darkness of the crucifixion day.

It must be this kind of faith that sustains many persons who take part in the struggle of today and maintain the vision of tomorrow. Here is a hymn to such faith from China where the struggle for freedom and human rights goes on as elsewhere in Asia today:

Gazing at the shining stars from the abyss of pitch
darkness,
Looking for a resting place for the spirit in a
vast desert,
Listening to the silent conversations of all that exists
on this small earth,
Coming to grips with oneself in the infinite passage
of time. . . .

This is faith—the purest in human life.
Faith is there at the end of all searching,
Faith begins when this transient life merges with
eternal life.[7]

Is this not a deeply religious faith? Is this not a vision of tomorrow struggling to be born out of the darkness of today?

This is faith! This must be faith from God—the power of God's love that does not leave us alone in the terror of yesterday and keeps us forever in the struggle of today. This must be faith from God—the creating and saving power of God's love that makes light shine in the darkness and calls life to rise out of death. This is the faith of resurrection. And the resurrection of all the human beings of yesterday, today, and tomorrow is the vision of tomorrow that theology in Asia must find and explore.

20

Mask Dance

CRITICAL TRANSCENDENCE

Masks, as a cultural object used in religious ceremonies and community festivals, have been made in all parts of the world in all periods since the Stone Age. In ancient Greece, they were used in tragic and comic drama. In China actors wear masks to identify the characters they represent. And when actors do not wear masks, as in Peking opera or a Japanese Kabuki play, they have their faces thickly painted to give the effect of a mask. Many native North Americans put on masks in their ceremonies. In ceremonial dances of the Hopi Indians, masked figures representing gods visit the villages, bring rain for the fields, and presents for the children. The devil dance of Sri Lanka is intended to frighten away diseases and evil spirits. The tribal peoples of West Africa, New Guinea, and the Amazon region of South America make some of the most dramatic masks.[1]

Is the mask dance just entertainment? Is it only for the pleasure of the eye? Does the mask ceremony relate only to a make-believe world of spirits and demons extraneous to real life? Certainly not. In this universal culture and religious practice of the mask dance is hidden and revealed at one and the same time emotions deeply engrained in human nature—emotions of anger, joy, awe, fear, sorrow, hate, love, hope. In the mask dance, persons laugh and weep, discovering themselves and their society, reacting to the prevailing religious mores and political situations. The mask dance is of course entertainment. It helps persons forget the toil of the day and the worries of tomorrow. The mask dance also creates community. It brings persons together out of their nuclear families to form a larger family, sharing jokes and gossip, hopes and woes.

But more importantly, the mask dance is a social and political event. It portrays the plight of the poor oppressed by the rich. It depicts the tragedy of powerless citizens under a tyrannical regime. It also inspires human resourcefulness in an unjust and merciless society. It records a good measure of the political wisdom of a people.

The mask dance is also a religious event. It tells of divine intervention in human affairs. It shows that human beings are never far from God's favor or disfavor. It weaves their faith in the life to come into the stories of here and now. The mask dance can be a cry, a plea, a prayer, of a community in trouble. In it one discovers popular political theology. Through it God must be working to comfort persons, to give them hope and courage, and to prepare and empower them for social and political upheavals.

The power of the mask dance comes from what is called "experience of critical transcendence":

> In and through the mask dance the *minjung,* the ordinary folk, experience and express a critical transcendence over this world and laugh at its absurdity. By satirizing the aristocrats they stand over against the aristocrats. By laughing at the old monk they stand above him. . . . They [also] laugh at and make fun of their own fate in this world, thereby transcending their own conditions. . . . They not only see correctly the reality of the world, which both the rulers and leaders cannot see because of their obsession with and separation from the world, but also envision another reality over against and beyond this one which too both the rulers and leaders cannot see.[2]

This is true not only of Korean mask-dance drama. It is also true of puppet shows in Taiwan and elsewhere. This is folk drama and folk play—the drama and play of the people. Through them persons transcend themselves and their social conditions. They come to grips with their problems and gain strength to solve them. There are redemptive elements in those dramas and plays of the people. Like parables and folktales, they invite theologians and Christians to reflect on them and to discover faith, hope, and love in them. Theologians in Asia must begin to do creative theological work based on them.

As an example, there is the Korean mask dance of Bongsan. It relates the reunion of an old lady, Miyal-Halmi, with her husband, Yeonggam. The scene begins with Miyal-Halmi looking for her husband. "She had been separated from him many years ago when there was a war on the Cheju Island where they used to live. Then an old man comes in searching for his long-separated wife. These two stage a reunion . . . begin to tell each other all the troubles they have been through."[3] They had a lot to tell each other after all those years of separation and hardship:

> *Miyal:* How have you got along and where have you wandered since we were separated from each other?
>
> *Yeonggam:* Since the tumult separated us, I wandered here and there and experienced many difficulties.
>
> *Miyal:* What's the hat you're wearing?
>
> *Yeonggam:* Do you want to hear the story of this hat? I wandered here and there through the southern provinces. At that time I had no way or

means of earning a living. So I got a set of soldering tools and wandered around. One day I encountered a Sandai-Dogam [official in ancient Korea in charge of mask-dance drama]. He said to me: "There is no one who isn't afraid of the tigers of Mount Inwang [on the outskirts of Seoul], and there is no solderer who isn't afraid of Sandai-Dogam. You must pay the tax allotted to your work." I asked how much it was. He said the tax was one don and eight poon. It was too heavy for me. I earned eight poon a day at that time. If I paid the tax, I would go into debt at the rate of one don a day. So I said I could not pay the tax. On hearing this, he suddenly attacked me, and we began to fight. As a result, my clothes and hat were torn. I looked into my toolbox and found the skin of a dog. So I made a coronet of it and wore it. Don't I look like a Dongji [government] official?

Miyal: Dongji, Dongji, Dongji of bears! You could never be an official, could you? eh! [she cries]. Jeol, Jeol, Jeolsigoo [in the tune of a song]! Look at the man's miserable appearance, ladies and gentlemen! . . . Yeonggam! Your face looked as clean and white as silk when you lived with me. But now it looks like a withered branch. What has been the matter with you?

Yeonggam: Nothing was the matter with me. But acorns and potatoes are all that I have eaten till now. How have things been with our children? Is Moonyeol [their oldest son] doing well?

Miyal: Oh, no! As we were very badly off, I had him go out to gather firewood and he was eaten by a tiger in the woods.[4]

There is humor in the mask dance, to amuse the audience. There are jokes that lighten the hearts of spectators. But in the midst of jokes and humor the misery of the old husband and wife must have driven home to any audience the cruelty and mercilessness of government officials.

Spectators must be moved by this seemingly ordinary tale of separation and reunion. As the old husband and wife recount the troubles they have gone through, tears must begin to flow behind the masks. And the voices coming through the masks must turn into wailing. Those in the audience cannot sit there unaffected. They must find it difficult to hold back their own tears. It is all because of government cruelty! The youthful years of the husband and wife are gone forever; the wrinkles on the masks make that sadly evident. Their zest for life is gone; the gray hairs on the masks make that painfully obvious. And their hope for tomorrow? It seems all buried in the yesterday that will not return.

They have gone through a lot, this old couple. Besides the pain of separation, they suffered much at the hands of government authorities—tax officials from the ruthless ruling power whose pleasure seemed to consist solely in making others' lives miserable. They were reduced to dire poverty. The old woman had to send her son out to the mountain to gather firewood.

But tragedy is not content with paying a single visit, as a Chinese saying goes.

Their eldest son, their hope and their future, was killed by a tiger. The killer-tiger alludes, of course, to those brutes in high places who drain to the last dregs the lifeblood of the poor.

The mask dance has projected onto the stage of life a clear image of the human person over against that of oppressive power. "Human person" is not a matter of definition, but a matter of life with deep involvement in the tragic affairs of society. "Human person" is life abused, the spirit crushed, the mind benumbed—in short, humanity under the unbearable weight of inhumanity. "Human person" is the image of God that evil forces in the world are out to stalk, overpower, and destroy.

JESUS: THE MASK OF GOD

But strangely, the more the masks of the old husband and wife in the mask dance become contorted with pain, agony, and tears, the more their humanity cries out from them. The masks are now exploding with the power of anguish restrained behind them until now, holding both actors and audience spellbound in a communion of suffering and sorrow. The spectators have become absorbed into the masks. The audience participates in the sad story. This is their lot in this world. In a world where aristocrats rule, it is the people who suffer hunger, separation, exploitation, beatings. . . . There is no escape! And yet both performers and audience participate in the storytelling with jokes and laughter. "[They] weep and laugh at the same time."[5]

So, the masks are the audience themselves. The story told in the mask dance is their own story. The tragic drama performed on the stage is their own drama. The pain of the masks is their pain. The wrinkles on the masks are their own wrinkles. The sighs coming from the masks are their own sighs. And the tears from the eyes of the masks are their own tears. A communion of persons in suffering is created by the mask dance.

There must be some Christians in the audience. They must also take part in this communion. For them a transformation may be taking place as the mask dance moves to its climax of sorrow and suffering. To them the masks of the old husband and wife begin to remind them of that ugly, painful, and helpless cross that once stood on a hill in the faraway place called Golgotha. The reminder may be so compelling that it does not appear to be a matter of coincidence. A mysterious hand seems to bring together the mask and the cross. The cross transcends its particular space and time to become present in the mask. The mask too seems to break out of its spatial and temporal framework to be transposed into the cross.

Transposition grows stronger as the mask dance reaches the height of the tragedy. There in the mask dance Jesus, a man of sorrow, seems to appear. In the pain of that old husband and wife one perceives the pain of Jesus. In the audience moved to tears by the mask dance one seems to catch sight of the suffering Jesus. The communion of suffering emerging from the mask dance is a communion of performers, audience, *and* Jesus. Is this just a coincidence? If it is, it must be an extraordinary coincidence. And what is an extraordinary coincidence if not divine providence?

Why does Jesus who suffered on the cross appear in the mask dance? Why is he in the puppet show? Why is he encountered in the stories and dramas of ordinary persons' lives? Why is he not confined to Palestine where he was born, lived, worked, and died? Why was he not bound to the pages of the New Testament that testify to his birth, death, and resurrection? Why is he not restricted to the territorial space gained by Christianity through witnessing to his message? And why is he not limited to the understanding and interpretation of him meticulously, scientifically, and exhaustively done by the teachers and theologians of the Christian church all this time?

Why? Because Jesus is the mask of God and not simply the mask of the faith embraced, interpreted, and proclaimed by the first generation of Christians and by succeeding generations. He is the mask of God who created heaven and earth. He is the mask of God whose ultimate concern is the redemption of creation in its entirety. Jesus is the mask of this God. The witness of the Bible and of the Christian community in every age should enable Christians to recognize that mask of God beyond the confines of "their" Christianity worked out in their particular space-time framework.

Philip, one of Jesus' disciples, once asked him: "Lord, show us God and we ask no more." There was a tone of earnestness in Philip's request. But Jesus was disappointed. He did not conceal his disappointment when he answered: "Have I been all this time with you, Philip, and you still do not know me? Anyone who has seen me has seen God" (John 14:8–9). Jesus' disciples must have been puzzled. They were looking for a God wearing the mask of a warrior-king who would drive out the Roman armies from their land and lead their humiliated nation to new glory. The religious authorities who treated Jesus with contempt and hostility must have become angry at those words. Anyone who claims to be an alter ego of God commits the heinous sin of blasphemy and deserves to die. The Roman rulers too must have been greatly worried when they heard what he had said. Someone who declares openly that he is an alter ego of God could be a dangerous political demagogue. That person must be done to death as an enemy of the empire.

But Jesus is the mask of God. Those who hear him hear God. Those who see him see God. Those who are touched by him are touched by God. God is not hidden in a sanctuary out of sight of the people, but out in the open among the people. That God is not especially fussy about all those religious laws and taboos handed down from one generation to the next. That God does not hesitate to ignore human traditions when persons tormented with disease and beset with danger need immediate help. That God is not very much concerned about remaining within the fixed boundaries of faith and religion, but wanders out of it from time to time, recognizing and commending Gentiles who show faith in God. That God is the God of the poor, the lost, the outcast, the God of those whose hearts have been broken in this world of suffering and pain. Jesus is the mask of this God.

This is something so startlingly new that Jesus' first followers, including his disciples, must have learned it only with great difficulty. But learn it they had to. This is also something so strange to many Christians today, including theologians, that it is still not easy for them to accept. But accept they must. Particularly Christians and theologians in Asia must dedicate themselves to this new learning—learning that the God of Jesus is the Lord of all space and time, the Lord of creation, that this God has never ceased to be the Lord of Asia since the beginning of time and will remain so until the end of time. How exciting to do theology with this God!

But Jesus is not merely the mask of God—a mask perhaps beautifully made of wood, marble, or precious metal, hanging in a place of worship to be revered as a religious object and admired as a cultural masterpiece. This is what has often been done to Jesus as the mask of God. Many cathedrals in Europe, which have become historical monuments for tourists, contain magnificent masks of God in paintings and in sculptural forms. Do these masks of God inspire us to envision the Jesus who radically departed from the religious ways of his time and opened up a new path of faith among those outside the synagogue, the temple, and outside his own religion? One has to have a strong imagination to visualize that Jesus, the true mask of God, in those cathedrals, churches, and museums.

But Jesus is not just the mask of God. He is the mask dance of God. He dances and dances until the mask dance of God becomes the mask dance of the people. He continues dancing the mask dance of God until persons realize God's presence with them and God's reality in them. He stages the mask dance of God so that they can hear, see, and touch God. And as Jesus goes on dancing the mask dance of God, he creates a community of hope—a community with a capacity for suffering as well as for rejoicing, a capacity for pain as well as for comfort, a capacity for tears as well as for laughter, a capacity for despair as well as for hope, a capacity for dying as well as for living.

Jesus begins his mask dance of God and the people with a solemn declaration in the synagogue of Nazareth, his native town, quoting Isaiah, that towering prophet in ancient Israel:

> The spirit of the Lord is upon me because he has anointed me;
> he has sent me to announce good news to the poor,
> to proclaim release for prisoners and recovery of sight for the blind;
> to let the broken victims go free,
> to proclaim the year of the Lord's favour [Luke 4:18].

This is a message of hope. This is a proclamation of the arrival of a new day. This is a declaration of the presence of God's reign.

This sounds familiar, does it not? It reminds us of Mary's Magnificat. Jesus' mask dance begins in fact with the Magnificat. It began, in other words, when Jesus was still in his mother's womb. The message of God's reign is a message from the womb, from the very depth of the creation of life, where the savior is conceived. It is a message from the womb of hope and life. Is not something very important disclosed to us here? It is this: the womb of despair is the womb of hope! The womb of unrequited bitterness becomes the womb of God's promise come true! That is why out of that womb we hear not only sorrow but also joy. From the pain of birth we also hear the joyous cry of new life. From the abyss of suffering we also see light.

Death, then, does not have the last word. When Jesus becomes fatally exposed to human sin, God overcomes it with forgiveness. When Jesus succumbs to pain and thirst, God heals and quenches with love. And when death finally comes, God gives birth to a new life that will never die. From that cross of death these words of life are heard from Jesus: "I am the resurrection and I am life. If a man has faith in me, even though he die, he shall come to life" (John 11:25). Jesus' mask dance of God is the mask dance of life and resurrection.

THE APPROACH OF DAWN

Jesus' mask dance of God is a mask dance of faith—faith that his followers are not left alone to cope with their misery. It is the faith that creates communion with a strong sense of divine presence. It is the faith that empowers his followers to go on living and hoping in the midst of suffering. It is the faith that enables them to laugh while their hearts are filled with sorrow. It is also the faith that makes it possible for them to exchange jokes and stories with one another even though life is so difficult. Knowing it or not, they become actors in the mask dance of faith.

It is this mask dance of faith that the sensitive mind of Christians watch today in Asia. It has different plots. It plays to different tunes. And it is performed by actors wearing different masks. But it is the same mask dance of faith. A poem from China, written by someone struggling for freedom and human dignity, is such a mask dance of faith. It is entitled "Believe in Life!":

> While I am imprisoned in a cage of pitch darkness,
> Still able to endure the pain from torture,
> I will struggle to rise up, bite open my fingers,
> And with my blood write on the wall: Believe in Life!
>
> After I have gone through all hardships of life,
> Dying at dawn surrounded by my posterity,
> I will summon my last breath with all my strength,
> Crying as loudly and as clearly as I can: Believe in
> Life! . . .
>
> If the earth goes round and round without ceasing,
> If history has a new journey to make,
> If my children and grandchildren go on living,
> Then I believe in the future. Believe in Life![6]

What a mask dance of faith! We do not know whether that poet is a Christian or not. We do not know whether the poet believes in God. But does it matter? The faith that fills that poem is a witness to God. That faith is stronger than the faith of many of us Christians.

This is a powerful hymn of light in the midst of the darkness. It expresses strong faith in tomorrow despite the suffering of yesterday and today. It expresses magnificent hope in life faced with the threat of death. This is a hymn of the people, a hymn of their faith. From past darkness we catch a glimpse of the radiance of the future; in the hell of cruel inhumanity we find signs of humanity.

Mary and Jesus, the Mother and the Son, the Magnificat and the proclamation in Nazareth! The creative force of God and that of the people become united in a message of hope for the blind, the poor, the outcast, the broken victims of oppressive powers. The mask dance of God is the mask dance of the Magnificat. This is Jesus' mask dance. And it is the mask dance of the people.

The cross is the grand finale of this mask dance of God danced by Jesus. The actors on the stage are Jesus and God. The humor is gone, the laughter is ended. All movement comes to a standstill. The mask dance develops into an intense dialogue between the two actors—a dialogue to probe the meaning of this deep suffering, a dialogue to scale the mountain of pain and agony, a dialogue to make a breakthrough from the dark Friday to the bright Sunday:

> *Jesus:* Father, forgive them; they do not know what they are doing [Luke 23:34].
>
> *God:* [Jesus said to the woman]: "Your sins are forgiven" [Luke 7:47].
>
> *Jesus:* Mother, there is your son; there is your mother [John 19:27].
>
> *God:* [Mary said]: "God's mercy sure from generation to generation" [Luke 1:59].
>
> *Jesus:* Today you shall be with me in Paradise [Luke 23:43].
>
> *God:* [Jesus said]: "How blest are you who are in need; the kingdom of God is yours" [Luke 6:20; par. Matt. 5:3].
>
> *Jesus:* My God, my God, why hast thou forsaken me? [Mark 15:34; par. Matt. 27:46].
>
> *God:* Thou art my son, my beloved; on thee my favour rests [Mark 1:11; par. Matt. 3:17; Luke 3:22].
>
> *Jesus:* I thirst [John 19:28].
>
> *God:* [Jesus said]: "Whoever believes in me shall never be thirsty" [John 6:35].
>
> *Jesus:* It is finished [John 19:30, RSV].
>
> *God:* [Jesus said]: "They will kill [the Son of Man], and three days after being killed, he will rise again" [Mark 9:31; par. Matt. 16:21].
>
> *Jesus:* Father, into thy hands I commit my spirit [Luke 23:46].

This is a painful finale. It is also a magnificent beginning. The mask dance of God cannot end on the cross. It must move on to the resurrection.

The mask dance of Bongsan does not end in despair. It ends in the hope for a new dawn. How else are we to understand the advice of a village elder at the end of the mask dance: "Children," he calls to those deeply immersed in the agony of their past and present, and dreaming a dream of a different future: "Awake! The dawn is approaching from the east and the south."[7] It has been a long night. The tragedy of life lasts long. It is as long as the night. The people must be tired. Many children have fallen asleep on the ground. And babies are sound asleep in their mothers' arms. It is time to wake up and brace oneself for the work and problems of another day.

But this is also a call of hope. The night must yield to the dawn. The darkness must give way to the light. Despair must lead to hope. And death must be overcome by life. One seems to hear faintly in this call of the village elder the call of the cross in the depth of suffering humanity to the resurrection in the heart of the living God. In fact the risen Lord is already present at dawn on that resurrection day. Mary of Magdala was so close to him. But the weariness and sadness of those last few days cast a thick veil over her mind's eye. She saw the tomb empty. Someone must have removed the body of Jesus from the tomb. She was overcome with grief again and began to weep. But the risen Christ was right beside her. The dawn of the resurrection day had already arrived. "Mary!" Jesus called her. The call came from beyond the empty tomb. It was a call from beyond the cross. She must have understood at once why the tomb had to be empty, why the cross was not the end of the future. "My Master!," she exclaimed. Her mission was to bring that message of the new dawn, the good news of new life, to Jesus' disciples.

The vision of tomorrow is the vision of faith. With that faith one can endure the suffering of today. With that faith one can live tenaciously, hope against hope, and stride forward without yielding to despair. And with that faith one can be together with others to become part of the redemptive force of God's love working in human community. It is that vision of faith that one sees in the poem of a Tamil teacher working among estate workers in Sri Lanka. He calls his poem "For Sure the New Age Will Dawn":

In the distance I see a new vision.
Won't you come quickly and see?
Look, its scattered glow is everywhere!
Look, I will sing a new hope.

We are the free ones in slavery,
Flowers duped into withering;
Let us all join together and fight,
Let us in dying seek life.

The desolate places we turn into oases,
Made tender green shoots come up;
Yet we have nothing saved for the future,
Nor have we hate in our hearts. . . .

Enough that others lived by our blood,
Now a new generation must live;
If they come to harm us we'll not cringe,
We'll stand ready to resist.

Burnt daily by the heat of the sun,
We are shrivelled human forms;
Yet, no longer shall we wilt in fear,
For e'en God weeps with our pain.

Now, in these blackened souls there is life,
In our eyes there's a new flame;
It will burn as unquenchable fire,
For sure, the new age will dawn.

It's our task now to kindle a light,
To burn in the eyes of the poor;
We shall live no longer as cowards,
For in victory our thirst will be quenched.[8]

The new vision of a new age comes from faith that has strength but no hatred. Believing in life, it faces death. It still has evil forces to resist but is aflame with hope for the generation to come. This is a song of victory in the midst of pain, comforted and emboldened by faith in the "God who weeps with their pain." Do we not hear in this song of victory the voice of Jesus saying: "In the world you will have trouble. But courage! The victory is mine; I have conquered the world" (John 16:33).

Theology is born out of such faith. It draws its strength from the faith that gives rise to a vision of tomorrow both inside and outside the church. Theology is a testimony to that faith in the love of God who makes life and world new. It grows out of the faith that hears a loud voice proclaiming from the throne: "Now at last God has his dwelling among men! He will dwell among them and they shall be his people" (Rev. 21:3). Can the vision of Christians and theologians be less than the vision of God dwelling among all peoples? And how can we have such a vision unless we are able to attune ourselves to that resonance, that *hibiki,* that echo, of God among persons both inside and outside the church?

Theology is poetry of God in the prose of the people. It is God's hymn in the songs of men, women, and children. It is God's story in the parables and folktales of our brothers and sisters. Theology is God's mask dance played in the mask dance of those who, in the darkness of night, long for the approach of dawn. Theology is confession. It is witness. It is testimony. And above all, theology is prayer: "God's will be done on earth as it is in heaven."

Notes

INTRODUCTION

1. Richard M. Dorson, ed., *Folktales Told around the World* (Chicago: The University of Chicago Press, 1975), pp. 253–257

1. LIFE IS CODED

1. *The New Caxton Encyclopedia* (London: Caxton Publications Limited, 1979), Vol. 19, p. 281.
2. *World Book Encyclopedia* (Chicago: Field Enterprises Educational Corporation, 1960), Vol. 19, p. 400.
3. See Johannes C. Anderson, *Myths and Legends of the Polynesians* (Rutland, Vt./ Tokyo: Charles E. Tuttle Company, Publishers, 1969), p. 353.
4. See Mircea Eliade, *From Primitives to Zen, a Thematic Sourcebook of the History of Religions* (London: Collins, 1977), p. 110.
5. See *Modern Chinese Poetry,* trans. Harold Acton and Ch'en Shih-Hsiang (London: Duckworth, 1936), pp. 74–75.
6. Eliade, *From Primitives to Zen,* pp. 34–35. Hiranyagarbha means "golden germ (garbha)." Prajapati is lord of creatures.

2. SIGNS OF THE TIMES

1. See Szuma Chien, *Records of the Historian,* trans. Yang Hsien-yi and Gladys Yang (Hong Kong: The Commercial Press, 1974), pp. 233–35.
2. Gandhi, *Satyagraha in South Africa* (Madras: S. Ganesan, Publisher, 1928), p. 173. Quoted in Nirmal Minz, *Mahatma Gandhi and Hindu-Christian Dialogue* (Madras: The Christian Literature Society, 1970), p. 7.
3. Quoted in Minz, *Mahatma Gandhi and Hindu-Christian Dialogue,* p. 18.
4. Minz, *Mahatma Gandhi and Hindu-Christian Dialogue,* p. 7.
5. Gandhi, *India of My Dreams* (Bombay: Hind Kitab Ltd., 1947), p. 14. Quoted in Minz, *Mahatma Gandhi and Hindu-Christian Dialogue,* p. 14.

3. PORTENTS OF OUR DAY

1. *Time,* March 29, 1982, p. 17.
2. *Comprehensive Study on Nuclear Weapons,* Report of the Secretary General, United Nations General Assembly, 12 September 1980, p. 10.
3. *Comprehensive Study on Nuclear Weapons,* p. 10.
4. *Time,* May 29, 1982, p. 17.

5. "A Pastoral Letter on Human Survival," in *engage/social action,* published by the Board of Church and Society, United Methodist Church, Vol. 6, No. 1, January 1978, pp. 27–28. Quoted in *Faith, Science and the Future,* Preparatory Readings for the 1979 World Conference of WCC, ed. Paul Abrecht (Geneva: WCC, 1978), p. 114.

6. Cf. C. S. Song, *The Compassionate God* (Maryknoll: Orbis Books and London: SCM Press, 1982), pp. 22–25 for a different interpretation.

7. *International Herald Tribune,* December 13, 1982, p. 4.

8. *Asia 1979 Yearbook* (Hong Kong: Far Eastern Economic Review, 1979), p. 20.

9. Ibid., p. 21.

10. See "Hong Kong, A Special Report," in *International Herald Tribune,* December 16, 1982, p. 9S.

11. Ibid., p. 9S.

12. Ibid., p. 9S.

4. SPEAKING IN PARABLES

1. *The Interpreter's One-Volume Commentary,* ed. Charles M. Laymon (Nashville/New York: Abingdon Press, 1971), p. 348.

2. Cf. *Webster's New World Dictionary* (New York: The World Publishing Company, 1970), p. 1028.

3. Norman Perrin, *Rediscovering the Teaching of Jesus* (London: SCM Press Ltd., 1967), p. 87.

4. Perrin, *Rediscovering the Teaching of Jesus,* p. 82.

5. See *The Threefold Lotus Sutra* (New York/Tokyo: Weatherhill/Kosei, 1975), pp. 110–25.

6. See glossary in ibid., pp. 371–83.

7. *The Buddhist Tradition,* ed. William Theodore de Bary (New York: Vintage Books, 1972), p. 85.

8. Reproduced in Perrin, *Rediscovering the Teaching of Jesus,* p. 91.

9. See ibid., pp. 92–93.

10. Ibid., p. 94.

5. IMAGING THEOLOGY

1. Basho, *The Narrow Road to the Deep North,* trans. with an introduction by Nobuyuki Yuasa (London: Penguin Books, 1966), p. 43.

2. Ibid., p. 33.

3. See "Introduction" in ibid., p. 32.

4. Concerning covenant as a political as well as religious concept, see C. S. Song, *The Compassionate God,* pp. 32–35.

5. For excellent discussion of *han* in the Korean context, see Suh Nam Dong, "Towards a Theology of *Han,*" in *Minjung Theology,* ed. Kim Yong Bok (Singapore: Christian Conference of Asia [CCA], 1981), pp. 51–61. The quotation on *han* is found on p. 54.

6. See de Bary, *The Buddhist Tradition,* pp. 61–64.

6. RHYTHMS OF PASSION

1. Lin Yutang, *My Country and My People* (New York: Reynal and Hitchcock, 1938), p. 302.

2. These phrases are from ibid., pp. 387–38.

3. See Shoji Tsutomu, "Living in Christ with People," in *The Japan Christian Quarterly,* Fall 1981, XLVII/4, p. 199.

4. Quoted by Suh Nam Dong, "Towards a Theology of *Han,*" pp. 58-59.

5. Ibid., p. 58.

6. From *An Anthology of Taiwanese Popular Literature* (T'aiwan Minchien Wenhsieh Chih, ed. Lee Shiann-Chang, Taipei: Cowboy Publishing Co., Ltd., 1978), p. 21 (translation from the Chinese original by C.S.S.).

7. The story is titled "The Shrew." See *Chinese Literature, Popular Fiction and Drama*, ed. H. C. Chang (Edinburgh: University Press, 1973), pp. 32–55.

8. See *A Thousand Years of Vietnamese Poetry,* ed. and trans. Nguyen Ngoc Bich (New York: Alfred A. Knopf, 1975), pp. 206–7.

9. The four passages known as the Servant Songs are: Isa. 42:1–4; 49:1–6; 50:4–9; and 52:13–53:12.

7. WHAT DO STATISTICS MEAN?

1. See James Avery Joyce, *The New Politics of Human Rights* (London: The Macmillan Press, Ltd., 1978), p. 83.

2. *CCA News*, January 15, 1981, p. 3.

3. *CCA News*, May 15, 1981, p. 7.

4. The phrase is from the heading of the second chapter in *The New Politics of Human Rights.*

5. The story is told in *Convictions, Political Prisoners and Their Stories,* eds., Arthur Dobrin, Lyn Dobrin & Thomas F. Liotti (Maryknoll: Orbis Books, 1981), pp. 76–90.

6. This story told by Sheila Cassidy, an English doctor who herself was arrested later, is found in Chris Ledger, *Across the Currents* and reproduced in *CCA News,* October 15, 1981, p. 3.

7. Harry Anlonides, *Multinationals and the Peaceable Kingdom* (Toronto: Clarke, Erwin & Company Limited, 1978), p. 7.

8. See *North-South, a Programme for Survival* (London: Pan Books, 1980), pp. 16 and 50.

9. Kim Yong Bok, "The Power of TNCs in the Stories of the Asian People," in *The Clenched Fists of Struggle* (Hong Kong: Urban Rural Mission-CCA, 1981, pp. 17–40), p. 36.

10. In *Minangkabau! Story of People vs TNCs in Asia* (Hong Kong: Urban Rural Mission-CCA, 1981), p. 36.

11. Quoted in *CCA News,* November 15, 1982.

12. See *CCA News,* March 15, 1982, p. 6.

13. *CCA News,* March 15, 1982, p. 6.

14. George Orwell, *Nineteen Eighty-Four* (London: Penguin Books, 1954), p. 7.

15. Ibid., p. 68.

16. Ibid., p. 239.

8. STONES CRY OUT

1. Chen Hsiu-Hsi, *The Last Love,* a Collection of Poems, trans. Ching Hsiang (Taipei: Li Poetry Magazine, 1978), p. 39.

2. Jon Sobrino, S.J., *Christology at the Crossroads* (Maryknoll: Orbis Books, 1978), p. 213.

3. See *No Time for Crying,* ed. Alison Wynne (Hong Kong: Resource Centre for Philippine Concerns, 1979), p. 12.

4. See *No Time for Crying,* pp. 10–11.

5. See *Suffering and Hope, an Anthology of Asian Writings,* eds. Ron O'Grady and Lee Soo Jin (Singapore: CCA, 1978), p. 35.

6. This account is given by Kim San in ibid., p. 35.

9. BIRTH OF FREEDOM

1. The poem is by Cheng Chun-Ming, a Taiwanese poet, and published in *Li Poetry Magazine,* No. 91 (Taipei: Li Poetry Magazine, 1978), p. 24 (translation from the Chinese original by C.S.S.).

2. *Self-Determination* (New York: Formosan Christians for Self-determination), No. 1, March 1973.

3. *Self-Determination,* No. 9, December 1977.

4. Translated and adapted from the Chinese original by C.S.S.

5. Ann Ming, *Taiwanese Voice* (London: British Council of Churches, 1981), p. 16.

6. Ann Ming, *Taiwanese Voice,* p. 16.

7. The poem is by Lin Lin in *Li Poetry Magazine,* No. 93, p. 43 (translation from the Chinese original by C.S.S.)

10. PASSION OF THE WOMB

1. The poem "The Newborn Child" by See Yeon Yuen is reproduced in *CCA News,* Aug. 15, 1977, p. 12.

2. Chen Hsiu-Hsi, "The First Baby," in *The Last Love,* p. 15.

3. *Women and Men in Asia,* the Women Question in Asian Context (Hong Kong: Asia Regional Office-World Student Christian Federation, 1976), Part I, p. 102.

4. For the discussion here, see Phyllis Tribble, *God and the Rhetoric of Sexuality* (Philadelphia: Fortress Press, 1978), pp. 100–104.

5. Tribble, *God and the Rhetoric of Sexuality,* p. 102.

11. A CLOUD OF WITNESSES

1. Tribble, *God and the Rhetoric of Sexuality,* p. 104.

2. Cf. David Barrett, *World Christian Encyclopedia* (London: Oxford University Press, 1982), p. 782.

3. The poem is by Kirinji Thennavan. See *For the Dawning of the New,* eds. Jeffrey Abayasekera and D. Preman Niles (Singapore: CCA, 1981), p. 16.

12. COMMUNION OF COMPASSION

1. Akitagawa Lyunosuke, "Kumo no Ito" (The Spider Thread), in *Collected Writings of Akitagawa Lyunosuke* (Tokyo: Kadogawa Bookshop, 1953), pp. 83–84 (abridged translation from the Japanese original by C.S.S.).

2. Quoted in H. Wolfgang Schumann, *Buddhism, an Outline of its Teachings and Schools* (London: Rider & Company, 1973), p. 39.

3. See *The Interpreter's One-Volume Commentary on the Bible,* p. 665.

4. See C. K. Barrett, *The New Testament Background, Selected Documents* (New York: Harper Torches, Harper & Row Publishers, 1961), pp. 132–33.

5. See *The Wisdom of Buddhism,* ed. Christmas Humphreys (London: Curzon Press Ltd., 1979), pp. 83–85.

6. From "The Lotus Flowers of the Wonderful Law," in *The Threefold Sutra,* p. 326.

7. From Siksha-Samuccaya (pp. 256–7), complied by Santideva. See Humphreys, *The Wisdom of Buddhism,* pp. 143–44.

13. BROKEN HUMANITY

1. See Mircea Eliade, *From Primitives to Zen,* p. 31.

2. From *UNICEF Letter,* October 1979, reproduced in *CCA News,* March 15, 1980.

3. Schumann, *Buddhism,* p. 20. The book contains a number of reproductions of Buddha statues in various postures.

4. Ibid., p. 20.

5. Ibid., p. 31.

6. Ibid., p. 47.

7. From "To the Buddha—a Plea" by Kirinji Thennavan, in *For the Dawning of the New,* pp. 17–18.

8. See *Suffering and Hope,* p. 29.

9. From *The Sutra of Wei Lang* (Hui Neng). See Humphreys, *The Wisdom of Buddhism,* pp. 37–38.

14. STRUGGLE FOR WHOLENESS

1. Thennavan, "To the Buddha—a Plea," pp. 17–20.

2. See Humphreys, *The Wisdom of Buddhism,* p. 93.

3. From "Introduction" in Kirinji Thennavan, *For the Dawning of the New,* p. 2.

4. Reproduced in *From the Womb of Han, Stories of Korean Women Workers* (Hong Kong: Urban Rural Mission-CCA, 1982), p. 21.

5. The report is reproduced in *From the Womb of Han,* pp. 31–38.

6. See *From the Womb of Han,* pp. 68–69.

7. From *Letters from South Korea* by T. K. (Tokyo: Iwanami Shoten, 1976), p. 9.

8. By Gerald O'Collins, S.J., reproduced in *CCA News,* December 15, 1979, p. 8.

9. See *Voices* (Hong Kong: Urban Rural Mission-CCA), Vol. 6, No. 3, May/June 1982, p. 7.

15. GOD OF COMPASSION

1. Richard M. Dorson, *Folk Legends of Japan* (Rutland, Vt./Tokyo: Charles E. Tuttle Company, Publishers, 1962), pp. 37–8.

2. The novel was abridged and translated into English by Arthur Waley with the title *Monkey* (New York: John Day, 1944).

3. C. T. Hsia, *The Classic Chinese Novel* (New York: Columbia University Press, 1968), p. 117.

4. Quoted in "Hsi-yu-chi k'ao-cheng," *Hu Shih wen-ts'un* (Taipei: Chung-hua shu-chu, 1963; 4 vols.), Vol. 2, p. 357. Reproduced in Hsia, *The Classic Chinese Novel,* pp. 117–18.

5. See *Poems of the Late T'ang,* trans. with an introduction by A. C. Graham (London: Penguin Books, 1977), pp. 117.

6. From the preface to the *Heavenly Questions* in *The Songs of Ch'u.* Reproduced in Graham, *Poems of the Late T'ang,* p. 117.

7. Originally Kuan-yin was a male Bodhisattva called Avalokitesvara. The name consists of two parts: *"avalokita,* a past passive participle meaning 'seen' and *isvara* meaning 'Lord.' It is translated in various ways—'the lord who looks down,' 'the lord who is seen,' 'the lord of compassionate glances' " (Kenneth Ch'en, *Buddhism in China,* Princeton: Princeton University Press, 1972), p. 340. In Japanese Pure Land Buddhism, Avalokitesvara is the chief minister of Amitaba.

8. See "Introduction" to "Kannon Who Substituted" in Dorson, *Folk Legends of Japan,* p. 38.

16. REIGN OF GOD

1. Eliade, *From Primitives to Zen,* p. 86.

2. Ibid., p. 91.

3. Anderson, *Myths and Legends of the Polynesians,* p. 353.

4. The story was told by Bishop Julio Xavier Labayen in his D. T. Niles Memorial Lecture, "Asian Suffering and the Christian Hope," given at the Sixth Assembly of CCA, Penang, 1977. See *Testimony amid Asian Suffering,* ed. T. K. Thomas (Singapore: CCA, 1977; pp. 19–25), p. 20.

5. See "Children of War," a special report, in *Time,* January 11, 1982.

6. See *Testimony amid Asian Suffering,* p. 20.

7. See Ernie Regehr, *Militarism and the World Military Order* (Geneva: WCC, 1980), p. 33.

8. Joachim Jeremias, *Rediscovering the Parables* (New York: Charles Scribner's Sons, 1966), pp. 117.

9. Cf. ibid., pp. 116–17.

17. A MESSIANIC BANQUET

1. See *Minutes and Report,* Sixth Assembly, CCA (Singapore: CCA, 1977), p. 93.

2. See *Faith, Science and the Future,* p. 133.

3. Cited in *Faith, Science and the Future,* p. 133.

4. Ibid., p. 134.

5. Ibid.

6. *Towards a Church of the Poor,* ed. J. de Santa Ana (Geneva: WCC, 1979), p. 22.

7. Jeremias, *Rediscovering the Parables,* p. 146.

8. Ibid., p. 140.

18. SPACE OF SALVATION

1. Yoji Inoue, *Watakushi no naka no Kirisuto* (Tokyo: Shufu no Tomo Sha, 1978), pp. 131–32 (abridged translation from the Japanese original by C.S.S.).

2. For these statistics see *Asia Yearbook 1979* under the names of the countries cited.

3. Reproduced in *Asiaweek,* July 30, 1982, p. 55.

4. Suzuki, *Essays in Zen Buddhism,* Third Series, pp. 365–66.
5. Ibid., p. 366.
6. Reproduced in *Pintig, Poems and Letters from Philippine Prisons* (Hong Kong: Resource Centre for Philippine Concerns, 1979), p. 34.

19. VISION OF TOMORROW

1. The poem is by Amita Pritam from India. See *Voices of Women, an Asian Anthology,* Vol. II, ed. Alison O'Grady (Seoul: Asian Church Women's Conference, 1982), p. 62.
2. Endrang W. Supardan, "Women and Human Rights," in *Women and Men in Asia,* p. 40.
3. From *Suffering and Hope,* pp. 19–20.
4. See *Inheritors of the Earth, Report of the People's Forum on People, Land and Justice,* ed. Alison O'Grady (Hong Kong: Urban Rural Mission-CCA, 1981), p. 28.
5. By Kwan Soon Hi, in *Letters from South Korea,* pp. 379–80.
6. From *Taiwan Church News,* January 2, 1983, p. 6 (translation from the Chinese original by C.S.S.).
7. From *Documents on the Chinese Democratic Movement 1978–80,* ed. Claude Widor, Vol. 1 (Hong Kong: The Observers Publishers, and Paris: Ecole des Hautes en Sciences Sociales, 1981), p. 764 (translation from the Chinese original by C.S.S.).

20. MASK DANCE

1. See *World Book Encyclopedia,* Vol. 12, pp. 205–7.
2. Younghak Hyun, "A Theological Look at the Mask Dance in Korea," in *Minjung Theology* (pp. 43–50), p. 46.
3. Ibid., p. 45.
4. The dialogue reproduced here is abridged from the original script. I am indebted to Suh Nam Dong, a Korean theologian, for providing the English translation of the Bongsan mask dance drama from the Korean original.
5. Hyun, "A Theological Look at the Mask Dance in Korea," p. 45.
6. By Kuo Lu-Sheng, in *Peking Spring,* ed. Wei Ching-Sheng (Hong Kong: P'in-Ming Publishing House, 1980), pp. 293–95 (translation from the Chinese original by C.S.S.).
7. Hyun, "A Theological Look at the Mask Dance in Korea," pp. 45–46.
8. The poem is by S. Ismalika. See *For the Dawning of the New,* pp. 47–48.

Works Cited More Than Once in This Book

Abayasekera, Jeffrey, and Niles, D. Preman, eds., *For the Dawning of the New,* Singapore, Christian Conference of Asia (CCA), 1981.

Albrecht, Paul, ed., *Faith, Science, and the Future: Preparatory Readings for the 1979 World Conference of the WCC,* Geneva, WCC, 1978.

Anderson, Johannes C., *Myths and Legends of the Polynesians,* Rutland, Vt./Tokyo, Charles Tuttle Co., 1969.

Asia Yearbook 1979, Hong Kong, Far Eastern Economic Review, 1979.

Barrett, David, *World Christian Encyclopedia,* London, Oxford University Press, 1982.

Basho, *The Narrow Road to the Deep North,* London, Penguin, 1966.

Chen Hsiu-Hsi, *The Last Love: A Collection of Poems,* Taipei, Li Poetry Magazine, 1978.

Comprehensive Study on Nuclear Weapons, Report of the Secretary General, New York, United Nations General Assembly, Sept. 12, 1980.

de Bary, William T., ed., *The Buddhist Tradition,* New York, Vintage, 1972.

Dorson, Richard M., *Folk Legends of Japan,* Rutland, Vt./Tokyo, Charles Tuttle Co., 1962.

——. *Folktales Told around the World,* University of Chicago Press, 1975.

Eliade, Mircea, *From Primitives to Zen: A Thematic Sourcebook of the History of Religions,* London, Collins, 1967.

From the Womb of Han: Stories of Korean Women Workers, Hong Kong, Urban Rural Mission-CCA, 1982.

Graham, A. C., trans. and Introduction, *Poems of the Late T'ang*, London, Penguin, 1977.

Hsia, C. T., *The Classic Chinese Novel,* Columbia University Press, 1968.

Humphreys, Christmas, ed., *The Wisdom of Buddhism,* London, Curzon, 1979.

Jeremias, Joachim, *Rediscovering the Parables,* New York, Scribner's, 1966.

Joyce, James Avery, *The New Politics of Human Rights,* London, Macmillan, 1978.

Kim Yong Bok, *Minjung Theology,* Singapore, CCA, 1981. Revised edition published 1983 by Orbis Books, Maryknoll, N.Y.

Laymon, Charles M., *The Interpreter's One-Volume Commentary,* Nashville/New York, Abingdon, 1971.

Lin Yutang, *My Country and My People,* New York, Reynal & Hitchcock, 1938.

Ming, Ann, *Taiwanese Voices,* London, British Council of Churches, 1981.

Minz, Nirmal, *Mahatma Gandhi and Hindu-Christian Dialogue,* Madras, Christian Literature Society, 1970.

O'Grady, Ron, and Jin, Lee Soo, *Suffering and Hope: An Anthology of Asian Writings,* Singapore, CCA, 1978.

Orwell, George, *Nineteen Eighty-Four,* London, Penguin, 1954.
Perrin, Norman, *Rediscovering the Teaching of Jesus,* London, SCM, 1967.
Schumann, H. Wolfgang, *Buddhism: An Outline of Its Teachings and Schools,* London, Rider, 1973.
Song, C. S., *The Compassionate God,* Maryknoll, N.Y./London, Orbis/SCM, 1982.
Suzuki, D. T., *Essays in Zen Buddhism,* London, Rider, 1970.
Thomas, T. K., ed., *Testimony amid Asian Suffering,* Singapore, CCA, 1977.
The Threefold Lotus Sutra, New York/Tokyo, Weatherhill/Kosei, 1975.
T. K., ed., *Letters from South Korea,* Tokyo, Iwanami Shoten, 1976.
Tribble, Phyllis, *God and the Rhetoric of Sexuality,* Philadelphia, Fortress, 1978.
Women and Men in Asia: The Women Question in Asian Context, Hong Kong, Asia Regional Office, World Student Christian Federation, 1976.
World Book Encyclopedia, Chicago, Field Enterprises, 1960.
Wynne, Alison, ed., *No Time for Crying,* Hong Kong, Resource Centre for Philippine Concerns, 1979.

Index

Compiled by William E. Jerman